LOVE
+
RELASIANSHIPS

A COLLECTION OF CONTEMPORARY ASIAN-CANADIAN DRAMA

VOLUME I

FOR JEAN

Like all these playwrights who shaped the destiny of our theatre movement,
thank you for helping me shape mine.
You are (and will always be) the one and only fireball.

LOVE + RELASIANSHIPS

VOLUME I

Yellow Fever by R.A. Shiomi
Bachelor-Man by Winston Christopher Kam
Maggie's Last Dance by Marty Chan
Mother Tongue by Betty Quan
Noran Bang: The Yellow Room by M.J. Kang
The Plum Tree by Mitch Miyagawa

PLAYWRIGHTS CANADA PRESS
TORONTO • CANADA

Love and RelASIANships - Volume I © Copyright 2009 Nina Lee Aquino

Playwrights Canada Press
The Canadian Drama Publisher
215 Spadina Ave., Suite 230, Toronto, Ontario, Canada, M5T 2C7
phone 416.703.0013 fax 416.408.3402
orders@playwrightscanada.com • www.playwrightscanada.com

For professional or amateur production rights, please contact
Playwrights Canada Press at the address above.

The publisher acknowledges the support of the Canadian taxpayers through the Government of Canada Book Publishing Industry Development Program, the Canada Council for the Arts, the Ontario Arts Council, and the Ontario Media Development Corporation.

Canada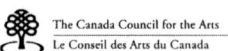

Cover Design: Leon Aureus
Production Editor: Micheline Courtemanche

Library and Archives Canada Cataloguing in Publication

Love and relAsianships / Nina Lee Aquino ed.

ISBN 978-0-88754-777-5 (v. 1).--ISBN 978-0-88754-779-9 (v. 2)

1. Canadian drama (English)--Asian Canadian authors. 2. Canadian drama (English)--20th century. 3. Canadian drama (English)--21st century. 4. Asian Canadians--Drama. I. Aquino, Nina Lee II. Title: Love and relationships.

PS8309.A75L68 2009   C812'.54080895071   C2009-901470-X

First edition: May 2009
Printed and bound by Transcontinental at Quebec, Canada.

CONTENTS

PREFACE
by R.A. Shiomi iii

INTRODUCTION
by Nina Lee Aquino vii

YELLOW FEVER
by R.A. Shiomi 1

BACHELOR-MAN
by Winston Christopher Kam 55

MAGGIE'S LAST DANCE
by Marty Chan 111

MOTHER TONGUE
by Betty Quan 163

NORAN BANG: THE YELLOW ROOM
by M.J. Kang 191

THE PLUM TREE
by Mitch Miyagawa 237

PREFACE

BY R.A. SHIOMI

I view myself as one of the pioneers of the Asian-Canadian Theatre Movement because my play, *Yellow Fever*, may have been the first professionally produced Asian-Canadian play (1983, by the Canasian Artists Group in Toronto). Certainly there have been Asian-Canadian theatre groups performing in Japanese and Chinese since the early twentieth century, but if there were any Asian-Canadian playwrights writing in English during that time, their work remains shrouded in history. And thus, this anthology represents a recognition of the first major wave of Asian-Canadian playwriting that has emerged since 1983. There are a number of possible reasons as to how and why this wave came into being.

In my own case, I can look back to my grandfather, who came to Canada in 1890. I have been told that as a child my grandfather loved to watch the travelling shows that toured the countryside in Japan. He brought that love of theatre to North America, and was the director of a kabuki-style community theatre company in Vancouver in the early twentieth century. The stage was never a place that my father desired to be, but the theatre bug was passed on to his younger brother, my uncle, who eventually performed contemporary Japanese plays in the thirties in Vancouver. I actually never realized this until I interviewed my uncle after my success with *Yellow Fever*. He spoke of performing in Japanese plays in the internment camps and told me of his obsession with Japanese television dramas in the sixties and seventies. It was tremendously comforting to realize that theatre was in my DNA, and I am sure that other Asian-Canadian playwrights could look into their family histories and find similar connections to theatre.

This understanding of my family history helped me to know where my own personal desire to write and tell stories came from. But growing up as a third-generation Japanese-Canadian (*sansei*) trying to assimilate into the mainstream culture through the fifties and sixties, I never felt empowered to write about Canadian society, and had no interest in writing about Japanese-Canadian community or history. So the key transformation, for myself personally, was my involvement in the Asian-Canadian community, including the political and cultural movement of the seventies and eighties, when I participated in such events as the Powell Street Festival in Vancouver, BC, and the National Redress and Reparations Campaign for Japanese-Canadians.

The Powell Street Festival is a Japanese-Canadian cultural event started in Vancouver in 1977. It was led by a combination of *shin-issei* (new immigrants) looking to revive the sense of a Japanese-Canadian community and *sansei* (third generation) young people searching for a connection to their community, history and culture. That festival was a success and has become an enduring focal point for the Japanese-Canadian community in Vancouver. For myself, my involvement in that festival, and with the Asian-Canadians involved in it, laid the groundwork of my understanding and acceptance of myself as a Japanese-Canadian. After all the years of growing up feeling oddly bereft, I found a new kind of belonging and importance. In fact, I often refer to it as my "eureka" moment, when I realized that so much of what I had thought were personal choices had actually been shaped by a history of political decisions steeped in racism and injustice. I had thought that being born Japanese-Canadian was a kind of curse, like an albatross around my neck, but it turned into my creative motherlode. It is my learning about Japanese-Canadian history that has been the philosophical and psychological foundation of my work as a theatre artist, as a playwright, director and artistic director.

My involvement in the National Redress and Reparations Campaign both in Vancouver and Toronto was a natural evolution from my work in the festival. And with this new acceptance of myself and understanding of our history, I felt I had something important to say about Canadian history and society. I simply had to find the right medium to communicate my ideas.

So there's DNA and the historical/community/cultural contexts, but there's also the need for a theatrical infrastructure. Back in the eigthties, there was no such infrastructure in any Canadian city, but there were Asian-American theatre companies in San Francisco, Los Angeles and New York. I had the good fortune to have a friend, Philip Gotanda, put me in contact with the Asian American Theater Company in San Francisco. It was through my work with the artists of that company, such as Marc Hayashi, Lane Nishikawa and Judy Nihei that I was able to write my first play. So the existence of the Asian American Theater Company facilitated my emergence as a playwright. The existence of fu-GEN and other companies is doing the same thing now for a new generation of Asian-Canadian playwrights.

But development of this infrastructure depends upon what I call the Leadership Quotient. One playwright, actor or director can come along at a time when there is not the right Leadership Quotient, and in most cases that one artist does not a movement make. And in the early eighties, though there were a handful of Asian-Canadian theatre artists around, we never quite had the ability to work together toward the kind of cohesive effort that would have resulted in the creation of an ongoing professional Asian-Canadian theatre company. There were efforts, like the Canasian Artists Group, which produced *Yellow Fever* in 1983, but that company had a wide range of artistic disciplines to support and could not survive many years beyond that production. There was Sansei Productions, which produced *A Song for a Nisei Fisherman* by Philip Kan Gotanda, but they lost the energy and enthusiasm for theatrical production. And companies like Cahoots in Toronto and the Firehall Theatre in Vancouver created larger frameworks within which Asian-Canadian work could be done, but then there was never quite the momentum and focus required to get the movement off the launching pad. And so, in the eighties, the idea of an organized Asian-Canadian theatre movement continued to germinate in the hearts and minds of a few individual artists. There were other groups that were in existence through this time, like Teesri Duniya in Montreal and the Carlos Bulosan Cultural Workshop in Toronto, but they tended to remain within the framework of their communities, and through the eighties and nineties did not rise to seriously break into the professional theatre scene. But it now appears that with fu-GEN and this anthology, there are indicators that the Asian-Canadian theatre movement is beginning to blossom.

Though I, myself, was not ready to be a part of an emerging leadership in Canada in the eighties, I became part of the emergence of a very successful company named Mu Performing Arts in Minnesota in the nineties. This could have been merely a matter of timing in terms of my career focus, but I also believe it reflected the desire and support for such a company within the Twin Cities (Minneapolis/St. Paul) community. And though, when I first started visiting Minnesota, I could hardly imagine a less likely place for an Asian-American theatre, there was a group of people ready to provide the leadership, and a very supportive funding community that wanted to see greater diversity within the Minnesota arts scene. Interestingly enough, I have always felt treated as an individual playwright in Canada but have been looked upon as an artistic and organizational leader in Minnesota. So I now live and work in Minnesota, having been the artistic director of Mu Performing Arts for the past fifteen years, overseeing its development from a handful of artists with a dream into a mid-sized company with a budget of over half a million dollars annually.

Having read the plays in this anthology, I feel energized by the wide range of writing styles and social/political perspectives exhibited by the playwrights. And as I read articles in the news on the playwrights and companies involved in this anthology, I can see the same hunger for understanding of who we are, how we got here and how we fit into this society. I can see it in artists like Nina Lee Aquino, David Yee, Richard Lee and Leon Aureus, who formed fu-GEN in 2002, with the desire to not only promote their own individual careers, but also to develop new artists, building something that could be far greater and more enduring.

Looking over the last twenty-five years, I can see the gradual emergence of a wave of Asian-Canadian playwrights, many of whom are represented in this anthology, and the Leadership Quotient is finally at the necessary level to give theatrical support to this first major wave. And that gives an old-timer like me new hope and energy.

So it is with pleasure and pride that I write this preface to the first anthology of Asian-Canadian plays. It is a collection that I hope not only lands in every library in North America, but also exists on the internet for the world to read and appreciate, for I believe it will bring a long-awaited recognition of the Asian-Canadian theatre movement.

INTRODUCTION

BY NINA LEE AQUINO
WITH TRANSLATION BY DAVID YEE

A NEW OUTLOOK

It took me quite some time to figure out the title to this anthology. In the end, I lifted it from fu-GEN Asian-Canadian Theatre Company's launch presentation entitled *love & relasianships*. Asians are known to be a lot of things: we're the mathematicians, the CEOs of corporations, the convenience-store owners, the typical nerds, doctors and engineers. We're submissive, quiet, very well-behaved (if bad drivers), intelligent and we're really good with computers and the violin or the piano. We eat rice and really, really hate disappointing our parents.

But I get the distinct impression that the general public doesn't really connect Asians and love. We can be obedient, loyal, patient, hard-working and ambitious… but not loving… in any capacity. Looking at the plays, trying to get a sense of what all of these plays were speaking to and about, I realized that, to me, all of them deal with love. Whether it's familial love or love for one's country or roots or love for oneself or love for Canada or loving one another or being a lover— Asians *do* love and we love deeply, and it's just as complex and complicated and mind-boggling as when everyone else does it.

As for "relASIANships"… I think this is what the plays are trying to do—form relationships within the community. Because we're so individualistic and disconnected, I feel that these plays become the little bridges to each other as a people, as a community.

I'd like to think that this anthology could be one of the many ways that could bring the Asian-Canadian community closer together, that the communities under this umbrella would get to know each other just a bit better, and a dialogue to better understand each other and respect/appreciate one another would ensue.

AN ANTHOLOGY OF ASIAN-CANADIAN DRAMA:
A NEW DIRECTION IN THE ASIAN-CANADIAN THEATRE MOVEMENT

You are about to read something vitally important to us—and by "us," I mean the Asian-Canadian community. You are about to read a collection of plays about us and, more importantly, written by us. You are about to read our stories.

This anthology marks a milestone in our community: we finally have a united, strong, artistic front. It is the acknowledgement that Asian-Canadians do have a form of expression; that we have a culture worthy of being witnessed, learned from, studied and critically analyzed by everybody—not just our own community.

This anthology is a definitive record of a theatrical movement, a movement that reflects a multiplicity of styles and genres, joined together by the singular fact that they are a series of plays written by us, for us… and for Canada. The pre-existing record of our presence in the Canadian theatrical milieu and the written dramatic canon is almost non-existent. And this could be indicative of the mentality of the Asian-Canadian theatre community in general. Our progress has been marked by fits and starts— historically a play written by an Asian playwright will get picked up by a "mainstream" theatre company, and once that production closes, we hope and pray that some other artistic director (who have, by and large, been Caucasian) will put us in their season or find a slot in some ancillary festival. There has been limited sustained activity to keep the work and the movement progressing at any pace.

The publication of this anthology marks a new direction in the Asian-Canadian theatre movement: a step toward sustainability, solidarity and a uniquely Canadian identity.

CHOOSING THE PLAYS

Collecting the plays to be included in this anthology was like the Asian-Canadian theatre movement itself—it was largely done piecemeal. I found some plays and playwrights in other drama anthologies (like Betty Quan and Marty Chan); some plays that were produced, especially in the early eighties, weren't saved in an electronic format and we were lucky enough to get a copy only through an actor who happened to be part of the production (like *Bachelor Man* by Winston Kam) and didn't throw away their script!

The selected plays are milestones in their specific communities and the Asian-Canadian theatre movement. Likewise, this anthology is intended to be the first milestone of the Asian-Canadian community at large.

Looking back, there were three major criteria for selecting the plays.

First, *geographically.* When I thought about "Asian-Canadian," the *Canadian* stood out, and I wanted to make sure that even though these playwrights were of Asian heritage, they all came from Canada, and that meant *all* of Canada. Trusty map by my side, I actively hunted down Asian-Canadian playwrights from east to west, north to south and collected the plays accordingly. It was of utmost importance that Asians all over Canada were represented.

Second, *chronologically.* Anthologies rarely include work of the "future." Typically, plays have to either already be published or produced at a mainstream full-production level… or both. For this anthology, I wanted to include at least one work that was *not* in line with that criteria—an unpublished play that had only been done in a festival setting. That play was *paper SERIES* by David Yee. As important as it was to reflect the past and present of Asian-Canadian drama, it was equally as important to me to include a work that was currently in progress, but had much promise should it progress to a larger-scale full production. I wanted this anthology to include plays that expressed the tone of what Asian-Canadian theatre was going to become.

Lastly, I wanted to strike a representative balance of the *Asian Diaspora*. *Asian*, specifically *Pan Pacific Asian*, is an umbrella term consisting of various communities—Filipino, Korean, Chinese, Japanese, etc. I really wanted to make sure that all the communities were represented both in the work and in the writer... and some were really interesting matches. Not all of the plays that dealt with Chinese issues were written necessarily by Chinese playwrights—like Filipino-Canadian Leon Aureus, playwright of *Banana Boys*—and not all Asian playwrights wrote plays that had any Asian content whatsoever—like Marty Chan's *Maggie's Last Dance*. And some, like Korean-Canadian playwright Jean Yoon, paint a bold portrait of "otherness" in our community that goes beyond culture—as she does in *Yes Yoko Solo*.

One thing I really want to highlight in regard to the process of choosing these plays: I didn't do it alone. Yes, ultimately, I had the final say of what was included in the anthology... but the process was special because instead of just me reading the canon of plays, they were read by committee. The reading committee I assembled consisted of emerging and established Asian artists, from actors to designers. We would get together once a week, read the plays aloud (stage directions and all) and have a discussion about it afterwards to compare our thoughts, insights, comments, etc. Finally, at the end of the reading, we would give the play a score within the context of inclusion in the anthology. At one point we had almost twenty artists coming back week after week, really looking forward to what play was going to be read next. There was much debate and (constructive) argument over the plays, and in the end it was the voices of the committee that made my final decisions informed.

THE FINAL CUT

First of all, I think all the plays chosen are good. Damn good. On their own, respectively, without the context of the collection, these plays are of excellent quality—strongly written, dramatically moving, with a strong sense of theatrical vision and relevant to the world we live in.

All twelve plays in this anthology are milestones for each of the communities they represent. Each play puts a spotlight on its relative community—makes us understand, listen, witness, break misconceptions or strengthen our perceptions of what those communities are all about. M.J. Kang's *Noran Bang: The Yellow Room*, for example, gives us a slice of Korean immigrant life and promotes a richer, deeper understanding of that life. *Miss Orient(ed)*, the play I co-wrote with Nadine Villasin, is not the first Filipino-Canadian play, nor was it the first play to come out of Carlos Bulosan Theatre. Carlos Bulosan Theatre had been around for over twenty years (as Carlos Bulosan Cultural Workshop) and has had a substantial collection of works written by Felly Villasin and Voltaire de Leon. The significance of *Miss Orient(ed)* is that it ushered Carlos Bulosan Cultural Workshop into the "professional" arena of Toronto theatre; it transformed Carlos Bulosan Cultural Workshop into what we now know as Carlos Bulosan Theatre. This was a conscious decision by Nadine Villasin, to make this play a watershed event in its community and for the new direction of Carlos Bulosan Theatre.

In selecting the plays, I also wanted to see if I could trace a trend in the issues that mattered to Asian-Canadians during the time they were written. I noticed that in the earlier plays (Volume 1), the hot topics were displacement, immigration, homesickness and questing to Gold Mountain. There's a sense of longing and nostalgia, a fierce connection to roots and the mother tongue and dreams of what could have been and what life is now. Then, somewhere in the middle (Volume 2), the writing started to go more inward. There's an acceptance of Canada as "home" and dealing with all the baggage of what that means. Often it meant negotiating feelings of displacement within ourselves, our identity and in Canada. The works that came out in the nineties had a lot to do with defining one's new identity, striding the hyphen that made up where you supposedly came from "originally" and your country of residence. The most recent plays, from the last decade, cover a much broader and explorative range of subject matter. There's a new wave of playwrights who are coming out writing about whatever feels relevant to them without connecting it in any obvious way to being Asian or Asian-Canadian. Stories run the gamut of modern experience: a group of boys learning what it is to be men (*Banana Boys*), a woman trying to find her place in the modern world (*Yes Yoko Solo*), isolated individuals chasing after the thing they love the most (*paper SERIES*), human beings coping with guilt and grief of past transgressions (*Tiger of Malaya*) or wanting to be free from the traditions that bind them (*China Doll*).

A WEALTH OF TALENT

We were all pleasantly surprised at the number of excellent Asian-Canadian plays out there. Some more familiar than others, but nonetheless of the highest artistic quality. We wanted to pack in as many plays as we could… however, a book can only hold so many pages, and the thicker the book got, the more expensive—and inaccessible—it would become… and of course that was not the point of creating the anthology. So we made the decision to release two volumes instead of just one.

The plays are arranged chronologically, starting with R.A. Shiomi's *Yellow Fever*, produced in 1983, and ending with David Yee's *paper SERIES* from 2007.

To be clear: this is not a "best of" collection or the "greatest hits" of Asian-Canadian plays. Very specific reasoning was used to collect these plays contained here and, if anything, they should be indicative of the calibre of work that exists outside the covers of this book. For instance: Terry Watada's *Tale of a Mask*, Mieko Ouchi's *The Red Priest*, Keira Loughran's *Little Dragon*, John Ng's *I*, Yung Luu's *I Chink*, Jared Matsunaga-Turnbull and Elyne Quan's *Lig & Bittle*, just to name a few. Between the time the plays were selected and this introduction being written, a slew of new, exciting Asian-Canadian plays have hit our Canadian stages: *Broken* by C.E. Gatchalian, *a nanking winter* and *The Madness of the Square* by Marjorie Chan, *People Power* by the Carlos Bulosan Theatre Collective, *Porn Life* by Bobby del Rio, *Singkil* by Catherine Hernandez, *The Blue Light* by Mieko Ouchi, *lady in the red dress* by David Yee, *Gas* by Jason Maghanoy, and *The Forbidden Phoenix* by Marty Chan spring to mind. Along with new plays, we have also seen a number of new, talented emerging playwrights taking matters into their own hands: Norman Yeung, Marie Leofeli R. Barlizo, Byron Abalos, Marie Beath Badian, Insurp Choi, Tricia Collins, Gein Wong and Romeo Candido are all actively creating new work as I write this.

THE FUTURE LOOKS BRIGHT

Looking toward the future of Asian-Canadian theatre I feel an overwhelming excitement. We're getting louder, bolder and more fearless in our choices; in how we tell our stories. My experience has always been that the Asian-Canadian community is a very insulated one—we work our butts off to put food on the table, keep a roof over our heads and set money aside to get our kids to university... and that's that. We're not really known to focus on the bigger picture; our visions are more personal and immediate. We tend to concern ourselves more with our immediate circles, and as long as they're okay, then we're okay. Then we wake up the next day and go on about our business. This has been *my* experience, when looking at my immediate and extended family, and perhaps it's generational.

Through the plays of this anthology, however, we are starting to see a new trend emerge in the kinds of stories we choose to tell. We are starting to broaden our scope, opening our eyes to the world around us and letting that world influence our storytelling. We are starting to realize that *we are all connected*. We cease to be afraid of disrupting the status quo. We are starting to make a scene. Our topics, our dilemmas, our generational baggage we've been handed down... we are starting to reveal them to the world outside without fear or shame. We are becoming less insular, more inclusive.

We can all learn from each other, deepen each other's understanding and enrich our lives as Canadians... our *identity* as Canadians.

Whether it's because you realize we are all connected, or because your preconceived notions of who we are have been broken, with the presence of these plays and these writers... chances are you'll never look at an old Chinese woman on the bus the same way ever again.

YELLOW FEVER

BY R.A. SHIOMI

ABOUT

R.A. SHIOMI

R.A. Shiomi has been one of the leading artists of the Asian-American theatre movement for over twenty-five years. His work as a playwright includes the award-winning *Yellow Fever*, which has been produced off-Broadway in New York, across North America and in translation in Japan. Some of his other plays include *Rosie's Café, Play Ball, Uncle Tadao, Mask Dance* and *Journey of the Drum*. Rick has also co-authored the book for two musicals, *The Walleye Kid, The Musical* and *Filipino Hearts*. In the nineties he wrote for Canadian television, including the CTV series *ENG* and the CBC series *Inside Stories*.

Rick has directed for Interact Theater in Philadelphia, the Asian American Theater Company in San Francisco and extensively for Mu Performing Arts in Minnesota. He is a member of the Asian American Theater National Steering Committee, which has organized national conferences and festivals. He is one of the founders and has been artistic director of Mu Performing Arts since 1993. He has received the Sally Irvine Ordway Award for vision in theatre and the award for artistic excellence from the State Council for Asian-Pacific Minnesotans.

Yellow Fever was first produced at the Asian American Theater Company in San Francisco on March 10, 1982, with the following company:

SAM SHIKAZE	A.M. Lai
NANCY WING	June Mesina
CHUCK CHAN	Dennis Dun
CAPTAIN KADOTA	John Nishio
SERGEANT MACKENZIE	Bob Martin
ROSIE	Suzi Okazaki
SUPERINTENDENT JAMESON AND GOLDBERG	Blaine Palmer

Directed by Lane Kiyomi Nishikawa
Set Design by Lane Kiyomi Nishikawa and R.A. Shiomi
Lighting Design by Wilbur Obata
Costume Design by Linda Obata
Technical Direction by James B. Chew
Produced by Rick Lee and Tom Wing Wu

Yellow Fever was produced in New York on December 1, 1982, by the Pan Asian Repertory Theater, with the following company:

SAM SHIKAZE	Donald Li
NANCY WING	Freda Foh Shen
CHUCK CHAN	Henry Yuk
CAPTAIN KADOTA	Ernest Abuba
SERGEANT MACKENZIE	Jeffrey Spolan
ROSIE	Carol Honda
SUPERINTENDENT JAMESON AND GOLDBERG	James Jenner

Directed by Raul Aranas
Set Design by Chris Stapleton
Lighting Design by Dawn Chiang
Costume Design by Lillian Pan
Stage Management by Eddas M. Bennett
Artistic Direction by Tisa Chang
Produced by Tisa Chang

The story for *Yellow Fever* was co-conceived by R.A. Shiomi and Marc Hayashi.

CHARACTERS

SAM SHIKAZE, forty-five, a nisei detective.
NANCY WING, twenty-five, a Chinese-Canadian reporter for a major
    Vancouver newspaper.
CHUCK CHAN, thirty-two, a Chinese-Canadian lawyer.
CAPTAIN KADOTA, forty-five, nisei policeman.
SERGEANT MACKENZIE, mid-thirties, a bluff policeman.
ROSIE, late forties, a kibei café owner.
SUPERINTENDENT JAMESON, mid-forties, a suave leader.
GOLDBERG, a Japanophile professor.

SETTING

Powell Street in Vancouver, British Columbia, Canada.

Stage right is an alley. Centre stage is a raised platform serving as SAM's office. There is an upstage window facing onto the alley. SAM's chair and desk are on stage right of the platform. There are windows with scrims as the backdrop for the office, with a door in the middle. There is a client's chair, a coat rack, a radio, a filing cabinet and a mirror in the office. Stage left is Rosie's Café. There is the café entrance upstage left with a kitchen exit curtain stage left of the door. There is a counter along the stage left wall with three stools and a table with two chairs downstage left. There is a coat rack and an extra chair extreme downstage left.

TIME

Act One: March 9, 1973, in the morning.
Act Two: Evening, a few days later.

NOTE ON GENERATIONS

Issei	First generation Japanese-Canadian (immigrants)
Nisei	Second generation Japanese-Canadian (born in Canada)
Sansei	Third generation Japanese-Canadian
Kibei	Born in Canada, but lived in Japan for many years before returning to Canada.

YELLOW FEVER

ACT ONE

Lights come up stage right and SAM enters upstage right, walking to downstage right and stopping in a spotlight, as if under a street lamp.

SAM   Monday, March 9, 1973, I walked down to my office on Powell Street. It used to be our main strip. Used to be snack bars, general stores, boarding houses, gambling joints, we had it all…. That was back in forty-one, when I was a kid running groceries for Mrs. Sato. World War II came and the government moved us out, sent us packing into the mountains, herded onto trains and dumped off in godforsaken ghost towns…. After the war it was never the same. They didn't let us back to the coast till forty-nine, and by then we were scattered east of the Rockies. A few of us returned, not just to Vancouver, but to Powell Street…. Times have changed, now my nisei friends tell me I should move downtown, forget the past and get a decent job. I just tell them I like the local colour…. Being a private eye doesn't give you that nine-to-five respectability, but you call your own shots and you don't have to smile for a living… and that's the way I like it.

> *SAM exits through the alley. Lights come up on the café setting. ROSIE is cleaning the counter and humming to herself. GOLDBERG is sitting at the counter eating.*

(entering the café door) Hi Rosie.

ROSIE   Irasshaimas-e. *[Welcome.]*

SAM   *(to the audience as he hangs up his hat and coat)* I stopped in at Rosie's Café, for some of her ochazuke *[rice soup]*. My folks died years ago and my sister moved to Toronto, so Rosie's like family to me. *(he walks to the table, sits)* She's my mama-san, my piece of the rock. *(ROSIE enters again with tea and ochazuke on tray.)* Well Rosie, another Cherry Blossom Bazaar's come and gone, eh?

ROSIE   Hai *[Yes]*, more year goodbye.

SAM   Good weather for a change, huh?

ROSIE   Honto, i tenki desu neh. *[Really beautiful weather.]* But I no see you at the bazaar. *(She serves the food.)*

SAM   Domo *[Thanks]*…. I was out of town.

ROSIE   Too bad, you miss everybody.

SAM   Tough luck, eh? *(He begins eating.)*

ROSIE   Hah, I think you hiding. Everyone ask, "Shikaze-san doko desuka? Shikaze-san nani o shiteruno?" ["Where is Shikaze? What's he doing?"]

SAM   They come down to Powell Street once a year and want to know what I been up to, eh?

ROSIE   Honto [Really], everybody wants to know.

GOLDBERG   (getting up to leave) Gochisosama deshita. [Thank you.]

ROSIE   (turning to GOLDBERG) Hai, domo arigato gozaimasu. [Yes, thank you very much.]

> GOLDBERG goes to the coat rack and stands there momentarily before exiting. ROSIE clears the counter.

Anata-no okasan [Your wife], I saw her at the bazaar. She's still very pretty in kimono, neh?

SAM   Not anymore. (He finishes the meal and sips his tea.)

ROSIE   Hontoni, kawaii desho. [Really, very pretty.] (returns to sit at the table)

SAM   Not my wife anymore, remember.

ROSIE   Ah Samu, why don't you try again? Everybody says she is so, how you say, delicato. Her family is high class and she knows ikebana so well, neh?

SAM   She always was arranging things.

ROSIE   I remember how excited you were long time ago.

SAM   A long time ago.

ROSIE   So young and crazy in love.

SAM   It was crazy.

ROSIE   Nanio shimashitaka? [What happened?]

SAM   It was like a fire, we burned out.

ROSIE   What burned? A house burns down, you can build another. Everybody has problems these days. No need to get divorce, like hakujin [white] people.

SAM   We threw in the towel ages ago.

ROSIE   It's hard to find a good wife.

SAM   It's a rough life, Rosie.

ROSIE   So neh, but you are not getting younger.

SAM   (gets up) You got me there. Old Man Time is the one guy I can't shake.... Gochisosama. [Thanks.]

ROSIE   *(walks to the coat rack to get his hat and coat)* You are so sad to get old by yourself, no family to take care of you. Look at all the ojisans *[old men]* living in hotels here; so poor and lonely and stubborn. You gonna be just like them.

SAM   *(takes his hat and coat)* That's life, Rosie. It' ain't so bad, lots of guys grow old, and I always got you.

ROSIE   That's what you always say, neh? *(clears the table, taking the tablecloth)*

SAM   Yeah Rosie, see you later.

> SAM exits out the café door. ROSIE laughs as she clears his table and exits to the kitchen. Lights cross-fade to SAM's office as he enters the office door.

Rosie was a real sweetie. She could dish out the advice without expecting me to take it. That was our understanding. *(He walks to the coat stand to hang up his coat and hat.)* My ex-wife was still pretty, but she needed the kind of attention I couldn't give her. She had big plans for us, too big for me. *(He opens the file cabinet to get a bottle of Canadian Club.)* We split up in sixty-three. Ten years married and ten years apart. *(He pours a shot and takes a sip.)* It's been a lot quieter since sixty-three. *(He turns on a radio that sits on a file cabinet.)* Her old man had the dough to keep her going in style. And me? I had the business. *(sits at the desk)*

> CHUCK enters.

CHUCK   You're back.

SAM   Yeah.

CHUCK   What was out in the Fraser Valley? *(takes off his overcoat)*

SAM   Con man selling phony insurance to some farming buddies, for their strawberries.

CHUCK   Sounds like easy pickings.

SAM   The farmers or the berries?

CHUCK   *(walks to the radio)* Who cares, huh?

SAM   Not you, eh?

CHUCK   *(switching channels to a pop music station)* All a matter of priorities, Sam. All a matter of priorities.

SAM   So what's up? *(SAM gets up and crosses to the radio.)*

CHUCK   *(sits down in the client's chair)* Just making my rounds.

SAM   Take advantage of the sunshine and fresh air, eh?

CHUCK   It's spring, Sam. Ever get the urge to clean this place up? *(SAM turns the radio off and CHUCK gets up.)* You could even splurge on a new hat. *(SAM goes *back to the desk.)* Might do wonders for your image. *(He takes SAM's hat off the rack and tosses it at him.)*

SAM   *(catches the hat)* Take it easy, I just got it cleaned.

CHUCK   Some people never change, huh?

SAM   What for? *(He finds a note inside his hat.)* Hmmm. Beware the Edes of March?

CHUCK   Ides, Sam.

SAM   Huh?

CHUCK   Ides of March, it's from *Julius Caesar*... you know, Shakespeare.

SAM   So what?

CHUCK   It's the warning an old man gave to Caesar.

SAM   Go on, it's just getting interesting.

CHUCK   The Republicans knocked him off on the ides, that's the fifteenth.

SAM   Yah ought'a be a detective, Chuck.

CHUCK   Not worth my time, least not the way you do it.

SAM   Yeah, you wouldn't spend a week saving a few bucks for a bunch of nisei farmers, would ya, Chuck?

CHUCK   You're too good for your own good. How much you charge those buddies? A hundred plus expenses? For a week's work? You run your business like a community service.

SAM   That's my business.

CHUCK   Having roots is fine, but you gotta grow, too. With your talent and my savvy, we could make a killing.

SAM   *(studying the note)* Tell me about it.

CHUCK   You're the detective, I'm the lawyer. You bring 'em in, I get 'em out. We get them coming and going. Like this divorce case I got now. Woman's suing her millionaire hubby for half the bundle. All we have to do is get some of his affairs in black and white.

SAM   Sure, but right now I'd rather figure out this little note.

CHUCK   So who's been fiddling with your hat?

SAM   Couple of people... naahhh.

CHUCK   What naahh?

SAM   Nothin'.

CHUCK   Somebody drops a threat on you and it's nothing?

SAM   Not yet.

CHUCK   Let me drop something else on you, care of my rounds. The Cherry Blossom Queen has disappeared.

SAM   Disappeared?

CHUCK   Gotta keep in touch, Sam.

SAM   So, who's been spreading the gossip this time?

CHUCK   Sergeant Mackenzie. He says she didn't make it home from the bazaar Saturday night. Her father's been calling the station by the hour. Funny thing is, Mackenzie and a couple of other cops dropped by the church that night, so she disappeared right out from under their noses.

SAM   They got big noses.

CHUCK   And they've put Kadota on the case.

SAM   Great, they're sending their tokens in after us, eh?

CHUCK   This is still the ghetto to them.

SAM   Funny, Rosie didn't say anything.

CHUCK   Kudo's trying to keep it quiet right now.

SAM   Gordon Kudo's kid is the queen?

CHUCK   Yeah, cute kid.

SAM   Too cute…. You check her friends out?

CHUCK   I'm not even on the case yet. This is your turf, I take over in court. Anyway, I got business to take care of.

SAM   Make hay while the sun shines, eh?

CHUCK   (heading for the door) That's only for farmers, Sam.

SAM   Yeah, thanks for the tip. (He turns on the radio to soft music.)

CHUCK   Any time.

SAM   Hey, how about dinner at Rosie's?

CHUCK   Sure, see you later. (CHUCK exits out of the office door.)

SAM   (standing by the cabinet, talking to the audience) I had to give Chuck credit. He ran a classy operation downtown and still had time for the people over here. (gets another file folder out of the cabinet) The dope on the Kudo kid was that she was some disco queen turning hakujin, hoping her crown would launch her into the mainstream modelling scene. (sits down at the desk again) I checked through her family file 'cause I had a hunch her old man would be calling me soon enough.

Phone rings. SAM turns off the radio before picking up the phone.

Sam Shikaze here…. Hi Gordon…. I just heard it…. It's my business to know, Gordon.

There is a knock on the office door. NANCY WING enters.

NANCY   Hi, I'm Nancy Wing of the *Sun.*

SAM   *(looks up)* Sorry, I'm busy.

NANCY   I thought you were Shikaze.

SAM   Huh…? *(into the phone)* Gomen, Gordon *[Excuse me, Gordon],* of course I'll take the case…. So when did you last see her?

NANCY   *(walking around the office)* Oh, about six o'clock.

SAM   *(into the phone)* You didn't think of taking her home?

NANCY   Her boyfriend usually did that.

SAM   What's his name?

NANCY   John Richardson

SAM   He belonged to the Phi Geta Bamma frat, eh?

NANCY   That's Beta Gamma, *(standing by the window)* and uh, don't you find it stuffy in here?

SAM   *(to NANCY)* Doesn't open… *(into the phone)* My window, Gordon… forget it.

NANCY   No problem. *(She bangs on the frame.)*

SAM   *(to NANCY)* Hey, take it easy!

NANCY   It's just stuck.

SAM   *(into the phone)* Gomen Gordon, I know you got a right to be upset.

NANCY   *(gets the window open a little)* See, it'll open some.

SAM   That's the way it is these days.

NANCY   It's better that way, isn't it?

SAM   *(into the phone but looking at NANCY)* Who knows, I'll get started on the case, and I'll get the window fixed. *(He hangs up the phone.)*

NANCY   So you're the Sam Shikaze. *(She extends her hand.)*

SAM   That's the name on the door, kid. *(ignores her hand and crosses to the window)*

NANCY   Quaint place you have here.

SAM   Most people call it crummy. *(closes the window)* What can I do for ya?

NANCY   You could let me in some fresh air.

SAM   You're fresh enough for me, kid. *(lets down the venetian blind and returns to the desk)*

NANCY   Are you always so friendly?

SAM   Not to strangers. *(She walks back to the desk and sits opposite SAM.)* So, what brings a big-time reporter down here?

NANCY   What do you mean by that?

SAM   Your kind only drops by when we turn out in kimonos.

NANCY   Anything else worth covering?

SAM   Guess not, eh? Just the skid row winos and us quiet Japanese.

NANCY   Not even many of you left, are there?

SAM   Let's get to the point.

NANCY   *(pause)* What's happened to Miss Cherry Blossom?

SAM   The grapevine's turned into a wire service, eh?

NANCY   We have our contacts.

SAM   So what's Miss Cherry Blossom got to do with me?

NANCY   The inside story. They say you know when a twig breaks on Powell Street.

SAM   You're barking up the wrong tree, kid.... You ought'a call the Gardeners' Association.

NANCY   I can see you're going to be a great help.

SAM   Help yourself, if you can open that window I'm sure you can kick in a few more doors.

NANCY   *(stands up to leave)* I will if I have to.

SAM   Good luck.

NANCY   *(pause at the door)* You wouldn't have a clue, or a suspect, would you? Somebody with an axe to grind?

SAM   *(looking up)* Listen kid, I'm getting an axe to grind.

NANCY   I mean, could she be the victim of feuding in the ghetto?

SAM   Where?

NANCY   The... ghetto... I mean Powell Street.

SAM   You know, for a second there you sounded like a princess in a garbage dump.

NANCY   Sorry, I didn't mean anything.

SAM   Sure, no water off your back, eh? Course its not all still waters running deep down here. Nobody says so, but there are some women who'd like to see Miss Cherry Blossom take a flying leap.

NANCY   Don't humour me. I came for the facts.

SAM   I thought they spoke for themselves.

NANCY   *(walks to the door)* Hell of a lot more useful than some people.

SAM   Yeah, then why don't you just run down the facts.

NANCY   Watch out, I might run you over.

SAM   I'll keep that in mind.

> NANCY opens the door only to have Sergeant MACKENZIE
> and Captain KADOTA enter.

MACKENZIE   Hello Sammy. Got hired help now? You must be movin' up in the world.

NANCY   Watch it, buddy, I'm from the *Sun*.

SAM   Look out Sarge, she might kick your drawers open.

KADOTA   Sam, we just dropped by to tell you we can handle this one.

SAM   What one, Kenji?

KADOTA   Captain, Sam… remember? I didn't get kicked out of cadet school. I made it.

SAM   That was a while back, Kenbo. What ya been doing lately?

KADOTA   More than cleaning out dirty laundry.

SAM   Least the boys come clean when I'm done.

MACKENZIE   Don't let him play about, Captain.

KADOTA   Listen Sam, stay out of the Kudo case, wakaru *[understand]*?

MACKENZIE   What's that, Captain?

KADOTA   Nothing, Mackenzie.

SAM   Don't worry Sarge, we're just playin' Japanese.

NANCY   He's a real character, isn't he? *(KADOTA turns to NANCY.)*

SAM   By the way, Kenji, this is my girl Sunday.

NANCY   I'm Nancy Wing, a reporter for the *Sun*.

KADOTA   You better look somewhere else for your story. *(sits in the client's chair)*

NANCY   Wait a minute.

KADOTA   This is off the record, understand.

NANCY   We're obviously not speaking the same language.

KADOTA   You Chinese?

NANCY   *(pulling out a microphone)* Does that bother you?

KADOTA   Shut that off! *(turns to SAM)* Get rid of her, Sam.

SAM   Come on, Kenji, I was just getting used to her.

KADOTA   Okay, Miss Reporter, we've nothing to hide. Just keep out of the way of our investigation.

NANCY   So, who's in the way? *(she steps away)*

KADOTA   Sam, listen to me, we deal with the criminals, you stick to the peep holes and petty thefts. None of this "we can take care of our own."

SAM   Should've told Sarge. He might have sneezed and blown the case wide open.

MACKENZIE   Now that's a bit much, Sammy!

KADOTA   For the good of the community.

SAM   We got a reputation to live down, eh?

KADOTA   We're Nihonjin, nah? *[We're Japanese, right?]*

MACKENZIE   We're what, Captain?

SAM   First time I ever heard you say "we" about us, Kenji.

KADOTA   Well, I'm telling you now.

MACKENZIE   Aye, we're givin' yuh fair warning, Sammy.

SAM   Real considerate of you boys.

KADOTA   This is no time for wisecracks!

SAM   Somebody leaning on you?

KADOTA   Nobody pushes me—

SAM   Sounds like election year to me. Mayor's out to clean out the ghettos, right kid…? With Captain Kenji Kadota leading the parade.

MACKENZIE   About time, eh?

KADOTA   Mackenzie!

MACKENZIE   I was just—

KADOTA   Interrupting me!

SAM   You two want to step outside?

KADOTA   Sam, I'm telling you, keep your nose out of this one.

SAM   Sorry Kenji, Kudo's already hired me.

KADOTA   Bakka! *[You're crazy!]*

MACKENZIE   Huh, Captain?

KADOTA   Nothing.

MACKENZIE   *(to himself)* Lot of bloomin' noise for nothin'.

SAM   We're just shootin' the breeze, Sarge.

MACKENZIE   Aye, well yuh better watch yer step Sammy, yer Chinese cousins may be behind this one here.

SAM   Sounds like you're hot on the trail.

KADOTA   We're doing our job.

MACKENZIE   Aye, we are at that. Ever heard of the Hong Kong Tong Connection?

SAM   That connected to the French one?

NANCY   Some detective we have here.

KADOTA   We've reliable sources that say the Tongs are expanding their operations, muscling in on your territory.

SAM   Didn't know we had anything left to take down here.

MACKENZIE   We all know how the Chinese like to trade in women.

NANCY   Now wait a second, buddy. Another line like that and you'll be on the front page and out of a job.

KADOTA   Watch your mouth, Mackenzie.

SAM   You talked to Chuck yet?

MACKENZIE   We have our doubts about him, too, 'cause he's one of 'em, ain't he?

SAM   One of who?

MACKENZIE   Don't muck us about, laddie!

SAM   There ya go, kid, front-page splash, "Terror of the Hongs."

MACKENZIE   Tongs, Sammy. Yuh think we're bloomin' idiots, don't cha? Think we ain't capable of doin' our duty here, eh?

SAM   I wasn't at the bazaar, so I don't know how you blew it.

MACKENZIE   Don't get perky now, we know how to deal with your kind.

SAM   So shit or get off the can.

MACKENZIE   *(reaches for SAM)* Why yuh!

KADOTA   *(grabbing MACKENZIE)* That's enough, Mackenzie!

SAM   Maybe ya better get a leash, Kenji.

MACKENZIE   *(lunges at SAM again)* By Jesus I'll bash his—

KADOTA   *(pulling MACKENZIE back)* Not here! *(to SAM)* and you shut up!

SAM   Sure, if you're finished with the small talk.

KADOTA   We are for now, but we'll be around. So don't try and get cute, nah?

SAM   I'm too old for that, and I never was good-looking.

> *KADOTA and MACKENZIE exit out the office door. SAM sits down to continue work at the desk. NANCY walks to the door.*

NANCY   You don't let up, do you?

SAM   Can't afford to.

NANCY   Tough guy all the way, eh?

SAM   Any last words, kid?

NANCY   The name's Nancy.

SAM   Sure, Nancy.

NANCY   Well I'd better get moving, no use—

SAM   Wastin' yer time here, eh?

NANCY   If I come up with anything I'll let you know.

SAM   Thanks, an old man like me needs all the help I can get.

> *NANCY exits out the office door. SAM clears his desk, gets up to put on his hat and coat.*

Kenji was whistling in the dark, and Mackenzie's warning about the Tongs was so much warmed-over B.S. As for the Wing kid, I'd seen her kind before. Another model minority expecting Powell Street to be a walk in the park, like she was doing us a favour by coming down to the dump. *(pause as he pulls out the note)* That only left his note to tie in. I figured the hakujin guy at Rosie's was in on the ides. If he had a hand in the disappearance of the queen... then I was in business.

> *SAM exits out of the office door and the lights cross-fade to ROSIE's café. ROSIE is cleaning the counter. CHUCK and SAM arrive. CHUCK has an umbrella.*

CHUCK   Hi Rosie.

ROSIE   Kombanwa. *[Good evening.]* *(She goes to get menus.)*

SAM   *(brushing off the water)* What's hot tonight, Rosie?

ROSIE   Have you heard, Samu?

SAM   No, that's why I asked.

> *CHUCK puts down his umbrella and goes to sit at the table. SAM hangs up his coat and pauses before deciding to keep his hat on.*

ROSIE   *(giving the menu to CHUCK)* Everybody is talking about Miss Lily Kudo. She's disappeared and no one can find her.

CHUCK   *(looking at the menu)* You think the kid's a runaway?

ROSIE   Well Watanabe-san says he heard Lily talking about going to Hollywood.

CHUCK   Doesn't sound likely, Rosie.

ROSIE   Sato-san says Lily ran away with her boyfriend-yo, because her daddy no like him.

SAM   *(walks over to the table, takes a seat)* Only problem is John's at home, all broken up. I'll take the special.

CHUCK   *(closes the menu)* Make that two. *(to SAM)* Who was the last to see her?

ROSIE   *(walking back to the counter)* Goto-san says she saw Lily go to the dressing room.

SAM   That was about six thirty. Goto-san left a few minutes later.

ROSIE   And nobody see her again.

CHUCK   What about the room?

SAM   The forensic boys had combed the joint by the time I got there.

CHUCK   I got some friends down at the labs.

SAM   You better get on them.

ROSIE   *(returning to the table to serve the food)* You think maybe somebody kidnap Lily?

SAM   That's possible, plenty of henna hakujin *[crazy white guys]* running loose, eh?

CHUCK   Looks good, Rosie.

ROSIE   Thank you, Chuck-san. You should come here more often. I cook plenty for you too.

SAM   He's on a diet.

ROSIE   Honto? *[Really?]*

SAM   Highballs and caviar at Chez Victor's.

ROSIE   Samu, you're pulling my leg again.

SAM   I've been meaning to do that for a long time. *(He taps ROSIE on the behind.)*

ROSIE   Oh Samu, kichigai neh! *[you are kinky!]* *(She walks back to the counter.)*

SAM   By the way, you remember that guy here this morning?

ROSIE   Ha *[Yes]*, he come here sometime. He was at the bazaar.

CHUCK   Got a suspect?

SAM   Just a hunch, about the ides note.

CHUCK   Oh yeah?

SAM   He was sitting right there when I came in this morning.

CHUCK   How'd he stuff the note in your hat?

SAM   He paused at the rack before he walked out, plenty of time to plant it.

CHUCK   You know the guy, Rosie?

ROSIE   He call himself Gold something… speak very nice nihongo *[Japanese]*.

SAM   Yeah, so I noticed.

CHUCK   Wouldn't be Goldfinger, would it? *(laughs)*

SAM   Go ahead and chuckle, Chuck, I'll bet on my hunch.

       NANCY WING enters with her umbrella.

NANCY   Well, we meet again.

SAM   You're on the job rain or shine, eh kid? *(CHUCK stands up.)*

NANCY   *(taking off her coat)* Don't let me interrupt you, I just dropped by for coffee.

CHUCK   *(to SAM)* You been holding out on me partner.

SAM   That's what you think.

CHUCK   Every man for himself, eh? *(He stands up.)* Hi, I'm Chuck Chan, Sam's legal advisor.

NANCY   Coffee please. I'm Nancy Wing, a reporter for the *Sun*.

CHUCK   Oh, I see.

NANCY   What?

CHUCK   Why Sam didn't introduce us.

NANCY   I'm sure he has his reasons. *(She sits in CHUCK's chair.)*

CHUCK   I call them grudges. He doesn't trust the press. *(He gets a third chair.)*

NANCY   So I notice.

CHUCK   Wing hmmm, you related to Wing Sum Chow by any chance?

NANCY   He's my great uncle.

CHUCK   Now there's a hell of a pioneer. I used to run into him down at the King Hong Café.

NANCY   I don't know him very well.

CHUCK   I haven't seen you in Chinatown, have I?

NANCY   It's not my usual beat, I grew up in Richmond… and just because I'm Chinese—

SAM   Don't mean nothin', right kid?

NANCY   Well it doesn't mean I hang out on Pender Street.

SAM   Wouldn't want to attract the wrong kind of attention, eh?

NANCY   You know, you have a way of saying things that can get on someone's nerves.

CHUCK   Don't worry about Sam here, that's just his sense of humour.

NANCY   I don't hear anyone laughing.

CHUCK   That's because it's not very funny…. Uh, you're new at the *Sun*?

NANCY   I started in January.

SAM   *(getting up)* Gochiso, *[Thanks,]* Rosie.

ROSIE   Domo Samu. *[Oh, thank you.]*

NANCY   Leaving already?

SAM   I got business to take care of.

CHUCK   You gonna talk to the other contestants?

SAM   Yeah.

NANCY   Might as well save your breath.

CHUCK   They disappear too?

NANCY   They're only talking to the police.

SAM   They didn't welcome you with open arms, eh?

NANCY   I suppose you know them personally.

SAM   Better still, I know their parents…. See you later, Rosie. *(SAM exits.)*

CHUCK   I got a cousin in Richmond. You know a Harry Chan?

NANCY   *(gets up)* There are a hundred Chans in Richmond.

CHUCK   Yeah…. You didn't touch your coffee.

NANCY   You can have it…. I gotta run.

CHUCK   Say, do you like Japanese food?

ROSIE   *(clearing table)* You want eat again?

NANCY   Thanks… but no thanks.

> *NANCY exits.*

CHUCK   *(puts on his coat)* Can't win 'em all, eh Rosie?

> *CHUCK exits and ROSIE goes out the kitchen curtain as the lights cross-fade to SAM's office where he's typing at his desk.*

SAM   The other girls talked all right, but they didn't have much to say. I wasn't worried because there were plenty of other witnesses to check out. There was always the chance that a lunatic had snatched the queen, but if the ides note was a threat to keep me off the case, then the disappearance was part of a bigger deal.

> *There is a knock on the door and NANCY enters.*

NANCY   Anybody home?

SAM   Look kid, don't you ever let up?

NANCY   I can't. This case is getting on my nerves.

SAM   It's getting on mine too.

NANCY   I saw the light on and wanted to check with you about the other contestants.

SAM   We partners or something?

NANCY   Couldn't we cut the sarcasm a little?

SAM   Look kid, ain't it a bit late for you to be out on the streets?

NANCY   I can take care of myself.

SAM   You put up a tough front, kid, but muggers take ya from behind. *(He gets himself a drink.)*

NANCY   I get the feeling your ideas about women are a bit dated.

SAM   Maybe they are, I gave up on them a while ago. *(returns to his desk)*

NANCY   So I've heard.

SAM   You been pumping Rosie or Chuck?

NANCY   It doesn't take much to get them going on you.

SAM   Yeah, well I better set them straight about talking to strangers.

NANCY   They went on and on about the crimes you've solved and how you didn't charge much.

SAM   I don't need a press agent, kid.

NANCY   I could do an article on the way you broke up the teenage gang snatching purses from seniors around here.

SAM   Forget it, it was just a couple of dumb kids.

NANCY   Aren't you interested in getting any credit for your work?

SAM   Word of mouth goes far enough down here.

NANCY   Have it your way.

SAM   That's the way I like it.

NANCY   *(pause)* I bet this late-night routine wasn't too popular with your wife.

SAM   My ex-wife…. Now, if the interview is over.

NANCY   You're always trying to get rid of me. I mean, for two days you've acted like I had some social disease. *(She sits in the client's chair.)*

SAM   I ain't used to having a woman waltz in here and shoot from the hip.

NANCY   What do you want, bound feet?

SAM   That's up to you, kid, but you'd get a lot further by paying a bit of respect to your elders.

NANCY   You're not that old, Sam. I mean, you don't look that old.

SAM   Thanks. *(finishes the drink)* I'm well-preserved.

NANCY   I get along with Chuck and I think Rosie even likes me.

SAM   Chuck's just a smooth talker and Rosie's the kind that takes in stray cats, so it's no use tryin' to use them to get to me.

NANCY   I'm not tryin' to get to you.

SAM   Then what have you been doing on my tail?

NANCY   I'm a reporter, and you're the only one who's got a handle on this case. At least this is the only place I can get my foot in the damn door!

SAM   It's tough getting inside when they know you want to get the story out there, eh? These people talk to me because they know I'll deal with it quietly.

NANCY   Do it the Japanese way?

SAM   *(walks to the window)* Think what you like, kid.

NANCY   But I'm trying to help. Getting the facts to the public can help. Somebody might read the story and have something click.

SAM   The only click the papers want to hear is the nickel in the slot, and they've never been fussy about the facts.

NANCY   You're paranoid. The whole community is paranoid!

SAM   We've been screwed by your kind before.

NANCY   Is that my fault?

SAM   You're only a stringer, kid. The editors call the shots.

NANCY   *(gets up to leave)* Thanks for nothing.

SAM   *(looking out the window)* Turn out the light.

NANCY   Huh?

> *She turns out the light. Window-shattering sound and SAM falls backward as if hit by a bullet. Then the sound of footsteps in the hall.*

Sam!

> *MACKENZIE and KADOTA rush into the office.*

MACKENZIE   Don't move!

NANCY   It's Sam, he's hit! *(She kneels by him.)*

KADOTA   Get the lights on!

MACKENZIE   Where's the switch?

NANCY   By the door, hurry, somebody call an ambulance!

SAM   No, I'm all right! I'm only cut.

KADOTA   *(turns on the light)* Mackenzie, check outside.

MACKENZIE   Aye, Captain.

> *He exits.*

KADOTA   You better get your nose fixed. *(He goes to the window.)*

SAM   *(sits in the chair, head back)* You should'a told me ya had the joint staked out. I'd've sent out for coffee and doughnuts.

KADOTA   I told you we'd be around.

NANCY   Here, let me help. *(She goes to the sink to get a wet cloth.)*

SAM   Thanks. *(He takes the cloth and wipes his nose.)*

KADOTA   Who did it, Sam?

SAM   That's confidential, Kenji.

KADOTA   You gotta play tough guy, nah?

SAM   I'll live longer that way… *(to NANCY)* Thanks…. So what have you got on the Kudo case? *(SAM gets up to walk to the sink and puts a bandage on his nose.)*

KADOTA   Nothing. A hundred witnesses and my own squad men at the scene, and the damn queen disappears!

SAM   Funny, eh?

KADOTA   Maybe people are talking to you. You've been down here long enough.

SAM   You make it sound like doing time.

KADOTA   Are you going anywhere?

SAM   I never did have your ambition, Kenji. You must be bucking for another citation.

KADOTA   You're so clever, nah?

SAM   Just my way of staying sane.

KADOTA   Well I'm telling you, Sam, if you're withholding evidence I'll make you pay for it.

SAM   You're getting edgy.

KADOTA   Maybe I am, just watch out.

          MACKENZIE returns.

MACKENZIE   Not a blasted thing to report, Captain. I did na see a shadow.

SAM   That's tough at night, eh Sarge?

MACKENZIE   Blimey, Captain, I'm gonna—

KADOTA   Call the lab boys, I want this place dusted for the bullet.

SAM   Maybe they could clean out my drawers, too.

MACKENZIE   Why don't we run Sammy here downtown. He's holding out on us, ain't he? I can tell that.

KADOTA   You can't tell shit from gravy, Mackenzie. Now get on the phone.

MACKENZIE   Now that's a bit much, Captain. There's no call to play high and mighty with me.

KADOTA   Who's running this investigation anyway?

MACKENZIE   I was just speaking me mind!

SAM   *(sitting down at the desk)* You two considered seeing a counsellor?

KADOTA   Mackenzie, do your job.

MACKENZIE   *(pause)* Aye Captain, I'll do a job. *(He picks up the phone.)*

SAM   Tough getting decent help these days, eh?

KADOTA   You keep quiet.

SAM   Sure.

MACKENZIE   Mackenzie here.

KADOTA   Man can't think with all that yapping going on.

SAM   So, how's Superintendent Jameson?

KADOTA   What?

MACKENZIE   Could yuh send over the lads from the lab?

SAM   I heard he paid you a visit today.

KADOTA   So what?

MACKENZIE   Sniper fire.

SAM   Heard he wanted to see how you were handling the natives.

MACKENZIE   Right, over at Shikaze's office.

KADOTA   He gave me his solid support.

SAM   And forty-eight hours.

KADOTA   You got big ears.

MACKENZIE   What's that?

SAM   Let's say I got friends…. What happens if you don't solve the case?

KADOTA   What do you mean?

MACKENZIE   Don't know, lad.

SAM   I heard you might get transferred to the vice squad. Who knows, we could be covering the same keyholes.

KADOTA   You're such a smart guy, nah?

MACKENZIE   Aye, you're right there.

SAM   Not me, Kenbo. I didn't finish cadet school, remember?

KADOTA   Yakamashi! *[Shut up!]*

MACKENZIE   *(hanging up the phone)* Captain?

KADOTA   Now what, Mackenzie?

MACKENZIE   They're on the way.

NANCY   Same for me, boys. *(She heads for the door.)*

SAM   Thanks for the nose job.

NANCY   Anytime.

KADOTA   You better not print anything you just heard.

NANCY   I won't, if I don't make my deadline.

           NANCY exits.

KADOTA   Let's go.

> *KADOTA and MACKENZIE exit. Lights come down to spot on SAM at his desk.*

SAM　The lab boys kept me up all night, turning the joint inside out. I showed them where the slug was buried, but they had to touch everything else too. Somebody was jumping the gun on the ides, and that was fine by me, 'cause nervous guys make mistakes and that's how I nail them. I spent the next twenty-four hours questioning every possible witness at the bazaar. It looked like a dead-end street till Rosie tipped me to a Mrs. Omoto.

> *Lights cross-fade to ROSIE's café. SAM enters as ROSIE prepares to take food out.*

Hi Rosie.

ROSIE　Ah Samu, can you watch café for me?

SAM　Sure, I always wanted to be a waiter.

ROSIE　Haha... domo.... Itekimasu. *[Thanks.... I'm going.]*

> *She exits and a beat later CHUCK enters.*

CHUCK　Hey, I heard you had a close call the other night.

SAM　Yeah, seems like everybody is trying to take care of me.

CHUCK　You bring out the urge in people.

SAM　Must be, huh?

CHUCK　*(goes to the counter)* Where's Rosie?

SAM　Running breakfast to a few seniors down the street.

CHUCK　Any cracks in the mystery? *(He goes behind the counter to get coffee.)*

SAM　I got a Mrs. Omoto who says she thinks she saw a hakujin man walk into the dressing room about six-thirty.

CHUCK　She thinks she saw?

SAM　The men's room is the next door down the hall. She can't recall which one he went in.

CHUCK　You know that won't stand up in court. *(returns to sit at the table)*

SAM　She's eighty-two with weak eyes and a bad memory.

CHUCK　Where'd you dig her up?

SAM　Through Rosie.

CHUCK　You ought'a put her on the payroll.

SAM　Yeah. *(pause)* You got the rundown on the other two cops at the bazaar?

CHUCK   Yeah, Jeff Hori is a sansei from Steveston. He just married his high-school sweetheart and talks like a young Kadota.

SAM   Another token, huh?

CHUCK   The flip side is Rolf Pendersen. His nickname is "The Swinging Swede" 'cause he likes to play Tarzan with the women.

SAM   Mrs. Omoto said the guy was big so Pendersen could be our man.

        NANCY WING enters.

NANCY   Well how goes the dynamic duo?

CHUCK   *(getting up to let her sit down)* That was some story in yesterday's paper.

NANCY   The public's got a right to know when the mayor's playing politics with ethnic issues.

SAM   From ghettoes to ethnic issues, eh kid? You're movin' fast.

NANCY   I'm doing my homework.

CHUCK   You've got the mayor and the superintendent dodging the media.

SAM   You may not have any friends soon.

NANCY   I'm not in this to make friends.

SAM   Pretty hard-nosed about it, aren't ya?

NANCY   How's yours?

SAM   It's still here.

NANCY   That's nice to see. It'd be difficult snooping around without one, wouldn't it?

SAM   Wouldn't know, I never tried it that way.

        ROSIE enters carrying an empty tray.

ROSIE   Ah, ohayo *[Good morning]*.

CHUCK   Hi Rosie.

ROSIE   Oh Nancy-chan, you looks so pretty, neh Chuck-san?

CHUCK   Sure Rosie…

NANCY   Coffee please.

        ROSIE exits to the kitchen.

SAM   *(to CHUCK)* Did Pendersen mention going to the john?

CHUCK   Yeah, he even said he bumped into Mackenzie on the way out.

NANCY   What are you getting at?

SAM   Nothin'.

CHUCK   By the way, the lab boys found traces of Shiseido face powder in the closet, the same type Lily used.

NANCY   You mean somebody might have put her there temporarily?

ROSIE enters with coffee for NANCY.

ROSIE   Who put Lily there?

SAM   If we knew that we'd all be celebrating.

ROSIE   I hope we celebrate sugu *[soon]*, neh? Everybody is crazy talking about Miss Lily Kudo…. Oh Samu, did you talk to Omoto-san?

SAM   Oh yeah, thanks.

NANCY   Who's Omoto-san?

SAM   A ninety-year-old issei widow.

ROSIE   *(returning to the kitchen)* Hachi ju ni. *[Eighty-two.]*

SAM   Eighty-two then.

NANCY   She know something, Rosie?

SAM   She sees things nobody else does.

NANCY   She a psychic?

SAM   Could be.

NANCY   Maybe I better check her out for myself, seeing as we're being so cryptic this morning.

SAM   Be my guest.

NANCY   You know where she lives, Rosie?

ROSIE   Hai, at the Lion Hotel, down the street. Be careful-yo, it's so kusai *[smelly]* in there, and full of junk. There's no room to sit down.

NANCY   Thanks, Rosie. Excuse me, boys, I got a story to cover.

NANCY exits.

CHUCK   She doesn't wait for anybody, does she?

SAM   You tryin' to make time with her?

CHUCK   You kidding? She hasn't got any to spare.

SAM   It'll take her some time to figure out Mrs. Omoto's story. The old lady doesn't speak a word of English.

GOLDBERG enters and takes a seat at the counter.

ROSIE   Ohayo gozaimasu. Irrasshaimasse. *[Good morning and welcome.]*

GOLDBERG   Ohayo gozaimasu. Ochazuke kudasai. *[Good morning. Rice with tea please.]*

>   *ROSIE exits to the kitchen.*

SAM   That's some fancy Japanese.

GOLDBERG   Sumimasen? *[Excuse me?]*

SAM   You speak English, buddy?

GOLDBERG   Oh yes, my name's Goldberg. I'm a Japanese specialist.

SAM   Fascinating, ain't we.

GOLDBERG   Well... yes, Japanese is. It has a certain simplicity and then yet the most subtle complexity.

SAM   So you're into things Japanese, eh?

GOLDBERG   I appreciate refinement.

SAM   How'd you like the Cherry Blossom Bazaar?

GOLDBERG   Oh, charming, not an authentic Japanese ritual, of course.

SAM   Chow mein and plastic lanterns, eh?

GOLDBERG   Unfortunately, but I do like to speak to the old people.

SAM   *(getting up)* By the way, you ever heard of the ides of March?

GOLDBERG   The what?

SAM   The ides of March.

GOLDBERG   That's not Japanese.

SAM   You're right there, buddy. *(walks toward GOLDBERG)*

GOLDBERG   Well I believe it's some sort of ancient pagan ritual.

SAM   Like kidnapping queens?

GOLDBERG   I don't know what—

SAM   And planting threats?

GOLDBERG   This is absurd!

SAM   *(face to face)* You wouldn't know anything about this here note, would ya?

GOLDBERG   What's the meaning of this?

SAM   Just what I want to know.

GOLDBERG   But I don't even know what it says.

SAM   What're ya gettin' nervous about?

GOLDBERG   I don't know.

SAM   Ya said that before.

CHUCK   Take it easy, Sam.

>   *ROSIE returns with a tray of food.*

GOLDBERG   *(getting up)* Uh, domo arigato *[thank you]*, I've got to be going.

>   *GOLDBERG exits.*

CHUCK   The guy doesn't even look like a kidnapper.

SAM   You tryin' to tell me something, Chuck?

CHUCK   I got a feeling the guy's okay.

SAM   Yeah, well I don't like the feeling I'm getting.

CHUCK   Maybe it's just coincidence.

SAM   What is?

CHUCK   The ides note and Lily's disappearance.

SAM   Could be, but that's not the way I see it.

CHUCK   Yeah, well it's your business, eh? *(gets ready to go)* Come to think of it, I better take care of my own.

SAM   You in a hurry?

CHUCK   Got a date with a half-million bucks.

SAM   Don't let me hold you up.

CHUCK   I'll drop by tomorrow…. Bye Rosie.

>   *CHUCK exits. Lights lower to black with only a spotlight on SAM at the table.*

SAM   *(to the audience)* The pieces were beginning to fall into place. The Omoto-san tip pointed at Pendersen but I still figured Goldberg was the wild card in the deck. I needed to nail one of them soon, 'cause I didn't want to face the ides without the kidnapper in my hands. So I figured it was time to take a walk downtown, into the heart of the jungle.

>   *SAM exits out the café door.*

>   *Blackout.*

ACT TWO

The Dover Inn, an English-style pub, in the same set as ROSIE's with all of her café items removed. There is a noisy pub soundtrack. SAM enters through the door.

SAM   I dropped by the Dover Inn, where Pendersen hung out. The joint was jumpin', so I eased myself into the crowd and waited for the Swingin' Swede to show up.

SAM takes a seat at the counter. MACKENZIE enters through the door and he walks to downstage left, not seeing SAM, and addresses the audience.

MACKENZIE   Hello lads, ready for the meetin' tonight? Good, the super'll give yuh a fine talk tonight, take me word for that... *(looks at his watch)* We better hurry though, eh? Drink up, we got plenty to do.

MACKENZIE exits out the curtain.

SAM   *(to the audience)* Mackenzie was up to no good, so I decided to tail him instead of waiting for Pendersen.

SAM exits out the curtain and the lights go to black with dramatic music. Lights come up in alley and SAM appears looking in a window in the stage left wall.

I followed the footsteps into a back alley. They were holding a meeting in a warehouse across the way. I was about to check out the action when I realized I wasn't alone.

Sound of footsteps. SAM backs away from the spotlight into the shadows and NANCY appears at the extreme right and begins walking cautiously left across the stage. SAM grabs her from behind.

Don't breathe or I'll bust yer arm.

NANCY bites into his hand and gives him an elbow in the ribs.

Owww...! Ough.

NANCY turns to swing at SAM who catches her arm and twists it back.

NANCY   Jesus, Sam, whose side are you on?

SAM   *(holding her hand)* You want to get hurt, kid?

NANCY   I wasn't planning on it.

SAM   That's quite a set of molars you got there.

NANCY   You scared me.

SAM   Shhhh…

> *SAM and NANCY look in the window as the SUPERINTENDENT and MACKENZIE enter from stage right and stop downstage right.*

SUPERINTENDENT   Everything shipshape?

MACKENZIE   Aye sir, I got them good and roused.

SUPERINTENDENT   How many lads?

MACKENZIE   Forty, sir.

SUPERINTENDENT   Good enough. Forty sturdy blokes could turn this city into a battlefield, right Sergeant?

MACKENZIE   Right sir.

SUPERINTENDENT   Right then, here we go.

> *He walks to centre stage, addressing the audience as if it were a warehouse crowd. He begins low-key and builds to a frenzy.*

Thank you, lads. I think you know who I am and what I stand for. And I know you wouldn't be here if you didn't share the same ideals and hope and faith. I know the thought of losing this land to foreigners gets your blood boiling, as it does mine. I know you're all sturdy blokes, ready, aye ready, to bash a few heads and send them packing across the Pacific. It was bad enough the Japs were allowed to return, but now we're being overrun by these Chinamen. They're taking our jobs, buying our homes, stealin' the very food from our mouths. Why, we don't even have a Chinaman's chance to survive if we don't raise our hands now to drive them out! Aye, this country is sick with yellow fever. They are a disease poisoning our bloodstream. And we are the saviours, the white blood cells, the first line of defence and the last hope of civilization! We are the Sons of the Western Guard, and we must drive them out! Drive them out! Now…! Thank you…! Thank you for this covenant of faith. Now let us kneel and give thanks to our Maker for blessing this gathering and your generous donations to the cause…. Thank you, Lord, for bringing our flock together in these troubled times, and bless all those who would be the soldiers of your faith, amen. *(aside to MACKENZIE who has stepped into the background)* Sergeant, pass the trays around and take care of the rest. I've another gathering to attend.

MACKENZIE   Aye sir. *(whispers)* When shall we move the girl?

SUPERINTENDENT   Saturday.

MACKENZIE   Right, sir.

> *MACKENZIE and SUPERINTENDENT exit and the lights cross-fade to stage left.*

NANCY   Do you know who that is?

SAM   He kicked me out of cadet school.

NANCY   He's a raving lunatic! What a scoop!

SAM   Keep yer shirt on, kid. This one ain't over yet. I'll tail the superintendent and you keep track of Mackenzie.

NANCY   Wait a second.

SAM   Got any suggestions?

NANCY   *(shakes her head)* I'll meet you tomorrow.

SAM   Just don't get caught or print anything I wouldn't, eh?

NANCY   Then what do I do for a living?

SAM   Sneak down back alleys.

> *SAM walks to stage right till the lights are black. Then he walks back to the spotlight for the monologue.*

(to the audience) The super slipped out the side door and took off in his limo. I tailed him all over town. He gave his little pep talk in a West Georgia office tower, an east-side factory and a British Properties mansion. *(While he talks, two figures search his office.)* The Sons of the Western Guard were on the move, an army of blue and white collars led by the likes of the superintendent and backed by bigwigs upstairs. The sons of bitches were everywhere and it was obvious that Mackenzie's remark meant they'd kidnapped the girl. I headed back to the office to check their file and think about their scheme.

> *The spotlight goes to black. Lights cross-fade to the office in low light as SAM enters, his hand groping on wall in the dark for the light switch.*

Goddamn switch.

> *He walks in the dark toward his desk. Two figures in ski masks jump SAM in the dark. One is MACKENZIE and the other can be the SUPERINTENDENT as a thug.*

MACKENZIE   Take that, yuh yellow bastard!

THUG   We'll give ya more than a bleedin' nose this time!

> *They beat SAM and throw him into his chair.*

MACKENZIE   Where yuh been, Sammy?

SAM   To see the queen, boys.

THUG   *(MACKENZIE hits SAM.)* Got any more smart answers?

SAM   *(pause)* Got any more questions?

MACKENZIE   Right, where's yer Kudo file?

SAM   This the Hong Kong Tong connection?

MACKENZIE   *(He hits SAM.)* Yuh best pay attention to me questions, Sammy, otherwise yuh might get hurt.

SAM   Bit early for the ides ain't it?

MACKENZIE   Yer blabbering again, Sammy. *(hits SAM)* Now where's the Kudo file?

SAM   *(pause)* The desk… bottom drawer.

MACKENZIE   Glad to see yuh show some common sense, Sammy. *(MACKENZIE goes to the desk and uses a flashlight to check the file.)* Nothin' here…. So yuh don't know a bloomin' thing yet, eh… not a bit of evidence to show for all yer snoopin' around. Why, I'm a bit disappointed, yuh know…. I was hopin' we'd have a reason to put yuh away.

SAM   Tough luck, eh?

MACKENZIE   *(hits SAM)* Ya should wise up Sammy and take a trip to yer homeland.

> MACKENZIE and THUG beat SAM then exit out the door.

> Lights fade to black then come up again on the office. It is the next morning. SAM gets up slowly and walks to the sink. There's a knock on the door.

SAM   Come on in.

> CHUCK enters.

Glad you could make it.

CHUCK   Somebody really did a number on you, eh?

SAM   Yeah, I feel like a bruised banana. *(He sits down.)*

CHUCK   Who did it?

SAM   *(getting himself a drink)* Mackenzie and a friend on a midnight ride.

CHUCK   What the hell was he after?

SAM   My Kudo file…. Wasn't much there so they tried a bit of muscle on me.

CHUCK   What's goin' on, Sam?

SAM   Plenty…. We hit the jackpot last night. The superintendent, Mackenzie and probably Pendersen are members of the Sons of the Western Guard.

CHUCK   You saying the Sons kidnapped the queen?

SAM   They were talking about moving the girl tomorrow.

CHUCK   That's gonna be tough to prove in court. You'll need the girl and plenty more.

SAM   That's where you come in, partner. Can you get a tail on Pendersen?

CHUCK   No problem.

SAM   I've heard Mackenzie and him are taking a fishing trip this weekend. It's a cover to move the girl, so I'm gonna get Kadota to keep Mackenzie in town. Meanwhile, we hope Pendersen leads you to the girl.

CHUCK   You better hope they don't get suspicious.

SAM   I'm gonna need a few bugs in here too.

CHUCK   I can get them set up this afternoon. What you got in mind?

SAM   Round two with Mackenzie tomorrow, where we get in our licks before the ides. *(He goes back to the desk.)*

CHUCK   You solve that one yet?

SAM   Not quite, but I figure we'll settle that tomorrow. How about your million-dollar divorce?

CHUCK   Oh fine, hubby wants to settle out of court, and we're in the money.

SAM   How'd you swing that?

CHUCK   We caught him red-faced with a babe in high heels and handcuffs.

SAM   He a cop?

CHUCK   No, a judge.

SAM   They got more weirdos up there than down here.

CHUCK   You might be right. *(He walks to the window.)* Nancy come by?

SAM   I'm expecting her. You looking for her?

CHUCK   Not particularly…. How are you two doing?

SAM   I was just gonna ask you that.

CHUCK   She's not interested in me.

SAM   I thought you were the big-game hunter.

CHUCK   She's sweet on you, Sam.

SAM   I'm old enough to be her father.

CHUCK   That's what I said.

SAM   Huh?

CHUCK   You've been around a long time.

SAM   Yeah.

CHUCK   She's sharp though. Different kind of woman.

SAM   I only know one kind.

CHUCK   You've been alone too long. Times have changed, so have the women.

SAM   I hadn't noticed.

CHUCK   You're still playing the rock, eh?

SAM   I've been alone all my life, even when I was married. The kid doesn't know me from nobody. Maybe she's got some nerve.

CHUCK   You're finally showing some respect.

SAM   But she's still hustling me for the big scoop.

CHUCK   *(He opens the briefcase and takes out a bottle of Canadian Club.)* You're as hard bitten as they come. Maybe this will soften you up.

SAM   Thanks... for the bottle.

CHUCK   *(walking to the door)* I'll get on the bugs and the tail... and you give my regards to Nancy.

      CHUCK exits.

SAM   *(to the audience as he sits at his desk)* You know, I had a hunch the kid was after more than one scoop. But the trouble with women is that they start out looking up to ya, then they move in and end up overhauling yer joint. They tell ya smokin's bad for yer lungs and sleeping in bed is good for yer back. I'd seen it all before, and if that's what the kid was after, she was in for a surprise. *(SAM picks up the phone to make a call.)* Captain Kadota please.... It's Sam Shikaze.... He's on his way over, eh? Fine... *(knock on the door)* Come on in.

      KADOTA enters.

KADOTA   What happened to you?

SAM   I was entertaining some friends last night.

KADOTA   I bet you've been snooping around, eh? And somebody jumped you.

SAM   Yeah, a pair of kangaroos.

KADOTA   I told you to let us do the job.

SAM   You already did.

KADOTA   Did what?

SAM   Nothin'.

KADOTA   You never learn, do you?

SAM   Oh, I'm learnin' plenty, Kenji.

KADOTA   What do you know?

SAM   Enough to get myself a citation.

KADOTA   Don't joke, Sam.

SAM   Would I kid you?

KADOTA   I'll give you a break. We put our evidence together and I'll make sure you get some credit in this case.

SAM   That's generous of you, 'specially with me holding all the aces.

KADOTA   You're so cool, nah? They shake you up and you're still a wise guy. I come here to make a deal and you laugh in my face.

SAM   Come on, Kenji, my time is short. *(He gets up to look in the file cabinet.)*

KADOTA   Your time? Who do you think you are, some big shot?

SAM   You're burning a short fuse, Kenbo.

KADOTA   I'm a captain, Sam, I got twenty years.

SAM   Don't tell me. *(sits down)*

KADOTA   *(gets up)* You got no idea how hard I worked.

SAM   Sure, I know it was a long haul.

KADOTA   You know! You know how much shit I had to take to make it. Smiling when they called me "Kamikaze Ken," never saying a word when they passed me over for promotions. Twenty years…! Seventeen citations…! I should be a chief inspector by now. The sons of bitches, that mayor and the superintendent. They tell me maybe somebody else can handle this case. Like I was dragging my feet. They give me this look like I'm covering up for the kidnappers. Like I was guilty too!

SAM   That's the way they think.

KADOTA   I don't solve this one and I'm washed up!

SAM   I know.

KADOTA   You know?

SAM   It's written all over your face.

KADOTA   I've sweat blood to make it, Sam, and I'll drag your ass downtown if I have to.

SAM   Don't threaten me, Kenji.

KADOTA   I'll run you through the wringer.

SAM   Chuck'll have me out in no time.

KADOTA   Not this time.

SAM   *(stands up to face KADOTA)* Look Kenji, all these goddamn years you been riding me, telling me I should play by the book, work my way up slowly like you. All these years I've been shrugging off your bullshit. So now that your ass is on the line, where are all the rules and regulations? Didn't you read the fine print where it says twenty years of loyal service don't mean piss in the wind, if you're nihonjin? *[Japanese].* You think they wouldn't put us away again if the chips were down? Don't you know they wrote the book for suckers like you!

KADOTA   Yakamashi! *[shut up]*

SAM   That's right, Kenji, turn it off!

KADOTA   And what have you got to show for your life? Everybody wondering how you live, divorced and working in this crummy joint. You should hear what your buddies really say about you. They call you an oddball... a loser!

SAM   They call me when they need me.

KADOTA   Sure, and later they say you're a weirdo, an embarrassment to us all.

SAM   Least they can't fire me.

KADOTA   You're not worth firing!

SAM   *(sits down)* So why bother with me?

KADOTA   We go back to the war, Sam. Doesn't that count for anything?

SAM   We never had it so good, eh?

KADOTA   What about my wife and my family? What'll I tell my kid?

SAM   Tell him the truth.

KADOTA   But he's a Boy Scout!

SAM   Maybe it's time you grew up.

KADOTA   Jesus, Sam, we're nihonjn *[Japanese]*!

SAM   *(stands)* What the hell does that mean to you? You ain't got the time of day for us, wouldn't be seen down in the dump without a clothespeg on your nose. Couldn't do an old man a favour till your fucking ass is in a sling... then we're "Nihonjin"!

KADOTA   They're putting the screws to me, Sam.

SAM   They always have been.

KADOTA   Don't talk crazy, Sam.... I need your help. *(He slumps into a chair.)* Give me a break.

SAM   *(walks to the desk to pour a shot for KADOTA)* Another break, huh...? Have a shot... *(He puts the bottle down on the desk.)*

KADOTA   Domo. *(He downs the drink in one gulp.)*

SAM   Okay… but ya gotta play the game my way.

KADOTA   *(pause)* Sure.

SAM   *(pause)* Mackenzie's off till Monday, right?

KADOTA   So what? *(SAM pours him another drink.)*

SAM   Never mind. Can you get him on duty tomorrow?

KADOTA   He'll be swearing up and down at me.

SAM   Don't worry about that.

KADOTA   What is this?

SAM   I'm calling the shots, remember? *(sits down at his desk)*

KADOTA   But who's the suspect? Give me a name and I'll pick the guy up myself. *(He stands up.)*

SAM   It ain't that simple. *(pause)* Has Mackenzie ever talked about Shakespeare?

KADOTA   Shakespeare?

SAM   Yeah, the writer.

KADOTA   Which paper he write for?

SAM   He never mentioned the ides of March?

KADOTA   He never talked about that.

SAM   Okay… I want both of you here tomorrow night.

KADOTA   I want the kidnapper, Sam.

SAM   You'll have him.

> KADOTA exits. SAM speaks while sitting at the desk, cross-fade to spot.

Kenji would never understand what was going down. He was the kind that believed the camps were a blessing in disguise. When they made it tougher on him, he put his nose to the wheel and pushed harder. Twenty years and seventeen citations later and they were still screwing him.

> Lights cross-fade back to the office. NANCY enters.

Well, glad to see you didn't get caught.

NANCY   *(staring at his face)* Are you all right?

SAM   I'll live…. You find anything out last night?

NANCY   That cop, Pendersen, showed up later. Mackenzie led them through a few songs and they broke up at eleven. I tailed Mackenzie home and that was it.

SAM   Not quite… but it doesn't matter.

NANCY   What do you mean?

SAM   Nothin'.

NANCY   What did you pick up on the superintendent?

SAM   *(gets up)* He's a busy guy. He had three more meetings to make.

NANCY   You got the names and addresses?

SAM   In my head. *(gets the file from the cabinet)*

NANCY   So give.

SAM   Not yet.

NANCY   Wait a second, I thought we were in this together.

SAM   That's what you thought.

NANCY   Look Sam, I held off today's edition because I thought we had a deal. I was getting a lot of pressure to print something, but I didn't… because I trusted you.

SAM   *(faces NANCY)* Then ya gotta trust me a bit longer.

NANCY   I could still make the Saturday paper.

SAM   Yeah, and blow our chance to scoop the bunch of them.

NANCY   More like blow the case wide open.

SAM   Sure kid, we tell them we got an eighty-two year old widow who's half blind and can't speak English as our key witness. We tell them we saw Sarge and the super at a social-club meeting. Hell, we can claim we heard them talk about moving a girl.

NANCY   Well why not?

SAM   That's hot stuff for a gossip rag like the *Enquirer*, but you better get your lawyers ready for a libel suit. We're close, but not close enough to make the charges stick. We don't nail them good and they cover their tracks better. You think these bruises are bad? Go ahead and break the story. *(sits down)* You may never type again.

NANCY   Don't try'n scare me.

SAM   I'm trying to protect you.

NANCY   So what do we do, sit on our hands till the sun shines around here?

SAM   In forty-eight hours you can deliver the whole scoop in the Monday-morning edition.

NANCY   What's the catch?

SAM   *(holds up his hands)* No strings attached.

NANCY   I got the urge to frisk you.

SAM   Give me a break, kid, I got more important things to take care of.

NANCY   Okay, it's a deal… but that makes us partners, right?

SAM   Sure, you'll have the kidnappers by the ides of March.

NANCY   Ides of March?

SAM   Yeah, you can call it my MO.

NANCY   You're a strange one, Sam. *(MACKENZIE enters.)*

MACKENZIE   Well now, ain't we as cozy as two peas in a pod?

SAM   Thought you had the day off, Sarge?

MACKENZIE   I do. Not like you, eh Sammy? Now when was the last time yuh took a holiday?

SAM   Thirty years ago. We all went to summer camp… in the winter.

MACKENZIE   Aye, well it's a sad thing yuh had to return, eh? Nobody was lookin' forward to seein' your kind around here again. *(sits down)*

SAM   Must have been a big letdown, eh?

NANCY   Jesus, Sam, you gonna put up with that bullshit from this oversized toad!

MACKENZIE   Yuh got a regular firebird for a sugar here.

NANCY   Watch your mouth before I stuff it with a story that'll make you choke.

MACKENZIE   Ah, yuh got another story for us, eh?

SAM   *(gets up)* Yeah, about a good cop who gets set up on the chopping block.

MACKENZIE   You're talking gibberish, Sammy.

SAM   Man serves twenty years on the force and suddenly the force ain't with him anymore. The top dogs tell him to solve a certain case or pack his bags and move down to the vice squad.

MACKENZIE   My heart's bleedin' for yer man, but if he don't know his bloomin' place, then he's gotta learn, ain't he? He can't be civil to the lads he works with, then maybe he's gettin' what's comin' to him.

SAM   You mean his partners are setting him up?

MACKENZIE   Now I didna' say anything like that. Yer puttin' words in me mouth again, turnin' 'em all around till yuh gets what yuh wants, that's it, ain't it?

SAM   *(stalking MACKENZIE)* But you wouldn't blame the partners if they did, would ya?

MACKENZIE   They did nothin' I'm tellin' yuh. And I'm warnin' yuh for the last time, Sammy, keep yer bleedin' nose outta this here case.

SAM   *(sneezes)* Achoo…! Damn nose…. Got a hanky?

MACKENZIE   Sure. *(He hands SAM his hanky.)* Better take care of yer health.

SAM   Beware the ides of March, huh?

MACKENZIE   Yer talking pretty fancy for your kind.

SAM   Too fancy for your kind, eh?

MACKENZIE   I knows me own language better than any foreigner.

SAM   You talkin' about English? *(He switches the hanky with another in his pocket.)*

MACKENZIE   Well now, yuh been very clever so far, and all it's got yuh is a bunch of bruises and funny sayin's.

SAM   *(sitting down)* Some guys think I'm cute.

MACKENZIE   Aye, we all know yuh got enemies.

SAM   Least I can tell my friends from my enemies now. As for you, Mackenzie, *(He extends his hand. When MACKENZIE reaches out, SAM puts the hanky in it.)* thanks for the hanky.

MACKENZIE   So take a tip from me, take some time off and let those marks heal up proper now. *(He stands.)*

SAM   I was hopin' they'd scar, give my mug some character.

MACKENZIE   Yuh never learn, eh Sammy? I go outta me way on me day off to give yuh some sound advice and I get no appreciation at all.

SAM   No use cryin' over spilt milk, Sarge.

MACKENZIE   Aye, I'll leave yuh with yer nursemaid here, and a warning. Why don't yuh save yerself a lot of trouble and take a long trip back to your homeland.

SAM   Beat the rush back, eh?

MACKENZIE   Yuh ken me words, eh…? Then yuh best take me advice.

    MACKENZIE exits.

NANCY   Sorry I almost blew our hand, but the goddamn nerve! *(turns away)* I bet he's even using the kidnapping to get rid of the captain, and that's only the beginning.

SAM   Things are coming together, eh kid?

NANCY   Look, I'm not a kid. Maybe I am new at this business, and I've made my share of mistakes, but I've figured some things out for myself.

SAM   Yeah, you've come a long way.

NANCY (*pause*) I never thought I'd hear that from you…

SAM You're doin' all right.

NANCY (*walking toward SAM*) I feel like I've touched a soft spot in the bedrock.

SAM Why don't we just stick to the story, you know, keep it simple.

NANCY I didn't mean to distract you… but don't you ever take time off? Just to relax and talk about things… or even watch TV?

SAM Yeah, at home.

NANCY But you're never there.

SAM Okay Nancy, what's on your mind?

NANCY (*walking away*) Jesus Sam, do you have to be so abrupt? Is everything so cut and dry for you?

SAM (*pause*) My wife said I'd dried up, that living with me was like dying of thirst in the desert.

NANCY She didn't pull any punches, did she?

SAM I heard a lot worse.

NANCY But it doesn't have to be that way.

SAM No, it didn't.

NANCY I mean, you care about people like Rosie and Chuck.

SAM That's different.

NANCY It's only another way of caring. Maybe it wasn't your fault. Maybe it was the relationship, or your wife.

SAM She had problems all right, but I was the biggest one. She wanted to entertain friends and take long vacations, have a big house in Shaughnessy with me playing the breadwinner. She had plans to turn me into a somebody.

NANCY I've talked to plenty of people around here, and they all look up to you. Not those stuffed-shirt nisei hiding out in the suburbs, but the people who live around here. You can't measure that in dollars and cents. Your wife couldn't understand what you were doing!

SAM So what are you getting worked up about?

NANCY I don't know.

SAM What'd I do now?

NANCY Nothing… that's the problem. Don't you feel anything through that thick skin of yours?

SAM Yeah, I've been here before…. I got a knack for upsetting women.

NANCY   Jesus Christ!

SAM   Look, Nancy, you're an attractive young woman.

NANCY   You sound like somebody's uncle.... Sam... I care about you.

SAM   *(pause)* Yeah, *(pause)* I could see you comin' a mile away. You were so busy winding yourself up for the big romance that you forgot one thing, you don't know me from nobody. To you I'm somebody who looks good in a back alley when you're scared. You want a hero but you're just setting yourself up for the fall.

NANCY   That's my business, Sam. You think you're the first guy in my life? I've been around and I can take care of myself. Maybe I am looking for a hero, somebody with character.... Who the hell isn't!

SAM   That makes great copy, kid, but what else have I got? A one-room walk-up with no closet space? You want to listen to music on a beat-up old radio? Make out on a lumpy mattress? You think we got a chance of lastin' five minutes beyond this case?

NANCY   It doesn't matter. I've got my own career and space. We don't have to live together. ·

SAM   You're the liberated type, eh?

NANCY   Does it have to be love and marriage, or love 'em and leave 'em? Isn't there room in your life for a mature relationship between consenting adults?

SAM   That was a mouthful, kid, and maybe that's your style, but I got my own way of doin' things.

NANCY   I can see that, but isn't there any room for the two of us to share?

SAM   Give me a breather, kid, we gotta think about this first.

NANCY   At least you're talking "we" now.

SAM   Why me? You could have your pick of the hotshots downtown. Chuck could go for you, and he's more your age.

NANCY   I'm looking for someone older, someone who's been around, knows the score the way you do.

SAM   What do you want, a father?

NANCY   That's not what I had in mind.

SAM   I'm getting nervous, kid.

NANCY   I mean it. You don't want or need the things most guys do to feel good about themselves. You don't need a flashy car or a new office or fancy women to stroke your ego. You don't need things to protect you from the world outside. You're different, you're weird.... You're down here on Powell Street because you want to be. You're not hiding out, you're just living here, like somebody who doesn't care if the world passes him by because the world isn't going anywhere!

SAM   Who would've believed this, eh? An old guy like me makin' time with someone like you.

NANCY   Sam, I'm gonna scream if you call yourself old again. You're in the prime of your life.

SAM   Maybe I'd rather not think about that.

NANCY   Why not?

SAM   *(pause)* 'Cause you start lookin' over your shoulder at how easy it used to be. You turn forty and you're still alone, and suddenly the old hot plate doesn't heat up enough to boil water. You get up and stare at the walls around you and wonder what's the use. You want to know why I spend all my time here? 'Cause this is where I live, this is what I call home…. This is all I got.

NANCY   Sam…

SAM   You want to know where these bruises came from? A couple of goons jumped me, right here in my own goddamned office! Twenty years ago I would have wiped the floor with their asses… and last night they kicked mine. *(pause)* The prime of life? Who're you kidding? It's the edge, and when you look out there it's dark, and fear turns your insides.

NANCY   But you don't change. You just go on.

SAM   You're too young to understand.

NANCY   You're not afraid of growing old alone. You're afraid of me, afraid of having to wake up and feel again. You want to go out like some dirty old butt! Look at you, look at this place! You've grown comfortable here, surrounded by "the community," by Mrs. Tanaka and her crazy son, by old-man Shimizu and his lost wallets, by Mr. Kudo and his missing daughter. You look at me and all you see is trouble, somebody who doesn't fit into your little world!

SAM   What the hell do you want?

NANCY   You! The guy that calls his own shots.

SAM   *(pause)* I don't know, it's been a long time. *(He walks to the spotlight.)*

NANCY   *(She walks up behind him.)* Not that long. *(pause)* You know you're pretty good-looking when you get going.

> Office lights come down as the spotlight comes up on them. SAM reaches out and pulls NANCY to him.

SAM   You don't let up… do you? *(They kiss as the music begins.)*

NANCY   I like to think I get my man.

SAM   You and the Mounted Police, eh?

NANCY   They got nothing on me.

SAM   Well you just about got this one.

NANCY   That's not good enough.

SAM   All right, I give up…

> *They kiss. The music continues as they exit out the office door. The lights go to black. A moment in darkness. A light comes up in the office and SAM enters.*

(to the audience) The kid was as good as her word. We started out in the office and ended up at her joint. It wasn't so bad after all. The only problem was we blew the rest of the afternoon and night. I figured the morning after was going to be rough, but the kid made a decent bowl of juk *[rice gruel]* to settle my insides. *(pause)* I dropped by the labs that afternoon to have them run a few tests on Mackenzie's hanky. If my hunch was right, the showdown wasn't gonna wait for the ides.

> *NANCY enters.*

NANCY   I still think we should go after the superintendent.

SAM   But Sarge is the weak link.

NANCY   And who's taking care of the queen?

SAM   Chuck is.

NANCY   What's that? *(looking at what SAM's working at)*

SAM   A bug, so just remember your lines and we'll nail his ass.

> *There is a knock on the door and MACKENZIE and KADOTA enter.*

KADOTA   Evening, Sam.

SAM   Evening, boys.

MACKENZIE   What's going on? I had a holiday comin' to me. I ought'a be out fishin' right now.

SAM   Hard-working Japanese don't believe in holidays. Right, Kenji?

MACKENZIE   What's yer game, Sammy?

SAM   I've decided to come clean.

KADOTA   Right, Sam.

MACKENZIE   Well ain't that a change? Tough guy turns law-abiding citizen. Yer sweetheart put yuh up to this?

SAM   Not this time, Sarge.

NANCY   You see, Mackenzie, we think Pendersen did it.

KADOTA   Pendersen?

MACKENZIE   Yer off the mark there. He's an honest sort of bloke if ever there was one. Why he's my drinkin' mate, and we was supposed to go fishin' together.

KADOTA   You know what you're sayin', Sam?

MACKENZIE   And how could he 'ave done it? We was there together with that Jeff Hori. Look to yer own kind, why don't cha! Now there's a sneakin' sort. Always smilin' and real quiet like. Walks like a cat, can't hardly hear him come up behind yuh. Can't drink without turnin' all red. Now he'd have a reason to snatch the queen.

NANCY   He had relatives at the bazaar who'll swear they were talking to him all the time.

MACKENZIE   How can yuh take their word for that? They're the same kin, ain't they?

SAM   Witnesses say Pendersen went to the john about six-thirty.

MACKENZIE   So now it's a crime to go to the convenience.

NANCY   He used the washroom as a cover. On his way out, after he ran into you, he ducked into the dressing room.

MACKENZIE   But the girl didn't scream.

SAM   Why would she, he was a cop.

MACKENZIE   Then I suppose he charmed her into a Houdini act.

SAM   That's where the hanky comes in. *(SAM pulls out a hanky in a plastic baggie.)*

MACKENZIE   Huh?

SAM   We figure it belongs to Pendersen. The lab tests show traces of ether and face powder. The ether to knock the girl out and the face powder matches the type she used. Then he puts her in the closet. *(He puts the hanky back in his pocket.)*

KADOTA   Honto! *[Really!]*

MACKENZIE   Very clever, Sammy. I always said yuh was the one to watch. But what next?

SAM   Everybody, including Pendersen, leaves. The bazaar is over, the father thinks the boyfriend took her home. All is quiet in the church. Then Pendersen gets off duty an hour later and returns to pick up the girl.

MACKENZIE   That's as sweet as a cup of tea. Only Pendersen ain't the type to kidnap women.

SAM   Right, they were usually after him.

MACKENZIE   Aye, he had a knack with them.

NANCY   We dug up another angle. He's a member of the Sons of the Western Guard. You're familiar with them, aren't you?

MACKENZIE   I knows something about them.

SAM   Yeah, I suppose you do, seeing as how you organize their meetings.

MACKENZIE   This is a free country, ain't it? Man's got a right to join a social club.

NANCY   One that proclaims the supremacy of the white race? That proposes Canada should purge itself of alien races, like Asians and Jews and Native Canadians?

MACKENZIE   I got a right to me own opinions, and what's that got to do with the kidnapping?

KADOTA   Yeah Sam?

SAM   We found out the superintendent is also an organizer for the Sons, the kind that goes around and gives pep talks to the faithful.

KADOTA   Now you're going too far, Sam.

MACKENZIE   Oh, yer very thorough now, ain't cha Sammy?

SAM   Pendersen and the super hatched the plan to get rid of Kenji here.

KADOTA   Naniyo? *[What?]*

MACKENZIE   Yer talkin' gibberish, man. Who's gonna believe this wild goose chase about hankies and social clubs and plans to get rid of the Captain here?

KADOTA   *(to himself)* Mackenzie?

SAM   Speakin' of hankies, this one's yours. *(He pulls out a hanky from a bag and reveals the initials.)* Got your initials on it.

MACKENZIE   *(He checks his own pocket to find the wrong one.)* This one ain't mine. Why yuh sneakin' yellow bastard!

KADOTA   Mackenzie! My own partner.

MACKENZIE   *(draws a gun)* Aye, I was yer partner, and a bit o' hell it was. Takin' orders from your kind. That weren't right at all. So we decided to fix yuh up good.

SAM   You and the super and Pendersen.

MACKENZIE   Aye, we're the Sons, and proud of it…. We've been letting yer kind push us around long enough. Now we're gonna start pushing back.

SAM   You kidnap the queen, squeeze Kenji out of position and later pin the rap on the Tongs.

MACKENZIE   And that's just the beginning. Like the super says, we're gonna send yuh packin' across the Pacific.

NANCY   What happens to the girl?

MACKENZIE   Oh, she's in good hands. We was gonna take her fishin'.

NANCY   You bastards!

NANCY and KADOTA step toward MACKENZIE.

MACKENZIE   Get back! *(They step back.)*

SAM   Things are getting complicated though, eh Sarge?

MACKENZIE   I was just thinkin' about that, and I thinks maybe we can fix up a bit of an accident in this here fire trap.

KADOTA   No, Mackenzie! *(He rushes MACKENZIE.)*

MACKENZIE fires and hits KADOTA but KADOTA knocks him off balance. SAM jumps MACKENZIE. Then NANCY rushes to help KADOTA while SAM and MACKENZIE struggle until SAM gets the gun.)

SAM   Back up, Sarge.

MACKENZIE   He was crazy!

SAM   You all right?

MACKENZIE   He jumped me, it was self-defence!

SAM   Don't worry, Kenbo, we'll get you to a hospital.

NANCY   I'll call an ambulance.

Enter the SUPERINTENDENT holding a gun.

MACKENZIE   I would na touch the tellyphone if I was you.

NANCY   What?

SUPERINTENDENT   *(at the door holding the gun)* Maybe you better call the morgue instead.

SAM   *(putting up his hands)* Shit.

MACKENZIE   *(taking the gun from SAM)* Excellent timing, sir. This is a bit of luck.

SUPERINTENDENT   Luck my arsehole. Now get on the phone and ring up the mayor. *(taking the gun from KADOTA)*. Tell him we've had a bit of bad luck here, losing one of our best men.

MACKENZIE   Right-o sir. *(He picks up the phone.)*

SAM   He always was a favourite of yours, eh?

SUPERINTENDENT   And you're still the troublemaker.

SAM What ya gonna call this one, a double murder-suicide?

MACKENZIE *(into the phone)* Sergeant Mackenzie here, may I have a word with the mayor?

SUPERINTENDENT How does the Ides of March Massacre sound?

SAM Like your kind of dirt.

SUPERINTENDENT You should have heeded the warning.

SAM I got the message.

SUPERINTENDENT But you had to stick your nose in anyway, eh?

SAM Just for the record… who delivered the note?

SUPERINTENDENT You're dying to know, aren't you…? Well you should be more careful about getting your hat cleaned.

SAM I will.

SUPERINTENDENT Too late, Shikaze, this is the final act with you playing the aging Romeo in a story about two middle-aged rivals squabbling over this pretty young thing. Such an exotic ending, eh?

MACKENZIE Uh, Mr. Mayor, sorry to disturb you, sir.

NANCY That could be difficult to explain with Sarge's gun as exhibit A.

MACKENZIE Well we've had a bit of an accident.

SAM Better let Sarge in on the plans before he blows his lines.

SUPERINTENDENT Just tell him to get down here!

MACKENZIE At Shikaze's office, sir. Uhuh.

SAM You're wastin' yer time, Sarge, he's not coming.

SUPERINTENDENT You're bluffing, Shikaze.

MACKENZIE But sir, we need yuh here.

SUPERINTENDENT Tell him it's a multiple murder.

SAM Tell him we've solved the kidnappings while you're at it.

MACKENZIE No sir, yuh don't understand… I got nothin' to do with it!

SUPERINTENDENT What's he saying, Mackenzie?

MACKENZIE Could yuh hold the line for a bit?

SAM You boys want to hand over your pieces?

SUPERINTENDENT One more word out of you and it'll be your last.

MACKENZIE *(to SUPERINTENDENT)* Jesus… it's all over, sir!

SUPERINTENDENT   What are you blubbering about?

MACKENZIE   He says they got us surrounded…. What'll we do?

SAM   Stiff upper lip, Sarge.

SUPERINTENDENT   Get over to the window, we've still got hostages.

> *CHUCK appears at the door with a gun.*

CHUCK   Get 'em up, boys.

SUPERINTENDENT   *(turning)* Chan!

SAM   *(taking the SUPERINTENDENT's gun)* Relax, Jameson.

SUPERINTENDENT   What's this about?

SAM   Shakespeare, buddy.

SUPERINTENDENT   But I was about to get Mackenzie to lead me to the others.

MACKENZIE   What?

SAM   Nice try, but you aren't calling the shots anymore.

SUPERINTENDENT   This is ridiculous. I'm the superintendent of police!

MACKENZIE   Aye, and the clan leader.

SUPERINTENDENT   This man is obviously a lunatic!

SAM   What does that make you?

SUPERINTENDENT   Listen to me… I can prove I've infiltrated the organization known as the Sons of the Western Guard.

MACKENZIE   Infiltrated? Why he's the bloody preacher, selling us all on his fire and brimstone ideas… he's the real looney bird.

SAM   Keep talkin' boys, I'm all ears.

SUPERINTENDENT   We're closing in on the highest level of command.

MACKENZIE   Why the dirty ferret.

SUPERINTENDENT   I can't name names right now.

CHUCK   That's pretty convenient, eh?

SUPERINTENDENT   We can't trust anyone… their agents are everywhere… even among your own people!

NANCY   This could be the tip of the iceberg.

SAM   That's what I don't like.

MACKENZIE   He's a sly one, Sammy.

SUPERINTENDENT   Believe me, this blundering simpleton is only the willing tool of the powers that be.

MACKENZIE   Why yuh sneakin' weasel! *(He lunges at the SUPERINTENDENT.)*

SAM   *(grabs MACKENZIE)* Get back! Another move and I'll bust yer ass, 'cause I owe you, Sarge.

SUPERINTENDENT   Take my word for it, gentlemen, his kind are dangerous. So we must move quickly. Pendersen still has the girl.

CHUCK   You mean he had the girl.

SUPERINTENDENT   What…? Well, jolly good work, but you've wiped out six months of careful investigation.

SAM   We didn't mean to get in the way.

SUPERINTENDENT   You've caught their thugs and saved the girl, but you've let the bigger fish out of the net.

CHUCK   We've got you.

NANCY   Who are you working for?

SUPERINTENDENT   Too much is at stake to expose the operation. Blowing my cover is not the only problem. There are others in more sensitive positions.

CHUCK   *(picking up the phone)* Why don't we call up the attorney general and find out who's giving the orders.

SUPERINTENDENT   Wait…! I didn't want to say this, but the attorney general is—

SAM   The honorary past president, right.

SUPERINTENDENT   You must take this seriously, we are sitting on a bomb that will rock the government!

NANCY   This is one hell of a story.

SAM   Yeah, if we can get it straight.

MACKENZIE   Yuh can't even trust your own kind anymore.

SUPERINTENDENT   In twenty minutes I have a meeting with the Sons' national director. If you want to get the kingpins behind the organization, you'll let me continue my work.

CHUCK   Your move, Sam.

NANCY   You think the attorney general's in the Sons?

SAM   Could be…. *(takes a gun out of his desk)* Okay, Jameson, we'll give you some rope to play with…. *(gives him the gun)* Here, ya might need this.

SUPERINTENDENT   What about mine?

SAM   I'm gonna run a check on it.

SUPERINTENDENT   Smart move. *(smiles and raises the gun)* But you can forget that.

NANCY   Oh no.

MACKENZIE   Christ Almighty, what's going on!

SUPERINTENDENT   I've saved our cause you idiot! Now get their guns!

SAM   *(raises the gun)* Don't bother, Sarge.

SUPERINTENDENT   *(pulls the trigger on the gun)* Huh?

CHUCK   Looks like the rat went for the cheese.

MACKENZIE   Blimey, Sammy, yuh got us again!

SAM   *(taking the gun)* Sorry, Jameson, they only work when they're loaded.

SUPERINTENDENT   You slithering bastard.

SAM   I ain't the one that's squirming, buddy.

CHUCK   That wraps it up, eh?

SAM   Almost.

NANCY   We'd better get the captain to the hospital.

SAM   Oh yeah, got to take care of our own, right Super?

Lights go to black with a siren sounding. All exit the stage.

SAM enters from the alley and walks into spot number one, downstage.

Monday, March 30, 1973. The ides had come and gone. Miss Cherry Blossom was back in the mainstream. The super, Mackenzie and Penderson were all plea bargaining in a case that was rocking the government. Chief Inspector Kadota was breaking in his new badge and Chuck was downtown, making hay while the sun shines. As for the kid, she won some award for her scoop on the Sons, and got a fat offer from *The Toronto Globe and Mail*. That meant moving east. *(pause)* And she did, saying she'd give it a year. *(pause)* Chuck was right. She was a different kind of woman. *(pause)* And me? I dropped by Rosie's for some ochazuke and the latest news on Powell Street.

He walks out of the spot into darkness. The spot comes down.

The end.

BACHELOR-MAN

BY WINSTON CHRISTOPHER KAM

ABOUT

WINSTON CHRISTOPHER KAM

Winston Christopher Kam was born in Trinidad in the West Indies and currently resides in Canada. Of Chinese descent, his influences are Chinese, Caribbean and Canadian. As such, his world view tends to be quite interesting and different (if not skewed, as observed by friends). He has written plays for stage and radio: *Bachelor-Man* (Theatre Passe Muraille, 1987), *Letters to Wu* (Firehall Theatre, 1989) and *Via the Rockies* (CBC radio, 1990). He has also had short stories and reviews published in various anthologies and magazines: *Many Mouthed Birds*, *Striking the Wok* and *Impulse Magazine*, for example. His short story, *Inside the Black Egg*, published by West Coast Line literary magazine, was shortlisted as one of the best short stories of 1996 by the Annual Western Awards. Winston is currently working on his new play, *MATTEO*, the story of Matteo Ricci, the first Jesuit missionary allowed into China in the sixteenth century.

A NOTE ON THE PLAY

On July 1, 1923 the Canadian Government passed the Chinese Immigration Act (Exclusion Act), which effectively barred the further immigration of Chinese to Canada. There were a few exceptions: diplomats, merchants and students. But for the majority (common labourers) it meant a life without their women and families.

The play is set in Toronto and takes place on July 1, 1929. Against the backdrop of the Exclusion Act and the Dominion Day Parade, a group of these bachelor-men are forced to re-examine their relationships with their women. They must confront their values as human beings.

The Exclusion Act was repealed in 1947.

THE LEGEND OF THE MONKEY KING
OR
JOURNEY TO THE WEST

The Legend of the Monkey King is a well-known and well-loved fable to the Chinese. It tells the story of the monk Tripitaka who travels to India in search of the Buddhist scriptures. Accompanying him on that journey were the Monkey King, Pigsy and Sandy.

It is a picaresque tale of adventure filled with history, folklore, religion and philosophy. Many scholars regard the fable to be a parable of man in search of a better world with the Monkey King as a symbol of rebellion and defiance.

Bachelor-Man was first produced at Theatre Passe Muraille in Toronto on November 12, 1987, with the following company:

ASI	Victor Wong
JOHN	Terry Barclay
GRANDAD LIAN	Ed Hong-Louie
KAO	Denis Akiyama
HUANG	Leonard Chow
KUNG	Robert Lee
MME WU	Jane Luk
QUEENIE	Brenda Kamino

Directed by Peter Hinton
Set Design by Stephan Droege and Denyse Karn
Lighting Design by Stephan Droege
Costumes and Props by Denyse Karn
Sound Design by Allen Cole
Choreography by Denise Fujiwara
Tai Chi Instruction by Albert Wong
Stage Management by Shawna Dempsey

CHARACTERS

The characters are common folk mainly of village stock. They live life on an instinctual level and rarely find cause to wonder at the "whys" of things. Those who do quickly find themselves on the outside in those intolerant times, and living in a foreign culture. Doing so is an act of supreme bravery that can lead to loneliness or death, or both.

JOHN (middle age) and **GRANDAD LIAN** (late sixties) are traditionalists in the worst sense of the word. They cling to all traditions, including those that are bad, such as foot binding. They share a further common bond in that they are both married with their wives still back in China. Subconsciously, they hold themselves to be above the others. They can be kind, although that too is an expression of their superiority. They are both practical men, doing what is needed to survive, and they choose to remain blind as to what the Gold Mountain could offer. The intolerance of the times drives them deeper into seeking the comforts of their old ways.

KAO (early thirties) lost an arm at Ypres during the war. Born in Canada but orphaned at an early age (his parents falling victim to disease), he is adopted by a white Christian family. Despite their care, he still feels alienated and unloved. He leaves as soon as he is able and joins the army, hoping to find a place where he can say he truly belongs. He does not find it there and turns to Chinatown where he finds resentment rather than acceptance.

KUNG (mid twenties) was also born in Canada of a Chinese father and a French mother. During this historical period, mixed parentage invited scorn from both communities. Kung seeks refuge in his books and knowledge and finds John's tea house to his liking because they respect what he knows. His self-esteem rises when he tells them that he can speak to the government and have them change the law so that their women can come to Gum Shan (Gold Mountain). He quickly realizes that he has bitten off more than he can chew. He is forced to face the men… and himself.

HUANG (early thirties) is gay. He was once married in China but the circumstances were horrible. He senses dark forces at play in village life. They cause him to ask questions that the villagers dismiss as the ravings of a troubled mind. Feeling stifled, he flees to the Gold Mountain, only to discover that it's not much better than his village. On a personal level, his "gayness" is an act of defiance to the way he's been treated back in China and in Canada. Psychologically, he's unable to perform with a woman as the act causes him to remember the horror of that marriage night, a horror that turns him against the villagers and sympathetic to women.

ASI is a teenager, fresh off the boat as a stowaway. Like the others, he came to the Gold Mountain to get rich but is discovering that it isn't what he was told back in his village. In fact, he learns more than he expected. He's like an empty vessel being filled with the experiences of the people around him.

MME WU (mid thirties) is a shy and retiring woman who has no sense of self. She stays indoors, afraid to venture outside and does everything her husband tells her. She is obedient to a fault. Yet beneath her timid demeanor, one senses a soul desperate to break free. But she does not know how, and even if she did know, she couldn't.

QUEENIE (middle age) has bound feet, a fact that the men are not fully aware of. They never cared enough to know. To them she's a prostitute, a hag, an object of humour not to be taken seriously. She's unlike any other woman that they have ever met; brash, rude, unafraid to speak her mind and intelligent. She is angry and, like Huang, defiant and finds in those the reasons for her existence. She roams about surviving as best she can, trying to make sense of her life and of a world that has cruelly mistreated her. Her experiences have made her bold, bitter and unafraid. Yet she is deathly afraid of what her ancestors might think of her, that they look down on her, and that even in death she will not be able to hold her head high to face them.

SETTING

John's tea house, restaurant and boarding house is the social centre for these men. Located in Chinatown, it is where they gather to chit-chat, gamble, eat, sleep, laugh, joke, gossip, complain and whine depending on the mood of the day. On July 1, Dominion Day (Independence Day), the mood is dark, especially when the parade starts. Feeling trapped, free and yet not free, they turn bitter and accusatory, and friendships are strained. For six years (1923–1929) it has been like this. But in this particular year it changes.

Stage left is a counter running parallel to the wall. Hanging on the wall are some menus written in Chinese. An altar hangs on the wall closer to stage front left. On the main stage are two or three tables and chairs as in a small inn. At the rear is a stairway leading to the upstairs where some of the men sleep. Near the stairway is a window and next to that is a door leading to the outside. The place is poor, rundown and sparsely decorated.

BACHELOR-MAN

ACT ONE

SCENE ONE

July 1, 1929

8:00 a.m. John's tea house

JOHN is wiping the table tops. He is tired and has just woken up. An alarm clock rings. He pauses, glances upstairs and lights a cigarette. He savours the smoke for one or two beats then with a large sigh ambles to the door, opens it, retrieves a newspaper, and after a quick look round re-enters, crosses to the counter where he puts the paper down without looking at it. He disappears behind the counter. There is a clatter of pots and pans then he re-emerges with a tray of cups and a teapot. He wipes his brow then pauses again. He spies the nearby money box and drops in a dollar. He shakes his head, sighs, then wipes his brow again.

Enter GRANDAD LIAN from upstairs. He stretches, yawns and looks around.

LIAN   Morning, John.

JOHN   Morning, Grandad.

LIAN   It's going to be hot today. You can feel the heat already… *(JOHN grunts.)* You're open early…

JOHN   Better to attract the customers. Business has been bad lately.

LIAN   Yes, I've noticed…

JOHN   It gets worse every year too. I wish I knew why. But today we'll see! When that parade starts everyone runs indoors.

> *Pause. LIAN slurps his tea, emitting a loud sigh of satisfaction. Next he lights a cigarette and picks up the newspaper. JOHN indicates the money box. LIAN obliges and drops a coin into the box.*

LIAN   Whose turn is it?

JOHN   Kung.

LIAN   It's a lot of money. I wonder what he'll do with it…

> *Pause.*

JOHN   What do you think, Grandad?

LIAN   *(intent on the newspaper)* About what?

JOHN   You're not paying attention! Why are the brothers staying away? What have I done? Did I say something? Tell me…

LIAN   Hah! I don't blame them. Look at this place. It's a dump. Even my rice-cooker could run it.

JOHN   When I'm rich I'll make this a real tea house. A home away from home! They'll come running back then.

LIAN   Your food is terrible.

JOHN   *(dismissively)* My food is excellent! The tea is even better and the company… *(thoughtful pause)* well, it's never boring…

LIAN   Now that is true…

> *JOHN lights incense, bows quickly three times at the altar and sticks the incense into a bowl of sand.*

Yes, praying should help…. I'm glad you still cling to the old ways, John. Have you seen Wu's altar? The one in his café? No wax candles and incense for him. Now it's plastic fruits and electric candles. His gods have gone modern… and he's a practising Christian too. Just like you…

JOHN   Practical, Grandad. Practical Christian. You never can tell, you know. These are strange times and it might be useful one day.

LIAN   Not likely. Listen to this, *(reads from the newspaper)* "Three wagonloads are taken in raid on Chinese Club"!

JOHN   Huh! They're raiding everybody nowadays. You'd think they have nothing better to do, the police. Whenever we get together they think we're up to no good. What do they expect from us? When they passed that immigration law they took away our women and families…

LIAN   Exclusion Act. It had nothing to do with immigration…

JOHN   It's all the same… without our families what are we supposed to do? So we get together in places like this, play cards, mah-jong, talk, socialize, and they call us crooks. Imagine that! They commit the crime and call us criminals. The world has turned upside down, Grandad. They'll drive us instinct…

LIAN   Extinct…

JOHN   That was a low blow, Grandad. So unexpected, too…

LIAN   It's the Gold Mountain. Many things are unexpected…

> *Enter ASI from upstairs, putting on his apron. He is in a hurry.*

JOHN   Asi, you're late. You know what day it is today. It's going to be busy.

ASI   Sorry, Uncle John.

JOHN   Save your apologies. Just get to work.

> *ASI begins clearing off the tables, sweeping the floor; he works throughout the scene.*

(*to LIAN*) Did I tell you I received a letter from my rice-cooker?

LIAN   Did you? That's wonderful! How is she?

JOHN   She's fine, I suppose. (*reaching into his pocket*) Here let me read it for you…

LIAN   (*setting aside the newspaper*) You sure you want to?

JOHN   Why not, Grandad? These are times when things must be shared.

LIAN   You honour me.

JOHN   (*reads*) "My dearest husband…" She always calls me that. What a loving woman. "My dearest husband, I write to you as if we're sitting face-to-face. You go abroad to seek wealth because we're poor. In your sojourn, do not sow wild oats…"

LIAN   Ha-Ha-Ha! Fat chance! (*JOHN eyes him coldly.*) Sorry…

JOHN   "… In your sojourn, do not sow wild oats. Before you departed I enjoined you to remember you have a wife and children at home. Please work diligently and be frugal with money. Two years hence, return home to sweep your ancestors' tomb. If not, then send for me…"

> *Silence.*

LIAN   Yes, she sounds wonderful.

JOHN   She still collects scraps of paper on the streets. It's how she makes a living. Selling them to tobacco factories to make cigarettes. That newspaper you're reading would be worth a fortune to her… I was just about ready to send for her when the government passed that law…

LIAN   Let's not talk about it.

ASI   When did you last see your rice-cooker, Grandad?

LIAN   Thirty years ago. When I went back for a visit. A daughter came of that.

JOHN   A small happiness…

LIAN   Yes… I never saw her. She's married now… with a family of her own. Never saw them either.

ASI   (*pours him tea*) You ought to go back, Grandad…

JOHN   Yes, you should…

LIAN   I don't want to talk about it.

JOHN   The Gold Mountain has betrayed you. You came here as a boy, you gave it your life, you built that damn railroad and look what's happened…! There's nothing for you here!

LIAN   There's nothing for me there either!

JOHN   But you may never see your rice-cooker again!

LIAN   *(angry outburst)* Will you shut up…! Why don't you go back…?!

        Enter QUEENIE, appearing only briefly at the door.

JOHN   Hey you! Get out of here! Go on! Get out! *(He chases her out.)* Smelly old hag…!

LIAN   Who was that…?

JOHN   Queenie. She sure is stubborn.

LIAN   *(chuckles)* You just chased away your first customer.

JOHN   That's not funny, Grandad. Her kind of business I don't need.

LIAN   Oh ho! High and mighty now, are we?

JOHN   Oh, keep quiet!

        Enter KAO, slamming the door behind him.

KAO   Morning…

JOHN   You're early.

KAO   …trying to avoid the crowds.

JOHN   Obviously you know what day this is. That why you're so cheerful?

KAO   Hah! Morning, Grandad. Asi… where's everybody?

JOHN   Upstairs. Still asleep.

KAO   Kung? Huang? *(JOHN grunts.)* What time is it?

JOHN   About eight.

        Pause.

KAO   *(pouring a drink)* It's going to be a long day… which reminds me. There'll be a lot of big noses around. They've never been to Chinatown before, never seen a place like this. You mind if I make some money?

JOHN   As long as I get my cut… and you behave yourself.

KAO   You'll get your cut.

LIAN   It's too early to drink, brother Kao.

KAO   *(with deliberate flair)* On the other side of this unjust world, people are drinking. It's discourteous and the height of bad manners not to join them. As for my behaviour, it's impeccable. Always has been. *(He raises the bottle.)* To health, wealth and happiness! May we all find them somewhere! Because they don't exist… here… or anywhere! *(he drinks)*

        JOHN and LIAN exchange knowing glances.

    You know what that means? Impeccable? It means "without blemish." I learnt that in the army where everything was spit and polish… and impeccable… except me…! Ha-Ha… *(He spies the tontine money box and puts in his share.)* Hey, how did brother Huang do last night?

JOHN   He did well. He found a new man-love.

KAO   Did he now? Who?

JOHN   Never saw him before. Ha-Ha-Ha! Poor Huang.

KAO   Leave him alone. He's a good man.

JOHN   Kai-dai…

KAO   So what if he's a man-love? What's a man to do when you take away his woman? What d'you say, Grandad?

LIAN   I don't understand these things.

JOHN   I say it's indecent.

KAO   What's that got to do with anything? A man's got to live. That makes everything permissible.

LIAN   You believe that, brother Kao?

JOHN   I do…

KAO   I…. Yes, Grandad. I do…

LIAN   You're very young.

KAO   I've been around. Where d'you think I lost this arm? I just think maybe Huang's right. I mean, look at us. We have our needs like healthy men everywhere. At least he's doing something about his. "Make love," he says, "wherever, whenever, with whomever because you never know what law they might pass tomorrow…"

JOHN   Are you man-love too? *(JOHN and LIAN laugh.)*

KAO   Your mother!

JOHN   And yours.

LIAN   Come, come! Let's not fight. It's too early in the day. Don't forget brother Kung?

KAO   What about him?

LIAN   Don't you remember? He's going to talk to the government today. He's going to make them bring our women back…. He's clever. I hope he succeeds. I want to see my rice-cooker again.

JOHN   Him and his books! I don't like these quiet people and their books. They think too much. That's a real tchap cheung for you!

KAO   Yes, it takes more than smart to deal with these foreigners. I should know. Look at you, Grandad. You've been here what? Fifty? Sixty years? Fifty years on the railroads, fifty years of hard work, of sending money back to your woman in China…. Fifty years of wisdom… and what do you have to show for it? No, it takes more than that to deal with the big noses…. They didn't pass that law because they thought we were stupid…

LIAN   Oh, very good! I like that. I must remember that. But you know, we're still alive…

KAO   So are maggots.

JOHN   You need a woman, brother Kao.

KAO   Don't we all.

JOHN   *(to LIAN)* Maybe we should find him one.

LIAN   Who? Where?

JOHN   How about Queenie?

KAO   Your mother!

> *They laugh at this. ASI laughs the loudest.*

What are you laughing at, boy? *(He darts upstairs.)* Kung! Huang! Time to get up! You don't want to miss that wonderful parade, do you?

> *JOHN and LIAN again exchange glances as KAO re-enters.*

LIAN   Why don't you go upstairs and lie down, brother Kao…

JOHN   Yes, you look tired…

KAO   Nothing wrong with me! I'm fine. The weather's fine… bright, hot and sunny. Even the air is sweet… no acrid smoke or mustard gas. Everyone will be puffed up in their finery off to some picnic or that damn parade.

JOHN   *(chuckles)* I knew it. It never fails. Every Dominion Day you come here feeling sorry for yourself. Well who told you to go fight in the foreigner's war?

KAO   Your mother!

JOHN   And yours!

> *Pause.*

LIAN You see, brother Kao. It's just that… don't get mad now… but we're tired of hearing the same story over and over again. Everyone knows it. You've said it so often it's become part of Chinatown lore…. First brigade, 52nd battalion…. You lost your arm at Ypres…

KAO No arm, no woman. Not that it'd make any difference. I couldn't even embrace her properly, could I? Do you understand? No, you don't. How can you…? *(He wipes his brow with his empty sleeve.)* Rotting in some poppy field in Belgium. It was my passport to the Gold Mountain… *(laughs)* I was born in this country and yet I needed a passport to live in it! And I watch you brothers clambering off those ships eagerly paying your five-hundred dollars to get to the Gold Mountain! And for what…? And you, Grandad, you told me you fled poverty and hardship in China…. What have you found here? More poverty and hardships! It's all the same! Fools…! *(pause)* The Gold Mountain owes me. It owes me an arm. It owes me a woman. A life…! Ahhh, I'm in the mood for fucking, brothers. And I don't care what I fuck. Be it a woman, the Gold Mountain or Chinatown… I just want to fuck… something…

JOHN Don't be so filthy or you'll have to leave.

KAO Spoken like a true Christian! They taught you well, didn't they? How to gracefully accept insults… *(pause)* Sorry, shouldn't have said that… it's just that… ha-ha-ha… I mean look at me. I'm over thirty and already a half man, a virgin man with cobwebs on my jade tendon. Women? None! Prospects? None! *(to ASI)* That's what it's all about, boy! A Bachelor-Man! Forever! Thank you, Emperor Mackenzie King! Thank you! For all of that I gave you my arm!

JOHN You're drunk.

KAO Yes, I've been drinking, but I'm not drunk.

LIAN You must try to put it out of your mind.

KAO Hah!

LIAN I'm not asking you to forget. We must always remember. All of us… this ghetto they pushed us into—yes! That's right! It is a ghetto! It reminds us who we are… where we belong. We must try to cope. Try to get on with living. We must try to ignore the pain.

JOHN You have to be practical…

LIAN Philosophical…

JOHN Why bang on doors already shut behind you?

LIAN …make do with what you have. The Tao teaches us to accept things as they are. It's our culture…

KAO That sounds cowardly. How can you ignore this… this… *(a sweep of the hand)* I can't.

LIAN Don't talk like that...

KAO There're too many reminders; the heat, the parade, July first... July first comes every year, you know. It's as certain as death. Only worse because it's always just around the corner waiting to mug you, and you know it. It's the waiting I don't like. Waiting for it to come... waiting for it to end.... It's going to be a long day, brothers. A damn long day...

> *QUEENIE appears at the door. JOHN rushes at her.*

JOHN Out! Get out! Shoo! Scat!

> *Lights fade to black.*

SCENE TWO

> *John's tea house.*
>
> *Same day. Late Morning.*
>
> *Spot comes up on ASI.*

ASI *(to the audience)* There is Heaven... there is Earth.
There is China... there is the Gold Mountain.
There is Dominion Day... there is Humiliation Day.

There is July 1, 1923, when the government passed a law that forbade my brothers and sisters from coming to the Gold Mountain. For those of us already here... it means a life without our women...

There is July 1, 1929... today and the Bachelor-Man...

There is a legend. A Chinese legend... of a mischievous little imp, The Monkey King, who wasn't afraid to speak his mind or point his finger and say the prime minister wears no clothes. Everywhere he went he created havoc.

There's The Monkey King... there is the Bachelor-Man....
There is havoc in Heaven... there is havoc in the Gold Mountain...

> *ASI segues into tai chi. Several beats. Lights come up to reveal GRANDAD LIAN also doing tai chi. KAO is standing near the altar with a cigarette in his mouth looking on. JOHN is at the door looking out.*

JOHN I don't understand it. It's getting on and still no customers.

KAO *(to LIAN)* Could I do one-armed tai chi, Grandad? Will I get the full effects of the chi, or just half a chi?

LIAN Show some respect for your culture.

KAO Culture? I thought it was an exercise. Amazing the things we call culture.

JOHN   Don't you go start again…

KAO   *(chuckling)* No seriously. This altar here is culture too, John? Honouring your ancestors? I thought you were a Christian.

LIAN   He's a practical Christian.

KAO   Practical? What's that got to do with it? It's faith, that's what! Just faith! That's what my parents told me.

JOHN   Your parents are Christian? Oh! I remember now. You were adopted by a foreign family.

KAO   *(reflectively)* They were good people. Very kind, took good care of me. I had lots of faith in them.

JOHN   So what happened?

KAO   They liked showing me off. They invited lots of people to their home to come see the little Chinese baby… *(heavily)* I was a pet. Not a real son. They were kind because it made them feel good about themselves. So I lost the faith…. No, I take that back. I had faith in the country. That's why I joined the army…

> *Lengthy pause during which he stares at LIAN and ASI doing tai chi.*

Hey Grandad, can I learn tai chi? You teach me?

> *Enter HUANG from upstairs.*

HUANG   Morning, brothers… *(They all reply.)*

KAO   You're finally awake.

HUANG   No thanks to you, loudmouth!

KAO   Sorry…. Where's Kung?

HUANG   Rehearsing his speech for the government.

JOHN   Ha-ha-ha! Tchap cheung!

HUANG   Leave him alone. *(tastes his tea)* Don't you know how to make coffee?

JOHN   This is a tea house. You want coffee? Go next door to Wu's. He'll give you coffee, knife, fork, roast beef and potatoes. He'll also treat you the way the foreigners treat us.

HUANG   *(puts a dollar in the money box)* I'll take the tea…. Where's everybody?

JOHN   You tell me…. You haven't heard anything, have you?

HUANG   About what?

JOHN   Why the brothers are staying away…

HUANG   Maybe if you served coffee.

JOHN   Your mother...

HUANG   They'll come running in when that parade starts. Nobody likes to be reminded it's Humiliation Day.

KAO   That reminds me! Grandad, you want to make some money? Do tai chi when I bring the tourists around. They like exotic things. It gives them something to talk about over tea and cucumber sandwiches. (*He mimics the action causing the others to chuckle.*)

HUANG   (*chuckling*) You'd better not. They'll think you've been doing opium. (*They laugh.*)

KAO   Brother John tells me you have a new man-love.

HUANG   John has a big mouth.

JOHN   It's true!

HUANG   See. He agrees with me.

JOHN   Very funny!

KAO   Well?

HUANG   Well what?

KAO   What's his name?

HUANG   Whose name?

KAO   You know who?

HUANG   He has no name, and you have a filthy mind.

KAO   Come now, everyone has a name. Even John has a name. What a wonderful Chinese name John is. Yes John? (*KAO and HUANG chuckle at this.*)

HUANG   He was just another tendon in the dark.

KAO   Tendon in the dark! Oh, I like that. Sounds like a song! Well...?

HUANG   Well what?

KAO   Was he... uh... I mean... tiny tendon?

HUANG   (*laughing*) You do have a dirty mind...

KAO   What do we care? We're not supposed to be decent. Not like outside...

HUANG   True.... Actually, he was... ample...

KAO   Ample?

HUANG   Well... maybe more than that... more like... uh... thunderous.

KAO   Ha-ha-ha! Thunderous? (*They laugh.*) You mean... a thunder tendon? (*They laugh louder at their private joke.*)

JOHN   You're disgusting! *(to LIAN)* He needs a woman too. *(HUANG rounds on him.)* Sorry! Just an expression. It seems appropriate… considering.

HUANG   True…

KAO   It's the law, isn't it? It made you a man-love.

HUANG   I don't want to talk about it.

KAO   I don't want you to end up like Yip. Remember him? No job, no money, no wife, no nothing. When they passed that law it broke his spirit.

HUANG   Killed himself, didn't he? Wrote a poem then did himself in. He started a trend. How did his poem go? Wait! Don't tell me, "Fellow countrymen, read the following poem quickly…"

LIAN   *(still doing tai chi)* "…Having amassed several hundred dollars,
I left my native home for the Gold Mountain.
I've always yearned to go to the Gold Mountain.
But instead I find it is hell and full of hardships.
I was detained in a prison and tears rolled down my cheeks.
My wife at home is longing for my letter,
Who can foretell when I will be able to return home.
I cannot sleep because my heart is filled with hate.
When I think of the foreign barbarians, my anger rises to the skies.
They put me in jail and make me suffer misery.
I moan until the early dawn, but who will console me here?
Not my wife, not my mother, not my sister, not any woman…. Then who?"

ASI   They say he chewed on his tongue and swallowed it. Did he really? That is so strange… *(stops doing tai chi)*

KAO   Not so strange. It's normal for men like us. *(pause)* They say the doctors found his loins filled with semen. And the semen had hardened. It was the pain that killed him…

> There are low groans all round.

JOHN   Speak to him, Huang. He's been talking like that all morning.

KAO   I'm fine…

JOHN   *(lighting more incense)* You know, yesterday I went to church. I don't know why I did. I just felt the urge. And I was glad I did… I felt at peace. Things were in their proper place. They made sense. Even this topsy-turvy world suddenly seemed well-ordered and livable. But that was yesterday. Today I have to contend with no-show customers and you, Kao. You make everything around you seem a living hell. I think it's you who chase my customers away. The way you behave, the way you talk…

KAO   Then throw me out.

JOHN   I have a mind to. But I'm a Christian…. Listen to me. There's something to be said for submitting to forces that are heaven-sent.

LIAN   Confucius couldn't have said it better.

JOHN   That's the trouble with you, Kao. You're confused. You have nothing to… to cling to. No past or tradition…

    Pause.

KAO   (*suddenly darts upstairs*) Hey Kung! It's time to talk to the government! It's time to bring our women back!

    Grandad stops his tai chi and glances upwards.

JOHN   He really needs a woman, Grandad. How about it?

LIAN   I don't know…. A woman creates as many problems as she solves.

JOHN   You heard him. (*He takes money out of his pocket.*)

LIAN   Oh… all right… (*He reluctantly hands JOHN a dollar.*)

JOHN   How about you, Huang? We're going to get him a woman.

HUANG   Don't be stupid! It will take more than that to help him.

LIAN   Oh? What do you know?

HUANG   Look, don't interfere. Just leave me out of it!

JOHN   He's your friend. Don't you care about him? Maybe you care too much? Ha-ha-ha!

HUANG   Leave me alone! Leave the women alone! For hundreds of years we've… we've…. Don't interfere, dammit! Don't interfere! Stay out of people's lives!

LIAN   (*to JOHN*) Now there's another oddball. For sure he needs a woman.

JOHN   I wonder if he's ever had one.

KAO   (*re-enters with KUNG*) Here he is! (*All except JOHN converge on KUNG.*)

KUNG   (*nervously*) Morning, brothers. (*They all reply.*)

KAO   It's a big day today, brother Kung!

KUNG   (*hesitantly*) Yes… it is…

ASI   Are you afraid, Uncle Kung?

KUNG   Of course not…

HUANG   Have some tea.

JOHN   Have wine instead.

KUNG   Oh, please no. Wine gives me too much courage. I'll have the tea…

LIAN   Your speech is finished?

KUNG   What…? Oh yes. Yes it is…

JOHN   Hurray for Kung! He'll bring our women back! Ha-ha-ha!

LIAN   Is it a good speech?

JOHN   Let's hear the speech, Kung!

ASI   Yes, Uncle Kung, let's hear the speech.

KUNG   I… I'd rather not…

JOHN   You do have a speech, don't you?

LIAN   Of course he has a speech. We're counting on you, Kung.

ASI   It's a good speech too! Not so, Uncle Kung?

KUNG   I… yes. Yes it is. It's just that… it may lose its spirit if I say it now…

JOHN   Meaning you don't have a speech!

LIAN   How can you say that? Don't you want him to get our women back?

KUNG   (defiantly) I do have a speech! It's… just that it's… rather long. You know how the English tongue is… there're many big words…

JOHN   You think we won't understand? You think we're stupid!

KUNG   (defiantly) I didn't say that! It's a good speech, very persuasive. And humble…

JOHN   Meaning it says who is master and who is slave. The round eyes will like that!

KAO   Why don't you leave him alone?! You don't want him to succeed, do you? Because if he does you're out of business! Ha-ha-ha!

LIAN   Come, come, come! Let's drink to Kung.

> They gather at the counter and prepare for a toast. JOHN forestalls KUNG from joining the others.

JOHN   Your name is being whispered about in Chinatown, Kung. Because they say you're going to bring our women back. And they believe it too. Never before has your name been shown such respect. And why? Because you give them vague promises…. Me? I give them things that matter, things that are real…. I make them forget their troubles. But here you are winning their confidence and gaining face for yourself because of vague promises. Not so? (No response.)

Listen to me. Not even you and all your books can deal with these foreigners. Do you know what Chinatown will say about you when you fail? You have no right to do this to these men. Giving them ladders without rungs…

KUNG *(feebly)* There is no result without effort…

JOHN You talk like a book. *(grabbing the money box)* Look! Here's the tontine. It's yours, it's your turn. Use the money to get Kao a woman. One for you too! Be realistic…

KAO Come on, Kung. Have a drink before you go.

ASI Uncle Kung is brave!

KAO He has the courage of the Monkey King. Wreaking havoc in Heaven!

HUANG Havoc in the Gold Mountain!

KAO Giving the bureaucrats what for! He'll bring our women back!

> *KUNG looks uneasily from JOHN to KAO.*

JOHN And if he doesn't—and I know he won't—I'll get you a woman! I'll put in a good word with Chen.

KAO That pimp! I want nothing to do with his whores.

LIAN Oh, you're high and mighty too…

KAO I'm not particular. I just want a decent woman. Chinese, virgin, pure. Preferably young with the freshness still oozing from her pores. She must have a healthy mind and not care about my one arm…

KUNG You might as well reach for the moon, brother Kao. *(to JOHN)* I hear they're smuggling in more women in San Francisco. Cheap too.

JOHN Are they? Hmmm, I must tell Chen.

KAO Enough of Chen! All he's got are French whores.

LIAN What's wrong with French whores? If it weren't for them, half of the brothers would be hanging from trees by now.

JOHN That's true… I like them… I find them to be kind and courteous and in their own curious little ways they're cultured… just like us. Too bad they're so clumsy though.

LIAN That's because they have big feet.

> *They laugh.*

JOHN Still, we ought to be grateful. They're the only ones friendly to us.

LIAN Why is that, I wonder?

KAO It's because they don't like the English either.

> *They laugh.*

HUANG Hey, listen to this, brothers. *(He reads from the newspaper.)* "Chinese learn joys of Western Picnic…"

KAO *(snorts)* The Western Front was no goddamn picnic…

HUANG Shhhh! *(reads)* "East and West met in a friendly way on Saturday afternoon… blah… blah… blah… at Exhibition Park…"

LIAN Friendly way! Hah…!

HUANG "…Pleasant-faced dads, proud mothers and happy children joined in the merriment, basked in the sunlight of an ideal June day…. Interested spectators questioned the Christian workers continually, anxious to know how many Chinese women had made their home in Toronto…"

They all burst out laughing except JOHN.

JOHN That's not funny, kai-dai!

HUANG It's right here! Page fourteen. Come read it.

JOHN I can't read English.

KUNG I thought the missionaries were teaching you.

JOHN Bible English. "Don't do this, don't do that. Don't say this, don't say that, don't think this, don't think that…"

KUNG Just like Chinese culture, eh? Hah! It says here, "There are between two-and-three-hundred Chinese children in Toronto…"

LIAN That many? Where did they come from?

KAO The only accurate thing in that newspaper is the date!

HUANG Monday, July 1, 1929… *The Globe*…

Suddenly the parade starts. They all stop and become attentive. Several beats as they listen, each occupied with his thoughts as they recall what the parade signifies.

KAO That damn parade's started.

JOHN Good! Now all the brothers will come rushing in. Get ready, Asi.

KAO *(as if to himself)* I can't believe it. On this very day they passed the Exclusion Act…

LIAN You know, come to think of it, Kung. I've never seen you with a woman. At least not in the year you've been here. You know, if you fail we can put in a good word for you too with Chen.

KUNG No, not for me, thank you. Not that I haven't tried…. It's just that… well… I'm not white enough for white women and I'm not Chinese enough for Chinese women. Even the whores have their own standards, you know, and of course I don't measure up…. No, I don't want any women. Anyway, I prefer my books. They don't talk back or insult me by making me feel like a half-skinned banana.

JOHN   What are you talking about?

> *There is an awkward silence as JOHN eyes KUNG. The parade grows louder.*

Shouldn't you be on your way…?

KUNG   *(very nervous)* I… yes, I should go now… *(He stands his ground looking for encouragement.)*

> *Silence.*

KAO   Good luck, Kung. *(shakes his hand)* If anyone can do it, it's you.

HUANG   Hear, hear. You can do it, Kung.

ASI   Yes, Uncle Kung. You can.

LIAN   Bring back our women, Kung.

> *KUNG hesitantly makes for the door. The parade grows louder.*

JOHN   You're afraid. Admit it.

HUANG   I'll come with you. I want some coffee.

> *KUNG moves defiantly to the door. HUANG accompanies him.*

JOHN   Let's see you wrap fire in paper, tchap cheung… *(with a laugh)* And tell the brothers I'm open early! Ha-ha-ha!

> *KUNG opens the door. The parade is louder. A shaft of light bursts in illuminating the darkened stage and framing KUNG and HUANG at the door. It is as if they're about to descend into Hades.*

> *End of Act One.*

ACT TWO

SCENE ONE

Darkness. The sounds of clicking mah-jong tiles. Spot comes on ASI.

ASI   *(to the audience)* There're about twenty-four-hundred men and one-hundred-and-fifty women in Toronto. Sixteen men to every woman…. Clearly the yin and yang are out of balance. The world is in disarray and disharmony abounds…. And that parade… listen to it… *(He listens.)* Reminding us what it's like to be on the good side of a bad law… it's enough to drive any man mad. But we keep our sanity waiting for the Monkey King…

> *Lights come up to reveal LIAN, JOHN and KAO at the table shuffling mah-jong tiles. ASI joins them. KAO gets up and paces restlessly.*

KAO   *(lighting a cigarette)* That damn parade gets longer every year.

LIAN   It's your imagination.

KAO   No, it isn't. They're taunting me.

> *QUEENIE enters, hobbling. JOHN goes after her.*

JOHN   Queenie! Out! Out, dammit! How many times…

QUEENIE   My feet are killing me…

JOHN   *(ushering her out)* So are mine! I'm on my feet all day! And stay out…! *(returning to his seat, laughing)* I thought she was going to say her back was killing her. Ha-ha-ha.

> *LIAN also laughs.*

KAO   You are cruel sometimes.

JOHN   What d'you mean? Oh, you mean her? *(dismissively)* Ahhhh! Come, sit down. Put your money in my pocket…

LIAN   Yes, we need another hand.

KAO   Is that supposed to be funny?!

LIAN   What? What did I say? Oh! I just meant we need another person, that's all. Don't be so touchy.

KAO   They're taunting me all right. I just know it. I mean listen to it! It's been like this every day for the past ten years. No matter where I go… it's all the same. Maybe I'll go to China. I've never been there before, you know… maybe I'll be welcome there. What d'you think? Will they welcome me? They don't welcome me in Chinatown, you know…

ASI   You should get some rest, Uncle Kao.

KAO   You're a good boy, Asi. A good boy…

ASI   I'll let you know when Uncle Kung returns. I'm sure he'll bring good news. I know he will.

KAO   *(brightening)* That's right! He is the Monkey King, isn't he…? He told me all about *The Monkey King*, Kung did. About the monk, Tripitaka, who went in search of the Buddhist scriptures; the three mythical knights who protected him on the way; the Monkey King, Pigsy and Sandy. They fought many battles on that journey. *(He picks up the broom, wielding it like a sword.)* With my nine-prong muckrake I fought the demons in the air and the evils of the world and I held them in abeyance! They were brave! Their bravery is carved in stone and their courage… their courage is impeccable…! *(brief pause)* I fought with them. Did you know that, Asi? And I too had courage. It was not for a lack of courage I lost my arm…

JOHN   Get him some wine, Asi. On the house. He's starting to ramble.

> LIAN exchanges glances with JOHN.

LIAN   I hope he doesn't go mad on us…

> Enter HUANG in a rush.

HUANG   The parade's going by! Come take a look!

KAO   What the hell for?

HUANG   Some of the brothers are in it.

JOHN   What! Marching in the Humiliation Day parade? I got to see this!

> All but KAO rush to the door where they stand and look.

ASI   There they are! You recognize them?

JOHN   No… wait. Yes, that's Lee over there. Dressed in a long gown and cap. Made of Chekiang silk, no doubt. Very expensive…

ASI   He has a pigtail.

KAO   A pigtail? In this day and age?

LIAN   He's traditionalist.

KAO   Like you? Ha-ha! What kind of tradition is that? Twenty years ago the pigtail was a sign of slavery. Well I guess some of us still enjoy being slaves…

HUANG   There's Wu…

JOHN   I knew he'd be there. You know he thinks he's white? Nothing worse than a Chinese who thinks like that.

KAO   Enough! I don't want to hear anymore. Shut the door…. Where the hell is Kung?

HUANG   I left him when I went to order coffee.

KAO   He's taking so long.

JOHN   You should know better than to trust a tchap cheung.

HUANG   I wish you wouldn't call him that. And behind his back, too…

LIAN   But he is a tchap cheung. His father was the village idiot and his mother was some poor white woman…

JOHN   Ha-ha-ha. And when she got pregnant he hightailed it back to China.

KAO   Fucking coward…

JOHN   Chinatown still talks about it.

KAO   Laugh about it, you mean! Ignorant peasants!

LIAN   What's come over you? Don't talk that way about your own people!

KAO   My people? *(to HUANG)* Ha-ha-ha! Did you hear that? My people… *(somberly)* They laughed at me when I enlisted. They mocked my uniform. Called me names when I lost my arm. Like children! They envy me for being born here…. Why? I fought for them, dammit! *(brief pause)* Have you ever walked on Yonge Street? Surrounded by foreigners? Suddenly you see a brother coming toward you. You try to catch his eye… but he turns away…! Why…?

LIAN   I don't blame them. The way you behave and talk. That's the trouble with people like you born in this country. You have no memories…

JOHN   That's right. Why, I remember when I first came over. An iron boat it was…. They packed us in… like sardines in a steel dungeon; no windows, no air, rancid water and maggoty food. You pissed and shitted where you slept and everywhere was the sweat and stink of men like yourself. But we didn't care, did we…?

LIAN   No! We were off to Gum Shan! To get rich! To better ourselves!

ASI   That's why I came. Back in my village everybody said how good it was here.

JOHN   They did?

ASI   Yes. Some of the villagers had relatives here. They sent back letters saying it was wonderful. How rich they were…

LIAN and JOHN laugh heartily.

JOHN   They lied. To save face! It's all a joke! The minute we landed on Victoria Island they put us in jail…! Oh! The shame! The humiliation! So unexpected!! *(pause)* And at nights the men would cry. Imagine that! Grown men crying! It was that bad! I'd shout and tell them to shut up! To put on a brave face and stop behaving like sissies! But they kept on crying, weeping for their mothers, wives… *(looks meaningfully at KAO and HUANG)* their women! I was as young as you, Asi…

ASI   Oh! I remember the custom guards. So frightening…! Like standing before white devils… and oh, the questions they asked: How many steps in front of your house? What's the distance from your front door to the village gate? How many people in your family? What's their names? Their ages? How many pigs? Goats? Chickens? It was so confusing… and… and if they didn't like your answer they wouldn't let you into the Gold Mountain. It was so stupid…. They… they made me feel like… like…

JOHN   Trickery! That's what! Trying to trick you so they can send you back!

KAO   Then why did you come? The Gold Mountain is a lie! And you're all fools for believing a lie.

JOHN   You fought for it. You lost an arm for it!

KAO   Oh, fuck off!

       Uneasy silence.

ASI   Is it always like this? Dominion Day…?

       Pause. No one answers him.

LIAN   When I was a waterboy on the railroads, there was this time we were camped on the beach. I remember it was quiet… we were tired. Numb and dazed and wondering why we'd come to the Gold Mountain. We wished we were all back home…. Suddenly there was a loud shriek! It was frightening! One of our brothers had jumped to his feet and flung a railroad tie across his shoulders… like so… *(He demonstrates with the broom.)* and he began walking into the ocean. *(pause)* I watched him till he was no more… I remember a full moon… a calm sea… and lights bouncing off the ripples where he had disappeared…. My baba told me the man had gone mad and was building a railroad under the ocean back to China. Sometimes I still see that man… under the ocean. Pounding spikes beneath those pounding waves. Building his railroad back to China… *(becoming testy)* It's men like him you mock, Kao. Men of great courage who suffered needlessly. So stop it!

       Pause. KAO, discomfited, lights a cigarette.

KAO   Ahhhh, you put a halo around your suffering and think you're somebody special. Well you're not. *(pause)* I saw my best friend killed, bullet straight to the head. Might've been a German bullet. Or English. Or French. Doesn't really matter, does it? All those fucking bullets look alike to me…. There he was lying in the trenches, covered with mud. I wanted to bury him, to make him decent. But that fucking sergeant screamed at me. "Leave the fucking chink where he is." No man deserves an epitaph like that. No man. Not even a "fucking chink." I'll always remember that. Especially today…

LIAN   There, you see! All the more reason not to talk against your kind!

HUANG   So let's stop arguing. That law has us squabbling…

LIAN   Yes, well, the foreigners are very clever, you know. Like Kao said, they didn't pass that law because they thought we were dumb.

ASI   What d'you mean, Grandad?

LIAN   It was because we were good. Everything we put our hands on we were good at. *(reflectively)* Remember the gold mines? The ones exhausted by the white miners? Well we brothers banded together, bought the mines and made them thrive. We found gold and the Gold Mountain took on real meaning then. But that didn't last. Those miners got mad and jealous and drove us off…

JOHN   I heard about that…

LIAN   The railroads? Ah, yes, the railroads…. You know it took those white workers two years to lay fifty miles of track? It's because every payday they went off and got drunk and wouldn't turn up for work the next day…. They turned to us and in no time we finished the hardest part of that damn railroad…

JOHN   What a price we paid…

LIAN   Yes. Many died. A very heavy price. I remember the mountains. The baskets carrying our brothers suspended in mid-air. *(He becomes excited.)* Explosions! Rocks! Pieces of flesh flying everywhere! Baskets tumbling down the cliff sides! Brothers screaming…! *(pause, softly)* And in the spring… in the spring… when the snow melted, we'd find them… stiff and still clinging to their shovels…

JOHN   And when it was all finished they drove us off, didn't they?

LIAN   That's right. So we moved on. Thousands of us, like nomads roaming the countryside looking for work and a bowl of food… anything! All we wanted was a piece of land to build a home, to grow food, to live in harmony with nature. The way of the Tao…. What do we care who runs the government as long as they leave us in peace… *(pause)*

Some of us went into farming. We reclaimed swamp and turned them into fertile fields and grew fruits and vegetables. We excelled and they found a reason to throw us out… *(pause)*

So we took up fishing. We built our own boats but because they looked different the foreigners passed a law forbidding foreign boats from fishing in their waters… because we were too good. It was as if someone was looking over our shoulders, approving or disapproving of what we did. So we moved on searching until all that was left were restaurants and laundries. Women's jobs! They haven't driven us out of those yet…

HUANG   *(sarcastically)* Ha-ha…. I just had a thought. You know why they passed that law? It's because we excel in screwing. Making lots of little babies! That's why there're so many of us… *(HUANG, LIAN and ASI laugh.)*

JOHN   That's not funny.

KAO   It's all very well what you say but you still don't understand. None of you! Chinatown thinks I'm nothing. It's bad enough being Chinese in a white man's land. It's downright degrading to be a nothing Chinese…. Explain that to me! Why they treat me this way?

> *There is an awkward silence. Only the parade is heard.*

> *(to himself)* Ahhh! That damn parade! Where the hell is Kung…?

JOHN   That's the trouble with you, Kao. Your mind is fevered. It's clouded your thinking…. I once knew a man like you…. He was full of hate, anger and bitterness. He walked around like a chip looking for a shoulder, wanting to get even with the rest of the world…. His problem was in his loins. So we found him a woman and ever since he's been happy…. We can do the same for you…

KAO   I won't argue with you, married as you are. *(pause)* What's it like to be married?

JOHN   Now you're talking!

LIAN   *(picking up the cue)* Now there's a man for you! How to describe a woman? Well… she… she's beyond description.

JOHN   *(like a salesman)* She makes you happy! Cooks your food! Washes your clothes! She happily inherits one half of your problems…!

LIAN   She gives you sons! The dream of every father! Sons…!

JOHN   Big happinesses…! *(seductively)* Imagine, Kao. Imagine lying next to her, feeling her warmth, her soft skin against yours, tufts of hair as fine as silk… and her breasts! Like mounds of rice flour…

LIAN   There's nothing like a woman, Kao. They were born to make us happy!

HUANG   God, what a load of lies!

JOHN   What do you know, kai-dai?

KAO   Yes, Huang, what do you know? You never had a woman before…. It's the law, isn't it? It made you a man-love. *(No response.)* I'm just trying to understand…

HUANG   Shut up!

> *Enter MME WU. A small, timid woman whose painful shyness hides a deep-seated fear; a fear of her husband, Mr. Wu. In reaction to this fear, she displays a reluctant fascination and attraction to the teahouse and its occupants. On her entrance the men react like mischievous school boys caught in the act. They come to attention, unconsciously preening themselves.*

MME WU   *(shyly)* I… I brought the coffee for elder brother Huang… *(No response.)* I brought the coffee…?

HUANG   *(with a start)* Oh! Oh, yes, of course. Coffee. I… I did order coffee, didn't I? I'd forgotten. Please… I'm sorry, Mme Wu.

LIAN   What's she up to? I've never seen her here before.

JOHN   Ssshhh…

MME WU   I… was delayed by customers. I'm sorry…

HUANG   Think nothing of it! As long as it's hot…

MME WU   Oh, yes! I heated it before I came…

HUANG   *(feeling the pot)* Yes, so it is…

> As they speak, JOHN circles MME WU, eyeing her with great curiosity. She is uncomfortably aware of this attention. JOHN rejoins LIAN.

KAO   How are you, Mme Wu?

MME WU   Fine, elder brother Kao… and you…?

LIAN   And how is brother Wu?

MME WU   Oh. Well… I suppose he's all right.

LIAN   Tell him we asked about him.

MME WU   You honour him too much, Grandad. *(Pause. She looks about uncertainly, then reluctantly.)* I must go now.

KAO   No! I mean… won't you stay a few minutes? It… it's so good to see a… you…

LIAN   Yes, why don't you, Mme Wu? Get her a chair somebody! *(There is a rush as ASI, JOHN and KAO oblige.)*

KAO   *(pushing forward)* Here…! *(imploringly)* Just for a few minutes…!

> MME WU glances demurely at him, then after some hesitation she sits facing the audience.

> Silence. The men stand behind her nodding their approval to one another. Some moments of indecision follow as they adjust to this new situation. Suddenly MME WU springs to her feet. Startled. The men jump back.

Don't go! Stay a few minutes more…! Please!

JOHN   *(indicating the chair)* Yes, Mme Wu, why don't you. *(Reluctantly yet willingly she sits.)* Would you like some tea!

KAO   I'll get it.

> Pause. She smiles shyly at JOHN and LIAN who return the smile then glance knowingly at each other.

JOHN   *(clearing his throat)* Your husband is a lucky man, Mme Wu, to have a loyal wife like you… *(she tenses)* a totally obedient wife…

> Suddenly she moans and covers her face with her hands. She trembles. Looks to HUANG for support.

LIAN   Mme Wu...?

MME WU   I... I must go...

KAO   Wait! Your tea...

> *Again, reluctantly yet willingly she stops, takes the tea from him. Their eyes meet and a brief moment passes between them.*

JOHN   Where are your manners, brother Kao? Ask Madame to sit...

KAO   Please... *(She does so.)*

> *Pause. Several beats during which she sips her tea, which appears to calm her. The men look at one another expectantly.*

MME WU   *(haltingly, trying to conquer her fears)* You know... I... I've never been in a place like this... never before.... There's many places I've... I've never... oh... *(chokes on her words and looks around, then in a clear voice)* It's so empty.... Our café is empty too. Nobody comes to our café.... Why is your tea house so empty, brother John? I thought everyone likes you. You know how to please people... *(She begins to ramble.)* I... Mr. Wu... my husband? He... he tries to please but he... he.... Why does no one come to our café? He's a... good... man.... That's what they told me when we married! But... he... he's marching in the parade, you know. He's very proud of that.... He wants to show his loyalty to the Gold Mountain so he's marching an entire block... a whole block. He told me so himself. He's so proud.... He... he says it will make his life better.... Oh! I hope so because then I... maybe I'll... *(pause)* It... it's always him... always him... always talking about himself... never... he... he... *(She chokes and suddenly darts for the door, fearfully.)* Oh! He'll be looking for me...!

KAO   No! Wait...!

> *She stops again, indecisively.*

I... I'll return the coffee pot...

JOHN   I'll come with you, Mme Wu. I want to speak with him.

> *They exit, JOHN flashing LIAN a knowing glance.*
>
> *Pause.*

KAO   How could she marry a man like that!

HUANG   Tradition...

LIAN   She is beautiful though, isn't she, Kao?

KAO   Yes, she is that...

HUANG   You think so? Cute maybe.... She looked like a tiny dumpling with duck's legs... but her eyes were sad like a bulldog's.... I've seen eyes like that before. It's not good...

ASI   She made me think of my mother.... When I was a baby, my mother used to put beet sugar on her breasts... and her milk would be sweet. I'll always remember that because when I grew up she teased me about it.... She said I never wanted to let go...

LIAN   She reminded me of my rice-cooker. My rice-cooker looked just like Mme Wu when she was young. A remarkable woman, my rice-cooker. A true Chinese wife: loyal, obedient, devoted...

KAO   I was standing that close to her. She had the fragrance of a flower garden... Chrysanthemums! That's it! She smelled like chrysanthemums.

LIAN   No, jasmine...

ASI   Beet sugar...

HUANG   She smelled like coffee to me.

KAO   (*huffily*) How typical! She honours us with her presence and beauty, and all you think about is coffee. No wonder you're a kai-dai.

HUANG   At least I didn't make a fool of myself mooning over her as you did.

KAO   I did no such thing!

HUANG   She's married for God's sake!

KAO   So...? She's second hand. So what?

HUANG   What a thing to say! You should show more respect...

KAO   Don't give me advice!

HUANG   Give him a drink, Asi.

KAO   I said I was all right!

HUANG   You're stupid like the rest of them. I expected better...

KAO   Don't call me stupid!

HUANG   You think a woman will solve your problem? It runs deeper than that, let me tell you. You'll soon see...

KAO   What do you mean?

HUANG   (*blurts*) Kung hasn't gone to the government!

KAO   What...?

HUANG   He's probably hiding somewhere. You honestly think he can talk to that government? You think this country's like China where you can go talk to the emperor? Well it's different! But you wouldn't know that because you don't want to know! I mean look at us! We lock ourselves up in this hellhole, afraid to go out, afraid of our own shadows. Like children! Kung will not succeed! But you'll

blame him. I know you will. You ought to blame yourselves! *(to KAO)* And you…
you ought to know better.

KAO   Oh, shut up!

HUANG   You, especially, should know better!

KAO   Shut up, you fucking faggot!

> *Silence. Several beats. HUANG quietly exits.*

Wait! *(But HUANG has gone.)* Did I say that? I didn't, did I? I couldn't have. It's
not me. I wouldn't say that. Not after what I've been through. It's just not me….
What's happening to me? Grandad? Tell me! *(No response.)* Asi? Then who can?
All my life it's been like this…

(brief pause) Like I'm lost in a storm, a winter storm. And all around me are
lights beckoning with the promise of welcome and warmth. I knock… but the
doors are slammed shut in my face so I move on, snow whipping at my feet, the
wind laughing at me…. Now there's an odd thing. Because I happen to love
winter and the snow and the cold wind blowing. I love the quiet streets and the
chill in the air because then I can wrap my scarf around my face and nobody'd
recognize me. No one would throw stones or call me names or spit at me. I can
hold my head high and feel like a man!

Winter makes me feel like a man! Yes it does! It gives me solace but no refuge.
Now that is curious! And what a queer country this is where you find solace only
one season out of four, and where the rest is a wrenching search for a refuge.

Summer is the worst… it's impossible to feel like a man in summer. The heat
strips you bare and leaves you naked. And everyone sees you for what you really
are… like today…

But that wasn't me! No, Huang. No, brother Huang, it wasn't me! I didn't say
that. It was the parade! July first! Middle of summer! Humiliation Day! It-was-
not-me! *(Suddenly he drops to his haunches and prances about, feverishly)* Whoop!
Whoop! Whoop! Whoop! Whoop! The Monkey King! I am the Monkey King,
and I would never say such a thing…!

> *KUNG enters. He is nervous. KAO sees him and comes to his feet, angry.*

You lied, Kung! You lied to me! How dare you lie to the Monkey King!

> *End of Act Two.*

ACT THREE

SCENE ONE

Spot comes up on ASI.

ASI *(to the audience)* It's so strange… walking the streets and seeing only the faces of men. Bland faces with dull, piteous eyes. Faces no different from your own…. After a while it got so that you couldn't stand seeing yourself anymore. So you walk with your head bowed low and all you see are feet. Your world has changed… from faces to feet. Hundreds of feet shuffling back and forth, monotonous, aimless feet… men's feet… and nowhere in sight… was The Monkey King…

> *Lights come up. The men are having supper. As ASI joins them, JOHN and LIAN come downstage and speak privately.*

LIAN Well how did it go? What did Wu say?

JOHN He's agreeable. He'll tell his wife what she has to do and…. We'll have to use one of my rooms, of course…

LIAN The price was good?

JOHN It always is when I do the bargaining.

> *They rejoin the others. Several beats as they eat, except for KUNG who finds it difficult.*

KUNG *(clears his throat, haltingly)* I… I'm just one man…. I can't talk to that government… no one can…. And today's a holiday. The government is closed… didn't you know that? Why did you believe me? Why did you think I could do it? Couldn't you see it was… impossible? So stupid! John was right…

JOHN Didn't I tell you? What will Chinatown say now? They'll be very disappointed.

LIAN You mean you knew from the start it was a waste of time? Then why? I remember the night you said you'd go. I believed in you. We all did.

KAO *(hurtfully)* He's a liar…

JOHN *(snidely)* It's because he's more learned than we are. He thought he'd have some fun at our expense. So he played us along… I wish you brothers listened to me…. You know what this means? We'll never see our women again, that's what. *(He reaches for his letter, maudlin.)* What do I tell her? This faithful woman who breaks my heart every time she writes.

KAO *(with pain and regret)* Why did you lead us on? Why? You gave me hope and did not deliver.

KUNG   You don't know what it's like… bounced from one world to the next… belonging to neither. Neither here, neither there, that's me. A half and half! An in between! A tchap cheung! *(pause)* This place was a godsend to me…. I felt at home here. As if I belonged. I could be myself. You called me brother. No one ever did that before…. I was so grateful I wanted to do something for you, all of you… to show my appreciation… that I was more than just a… a… half and half. *(pause)* It's so important to do something, you know, anything, as long as it's something. When I said I could talk to the government I… I knew right away it was a mistake…

HUANG   You could've told us.

LIAN   Yes, we can take the truth.

        Outside, near the door, comes a loud cackling laugh.

JOHN   *(rushing to the door, threateningly)* Queenie…! *(He returns grumbling.)* There should be a special Exclusion Act just for her…

KUNG   I'll pack my things and go…

ASI   But where will you go, Uncle Kung?

JOHN   Let him go. It's not right what he did.

ASI   But he tried. Isn't that good?

HUANG   Yes, it is. Much better than hiding in here whining all the time. Stay, Kung. Have a drink.

LIAN   You know what I think? I think we ought to show we don't give a damn. We don't care what they do to us. We can take it! We'll fight this to the very end!

ASI   I thought you said we should accept it. It's our way of life. Now you say we should fight. Shouldn't it be one or the other? How can it be both?

HUANG   Ha-ha. What have you to say to that, Grandad?

LIAN   He's just a boy.

KUNG   The young are to be held in awe, says the old proverb.

JOHN   You are in no position to speak words of wisdom.

KUNG   You're right. Look, when I said I could talk to the government and saw the eagerness in your faces… I felt… happy. I mean, you believed in me. You trusted me. You had confidence in me. It felt so good. I never felt that way before…. I just didn't want it to end…

LIAN   *(after a brief pause)* It will take you a long time to climb back up the ladder.

JOHN   Listen, brothers. It's not hopeless. True, we'll not get our women back but there're others. They may not be Chinese but…

KAO   *(hovering by the window)* Here comes Queenie.

JOHN rushes to the door to forestall her entrance.

HUANG   Let her be, John. At least she's a woman…

JOHN and LIAN laugh.

LIAN   Why not, John? She'll be good for a laugh.

QUEENIE enters.

QUEENIE   Evening, brothers. They tell me in Chinatown you need a woman. But then all of Chinatown needs a woman. So I walked all day, back and forth, looking for a customer. But no luck! You sure could fool me! Any customers here?

JOHN   Queenie, you old hag, not in here…

HUANG   Let her be. She's been hovering outside all day. She's got no place to go. Give her a drink.

JOHN   She has no ready money.

KUNG   I'll pay…

KAO   Let her stay. She'll help pass the time.

JOHN   Well… just one. Then she'll have to go. *(to QUEENIE)* And no soliciting.

QUEENIE   Thank you. You're so kind. Men are so kind. *(She sits. JOHN pours her a drink.)* I've been looking all day for a customer. A rich one this time. I'm tired of rancid rice and bitter tea. But there's nobody around. They're all inside… hiding… afraid of that parade…

JOHN   *(giving her a drink)* Remember, just one then you go.

QUEENIE   *(raising the cup)* Here's to kindness… *(She slurps noisily.)* Ahhh! *(then dryly)* Excuse my manners. But I'm no lady, as you can see. All that was stripped away from me a long time ago… *(She turns to see the men standing far away with amused contempt.)* So? What am I? A disease? *(The men laugh.)* You look like roosters staring at a hen… *(They laugh louder. So does she.)* I hear you went to talk to the government, Kung…

KUNG   Please…

QUEENIE   *(gently)* Don't worry! I'm not going to laugh at you like they. They did, didn't they? Ha! *(reassuringly)* No, I just want to look at someone who dared…

JOHN   Let's have no trouble today, Queenie.

QUEENIE   Pooh on you, John. Pooh on your ancestors, too! *(spying his altar)* That where you honour your ancestors? You're lucky. I have no altar. I have no ancestors. They've disowned me. Let me see what… *(She hobbles toward the altar.)*

JOHN   *(blocking her path)* I said no trouble today, Queenie.

QUEENIE   Why blame me for trouble that hasn't yet started? Eh? *(sits and rests her feet on a chair)* You know, if I had a place, I'd have an altar too, so I can honour my ancestors. Maybe they'll honour me. But I need money for that. So! Which one of you will it be?

JOHN   I said no soliciting.

QUEENIE   Soliciting? I'm just being practical, John. You're men, I'm a woman, its Dominion Day. We have our needs…

KAO   That may be, Queenie. But you shouldn't gild your mirror. We don't see what you see.

QUEENIE   *(sighs)* I know. Anyway, I'm just here to rest my feet and I'll be on my way.

KAO   Give her another drink, John.

HUANG   I'll pay for it…

JOHN   *(haughtily)* This one's on me! I feel generous.

QUEENIE   No, no! No generosity ridden with contempt! I'll work for it, thank you. *(She grabs the nearby broom.)* I'll sweep the floor clean. Give this place a woman's touch…

HUANG   *(taking away the broom)* Sit down, Queenie.

QUEENIE   *(grabs the broom back)* I'm still useful. *(emphatically)* I'm still useful.

> She hobbles around sweeping. The men exchange amused glances.

LIAN   You missed a spot over there.

QUEENIE   Oh, yes… *(She sweeps vigorously around the tables.)* It's good to be useful. *(several beats, then suddenly, mockingly)* Brings back memories, doesn't it? The men gathered about the wine talking important nonsense and I… I sweeping the yards, feeding the chickens and pigs…. I remind you of anybody? Your women perhaps…? *(They chuckle.)*

LIAN   Ha-ha-ha! Don't flatter yourself, Queenie! You're not in their class.

JOHN   And don't you insult my rice-cooker! Feeling sorry for yourself, are you?

QUEENIE   Who? Me? Oh, no. I've outgrown that. I leave the self-pity to you men. You plaster saints who've made it a way of life…. Next to beating your women self-pity is your favourite pastime.

LIAN   You watch your mouth, woman!

QUEENIE   Sorry, Grandad. I'm tired, that's all. I've been on my feet all day. Why don't you rent me a room, John? That way my customers can come to me and I won't have to walk so much…

KUNG   Yes, John, why don't you?

JOHN   I have my customers to think about.

QUEENIE   Tch. Tch. Tch. John! Customers? What kind of customers? Come on, I'll give you a good cut…

KAO   *(grinning)* Five percent, Queenie.

QUEENIE   That much? My volume isn't that great but… all right. If it'll save wear and tear on my feet. How about it, John?

KUNG   How about it, John?

HUANG   Yes, John.

JOHN   Queenie, if you were younger, no problem. But you're old. A dried up social flower…

LIAN   Not only that, you're poorly bred and you talk too much.

QUEENIE   But John, we have so much in common. I'm a freelance whore and you're a pimp…

JOHN   I'm not… that!

KUNG   *(chuckling to KAO)* He should hear what they say about him in Chinatown.

QUEENIE   But you are! Oh, I know! It just sounds different when someone else says it, doesn't it?

JOHN   *(becoming riled)* I am respected and admired!

QUEENIE   Because you have money! And no one has the guts to ask if it's honest money.

JOHN   That's enough! You've had your drink!

QUEENIE   Oh, I don't blame you. We must do what we must do. If we're lucky we'll get rich and buy our way out…. You can buy so much with money. You can even buy your way into the Christian heaven…. How many women will have to lie on their backs for you to get into your Christian heaven?

KAO   A-men!

LIAN   Why are you looking at me like that?

QUEENIE   You know why, old man. You told him that! *(postures)* "St. Peter will be standing at the Pearly Gates," you said. "Five hundred dollars to enter heaven, John Chinaman…"

LIAN   But it's true! I heard it said myself.

QUEENIE   Superstition! You come ten-thousand miles to Gum Shan bringing your stupid superstitions with you! And he believes it too, the rich fool!

JOHN   Don't call me a fool!

QUEENIE That's why he's running this… Christian whorehouse!

LIAN Damn you woman! Your tongue is loose!

QUEENIE And my feet are bound!

> *Using the broom as a support, QUEENIE puts one foot on the table.*
> *Shocked, LIAN springs to his feet, his chair making a loud clatter.*
> *The others come to attention. KAO, KUNG and ASI advance slowly,*
> *fascinated by the sight before them.*
>
> *A stunned and shocked silence. Several beats.*

Aren't they pretty? Almost perfect. Like works of art…. That's why they're always killing me. You ought to try it sometime, walking on bound feet chasing after men to give you a hot meal. The same men who bound my feet in the first place…

KAO Who did that…?

QUEENIE My little birdies, I call them. My little pets…

LIAN Throw her out, John!

JOHN Out you go! You overstayed your welcome! *(He ushers her out.)*

QUEENIE Don't push! I can still hobble…

KAO Did you see that…? Her feet…?

JOHN *(returning to the counter)* That's what happens when you're kind to people.

KAO Who did that to her?

LIAN *(to JOHN)* Insufferable woman!

KUNG *(to KAO)* I read about it. I never thought I'd see it.

JOHN *(to LIAN)* Her kind give all women a bad name.

KAO *(to KUNG)* Read about it?

LIAN *(to JOHN)* She does not behave like a woman.

KUNG *(to KAO)* It's not just her…

JOHN *(to LIAN)* Shameless behaviour.

KAO *(to KUNG)* What do you mean?

LIAN *(to JOHN)* Her ancestors would be ashamed.

KUNG *(to KAO)* Tradition…

HUANG Yes, tradition. Bad tradition! But she's lucky. At least she can hobble. I saw women who couldn't even do that. Their feet were destroyed… totally… useless stumps of broken bones and flesh… I never knew Queenie…

KUNG   (*to KAO*) Back in China she'd be run out of the village. There's no place for people who don't know their place…

KAO   Tell me more, Kung. I want to know more…

JOHN   (*dismissively*) Enough! She's not worth talking about. We give her too much face. She's the one who's keeping my customers away… standing outside the door all day… (*quickly*) Asi, go see if she's still there! (*to KUNG*) You told the brothers I'm open, Kung?

KUNG   What…? Oh, yes, I did…

JOHN   Well? What did they say?

KUNG   They snickered. They talk about you, you know.

JOHN   What about me? (*KUNG chuckles.*) What about me?!

KUNG   They're staying away because you let the wrong people live here. People like me. And Kao and Huang. But I know you don't mind. We have ready money…

JOHN   I don't believe it!

KUNG   It's true.

JOHN   I still don't believe it! You're lying…. Anyway, they wouldn't talk against me… (*pause*) How dare they? After all I've done for them? They wanted food, so I made my tea house a restaurant…

Enter QUEENIE quietly. She stands perfectly still until she's noticed.

…they wanted rooms to let, so I let them have rooms. I even gave them rooms for their women! And now they talk against me? That's gratitude for you! One day they're smiling at you, the next day they're badmouthing you…. What kind of people is that?

He finally sees QUEENIE.

Queenie! What d'you want now?!

QUEENIE   Mme Wu is dead…

HUANG   What…?

KAO   That can't be. She was alive an hour ago. She was standing right there where you are.

QUEENIE   Now she's hanging from the rafters. I was passing by, I saw the police… the ambulance… next door. Go see for yourself.

JOHN   If this is a joke, Queenie…!

KAO exits hurriedly.

LIAN   But… why? Why would she do that?

QUEENIE   She's a woman…

> *HUANG gives her a drink.*

You ought to see Wu. Silly little man! Running around in circles in the middle of the street, grieving for himself—not for her, for himself—arms flapping about like a crazy hen. He never knew how lucky he was until now. So stupid! Poor Mme Wu…. I wish I knew her. But I never had the chance. There was always that glass window between us…. Sometimes our eyes would meet and I would sense a need to talk. But Wu wouldn't let her out and he wouldn't let me in…

LIAN   She was a good woman. Obedient…

QUEENIE   Yes, she was good. Only good women die like that. Wicked women go on forever…. Like me… with my loose tongue and bound feet…. Not so, Grandad?

> *Enter KAO, pale, tense and angry.*

KAO   *(in a fury)* What kind of man do you think I am? *(He lunges at JOHN.)* What do you take me for?

> *HUANG and KUNG spring forward to restrain him.*

Let me go! Let me go! I'll kill him…!

KUNG   What is it?

JOHN   What's the matter with you? Where's your respect?

KAO   I can't believe it! I just can't! What kind of men are you?!

KUNG   What is it?!

HUANG   Let me guess…. They bought Mme Wu. For one night. For you, Kao. Am I right, John?

> *Shocked silence.*

KUNG   Wu agreed to that?

HUANG   Why not? That was normal… to him…

LIAN   You don't understand…. We did it for you, Kao. To help you. We don't want you to end up like the others… going crazy and killing yourself…

JOHN   Every day we watch you not knowing what to expect. You're always on edge. Doing crazy things, saying crazy things…. We were frightened for you. Can you blame us? We just wanted to help, that's all…. It's the law, that's what it is! That damn law! Blame the law…

> *Pause. Several beats as KAO looks around, pacing confusedly, looking for something to say but at a loss.*

QUEENIE   Ah! So that's it! The roosters merely wanted a hen. I should've guessed! Poor Mme Wu. A poor choice if any, too fragile. You might've asked me! I'm available. I'm cheap. Not to mention durable. *(to JOHN)* Why didn't you ask me? Don't you think I'm pretty…? *(she sashays)* Look at me…! *(parades herself in a mocking manner)* How about you, Kao? Well? What d'you think? Am I pretty? No? The look on your face says it all. What a shame! With your one arm and my bound feet I'd say we're meant for each other! How about you, Kung? Am I beautiful? No, of course not! You cross the streets whenever you see me coming…. Huang? Man-love that you are. Do you find me twice as pretty or twice as ugly?

HUANG   *(hurt)* Stop it, Queenie.

QUEENIE   You, Grandad? John? Don't you find me the least bit desirable? *(mockingly)* Oh, I am so sorry! Forgive me! I forgot! You're doting husbands! You have precious loyal wives… like Mme Wu! *(pause)* You'd think I'd be the most sought-after woman seeing its Humiliation Day. The day they took away your women… *(pause, then matter-of-factly)* That law has nothing to do with it, brother Kao. You're a victim of kindness…

KAO   Kindness? What kind of kindness is this?

QUEENIE   Man's kindness. Ask Mme Wu…

KAO   What are you saying?

QUEENIE   You really want to know?

KAO   Yes, I do. I must!

QUEENIE   *(regarding him with new respect)* Well, well, well! You're the first man to ever ask! *(brief pause)* Well, all right. Why not? I'll tell you. Like you said, "It will help pass the time." But promise me one thing. No more kindness. Buy me no more drinks and save your pity for Mme Wu… *(She picks up the broom.)*

You see, they said it was for my own good when they bound my feet. *(postures)* "You'll advance in the world," they said. "You'll have the prettiest of feet! You'll join the upper classes!" I'll be the most desirable of women! I'll stand on the palms of emperors! I'll be a concubine! Of the emperor! And if the Fates were kind I might become the empress! *(pause, tremblingly)*

So they broke my toes and curled them under… then they tied it tight with wet cloth so that when it dried it was even tighter…. Oh! The pain! The pus! The smell! You cannot imagine! They… they tried to soothe me. "The pain will go away," they said. "You'll get accustomed," they said. They lied! After all these years I'm still not accustomed…

LIAN   Who wants to know your life?

QUEENIE   But I was village born and not very pretty. I didn't belong to the cultured elite. Culture is very serious business, you see, and I was just a commoner who liked to talk and laugh…. No. I could never belong.

My parents were disappointed. So they married me off to a wealthy merchant. Money! They did it more for them than for me…. And so began my married life. What a sick joke! When he parted my wedding veil and I peered into his face, I knew I had married death! And my heart shrivelled to the size of my feet…

He was an old fart with a face like a dried prune and a tendon to match. But give the old bugger credit! Somehow he was able to get it up! I think my feet must've excited him to no end…! I remember his hands were coarse, his breath foul and he smelled all over like a mildewed carpet…

But within a year I gave birth to a baby girl. *(softly)* Oh! She was so pretty! *(Her voice hardens.)* But he wasn't happy! He wanted a son. A big happiness! She was still moist, the cord still tied to her when he grabbed her by her tiny feet and tossed her into the garbage heap…! Because she was a baby girl, a small happiness…! *(pause)* I had failed, you see, as woman and wife…

KAO   Why did you marry him? You didn't have to!

HUANG   Oh, yes, she did! There is no "yes" or "no" in their lives…

KAO   You know about this…?

KUNG   I've read such stories…. Baby girls drowned or strangled because they weren't wanted. Men beating women because they produced no sons…

KAO   What are you saying, Kung?

LIAN   Ah, nonsense!

HUANG   He's saying it's normal.

KAO   Normal?

QUEENIE   The next day he was on top of me again. Telling me I'd betrayed his ancestors because I didn't give him a son. I turned to my mother-in-law for help. She's a woman, isn't she? She'll understand! She'll help! But no! She took her turns beating me! Ordering me around! I'd made her lose face, you see! She went around the village telling everyone she was going to have a grandson…. The ignorant bitch! I never thought a woman could be such a bitch!

JOHN   They're all like that!

QUEENIE   Ah! The worm crawls out of the apple!

JOHN   You think you're the only one with a hard life? Look around you! It's been hell for us over here. The Fates have been unkind to all of us…

QUEENIE   Tell that to Mme Wu…!

LIAN   Ignore her, John!

HUANG   But you ran away, didn't you?

QUEENIE   Yes! Yes! I did! Like this! *(She hobbles around dragging the broom behind her.)* And the old fart came after me! With my bound feet and his wobbly legs we were evenly matched! So I ran faster! I'll show them! This is one piece of furniture you can't nail to the floor…! *(brief pause)* The old fart had a heart attack and fell dead! Ha-ha-ha! I wept for joy! I fell to my knees and thanked Heaven! *(She does so.)* There is justice in the world after all…. And you, John, when you get to your heaven, you ask St. Peter why such piecemeal justice for women like me…!

LIAN   She's crazy! Anyway, what's all this got to do with Mme Wu?

KAO   Shut up! Go on, Queenie…

    Brief pause.

QUEENIE   I ran, I walked, I hobbled all the way to the big city. Life will be better there. I would find woman-sisters and we'll comfort one another. I'll lose myself in the big city. There, all around, were thousands like me. That made me happy. Isn't that strange? That it would make me happy? But it was nice to know others shared my burden.

    (reflectively) Some of us became friends. And we survived as best we could in the gutters of Canton…. Our wits kept us alive! And our laughter gave us strength! Oh! We laughed at everything! When the men taunted us and called us loose women, we laughed in their faces. *(postures)* "How loose can a woman be with bound feet?!" That shut them up! They didn't know what to say. They never do. So they called us crazy…

    Sometimes at night… we'd gather around and talk. Small talk, woman talk…. We'd always talk about men… how strange they are. Then we'd laugh at their strangeness… *(pause)*

    Sometimes we even dared to dream! Then we'd laugh at the conceit of those dreams… then we'd fall silent and stare at one another… each knowing what the other was thinking but afraid to ask. *(lengthy pause)* That's why I wished I knew Mme Wu. We could've laughed together… and maybe… maybe she'd still be alive…

LIAN   *(quickly)* I don't believe this! Listen to you…! It's not as if every woman's life was the same. Look at my rice-cooker…

QUEENIE   Rice-cooker? Ha-ha-ha! Rice-cooker! What is your wife's name? Quick! Her name! *(LIAN is flustered.)* Ha-ha-ha! Can't remember, can you?

LIAN   Ah, you're useless! You understand nothing!

KAO   Kung, is this all true…?

QUEENIE   Sometimes even I wonder if it's true. Even as I sweep this floor on the Gold Mountain, I wonder. In the mornings I wonder. At night I wonder…. You never know for sure because it's so confusing. And it's hard to think because your mind is not made to think... because you're a woman. You're born numb, you're kept numb. You're aware, yet you're not aware. You remember and don't remember.... Things happen but you don't know what they are. You can't make head or tail of what's going on. Your mind has shut down. Maybe it never worked. And your thoughts? They're all over the place. There's nothing to bring them together because everyone wants a piece of you. You're like a bedpan for all the filth in the world.

JOHN   Oh, what nonsense! Don't listen to her! She's just babbling! All lies...

QUEENIE   *(snaps)* Tell that to Mme Wu! I know all about lies! *(postures)* "It's for your own good!" they said. They lied! "You'll move up in the world," they said. They lied"! Lie followed lie to excuse a wrong. Lies became so commonplace, common sense was not common anymore! That's what happened to us.

Why else would women be a part of this? It was the women; my own mother, my aunts, the village women who held me down as they bound my feet. How could they? Why? Aren't they women like me...? Couldn't they see it was wrong? Couldn't they see through my pain and know it was wrong? Couldn't my screams jar their minds and tell them it was wrong? Why couldn't they see it...? Instead they lied.

(sadly) What can you say when the victims take part in the crime? I couldn't understand these things so I blamed myself.... It was my fault I was treated this way. I had done something evil. I was paying for a wicked past life.... I wanted to die...

          Pause.

HUANG   Instead you fled to the Gold Mountain...

LIAN   All right! That's enough! Can't you see what she's up to? She wants our sympathy...

JOHN   Yes! Yes! That's right! She wants me to give her a room. You heard her say so yourself.... Exaggeration! That's what it is!

HUANG   Is it?! *(Lengthy pause. He looks around indecisively.)* You... you remind me of my wife, Queenie. *(They turn to him.)* Yes, that's right... *(pause)* she was just fifteen. I wasn't much older. Wasn't very bright either... I didn't even know what marriage was. But the village men told me I'd have a woman and she'd do things for me.... She'll make me happy, they said.... So they found me this girl. *(brief pause)*

She was small and pretty but her feet were not bound like yours, Queenie. She had to work in the fields... I remember during the ceremony she had to bow to me. She didn't want to so they forced her. I should've sensed something not right but... anyway, that night... when I parted that red veil and we saw each other for the first time, the most extraordinary thing happened.... She, she screamed! She pulled away from me! And before I knew it she ran smack into the wall! Cracking her skull open! I couldn't believe it! Was I that ugly?! I couldn't be that ugly! Could I? Then why…?! *(pause)* I found out later she never wanted to marry me. Or anybody! She was being forced…

KAO   Huang, I'm surprised. You never said a word…

KUNG   *(quietly)* In some villages, women were forced to marry boys. I read of one woman who had to marry a six-year-old. Later, she fell in love with a man… the villagers almost killed her…

QUEENIE   In other places, if the husband-to-be happened to die before the marriage, the woman still had to go through with the ceremony. Then she had to move in with his family; a widow and slave for the rest of her days…

        Brief pause.

HUANG   Anyway, the men came back and bandaged her and told me to get on with it… encouraging me with their dirty jokes. And I did. *(pause)* I didn't know any better! That's what happens when your world is a little village and your teaching a perversion… I shudder any time I think about it! I should've known better! But I didn't! I honestly didn't! It's like what Queenie said. Your mind just stops. I did what they told me…! As if… as if I had no mind of my own! My god! I didn't even know what was right or wrong!

    (angrily) The next morning she was dead! But they told me not to worry. I can get me another one *(He snaps his fingers.)* just like that! Like drawing water from a well! *(pause)* I did get me another one… another wife. But I couldn't… I kept hearing the screams… the blood pouring down that face… *(pause)*

    I… I could never do it with a woman after that. I sent her back to her parents. The villagers laughed at me. Called me all kinds of names. Troublemaker! Kai-dai! Soon the whole village was against me… *(pause)* I had to get away! Far away… so I fled…

KUNG   To the Gold Mountain… where it's not much better…

HUANG   *(sarcastic laugh)* Yes, here I am. Being what I am… on the Gold Mountain… I thought I could be happy here. But these whites are as ignorant as those villagers. They have a way of making you feel so dirty all over… *(brief pause)* It's no different here…

QUEENIE   It's the same all over…. No matter where you go, you wake up in the morning… afraid to face another day…

KAO   You're even afraid to go outside…. And if you do, you hunch down low… hoping your shoulders hide your face.

HUANG   You overdress… making sure every part of your body is covered…. Sometimes… you even avoid mirrors…

QUEENIE   You never shower... but you don't mind because dirt is nature's best disguise...

ASI   Oh.... You never shower, Queenie?

> *QUEENIE looks from KAO to KUNG to HUANG. Suddenly the four burst out laughing, finding a sense of camaraderie.*

KAO   How about some tea, Queenie?

HUANG   Coffee?

JOHN   No, no, that's enough. She's had her drink! It's time she left.

QUEENIE   Yes, yes, John, don't worry! I'll soon be leaving... *(wry smile)* I still have a customer to find...

HUANG   *(giving her some coffee)* Drink up...

> *Pause. Several beats. An air of expectancy. A silence crying out to be broken.*

KUNG   You're better than all my books, Queenie.

KAO   You make me wonder who's worse... whites or Chinese...

QUEENIE   I see only men. And they're all the same to me. Little boys with hair between their legs. Doesn't it frighten you? It does me. Everywhere I look around it frightens me... *(pause)* It's better not to talk about it. *(with a laugh)* Don't worry about me! I can take care of myself! I'm Queenie, aren't I?

The Queen of Dundas Street! Where the sidewalks are my realm! From the gutters of Canton to the sidewalks of Toronto! *(dryly)* I have moved up in the world! Ha-ha-ha! Isn't that why we came to the Gold Mountain? Ha-ha-ha! There's no telling what I can do now...!

KAO   But how can you live like this? Always on the go, roaming the streets. No shelter, no place, no one... I mean... don't you ever want a... a place to call your own? Somewhere... where you... you...

QUEENIE   Where I can hide? *(KAO looks away, embarrassed.)* Where can anyone hide when life chases you? Anyway, I didn't come here for that. I came chasing dreams, like everyone else. Only to discover they too were lies. *(brief pause)* What was the first thing you noticed when you landed, brother Huang?

HUANG   The first thing? Big... big country, big land, big cities, big towns. Everything big. Even the people... ten-feet tall! And they all wore these tall hats that made them look even taller...

QUEENIE   I saw feet. Big feet...!

KAO   *(laughingly)* You would, wouldn't you?

QUEENIE   Everywhere! Big feet! All around! And everyone had a pair of them too! Well! Imagine my surprise! I didn't quite know what to think! I thought it was some fashion craze…! *(pause)* I tried to make myself beautiful for the Gold Mountain… so I put on a corset. It made my waist small and my breasts large… and I almost suffocated to death…. That was no different than bound feet…

It told me I didn't belong here either. I belonged nowhere! And suddenly, suddenly my life was made so small there was no room for my dreams. *(pause)* I don't want much. I'm a simple woman… *(in a tired, far-off voice)* All I wanted was a place where I could walk the streets openly, where I didn't have to hug the sides of buildings or cling to the shadows. But here the buildings are so tall and the shadows so long, it's twice as hard to emerge into the sunlight…

(a sudden self-deprecating laugh) I had a woman's dreams! Fanciful! I dreamt of romance! Oh, the conceit of this old cow! To dream of romance! *(soft laugh)* I dreamt of a place where man is man and woman is woman; where that is understood with no deviousness, simple with no confusions. Where eyes can meet and nothing else need be said… *(short pause)* I dreamt of a place where the nights are silken and where a man's touch brings no pain. I dreamt of a place where the nights are like velvet and where there are welcoming shoulders for weary heads… *(tremblingly)* where there are no dogs barking and no baby girls on garbage heaps screaming for their lives! *(pause)*

Ha-ha-ha! I dreamt of love! Can you imagine me being loved? It's so important… to be loved… to know that you exist. I needed it… for my sanity… and to keep all the hate I have inside of me from oozing through my pores… I wanted it so badly I was desperate. It drove me to do wild things…. So at nights… I'd say to the men gathered outside my door, "Keep your money! I don't want it! Just tell me you love me… *(poignantly)* Unbind my feet and tell me you love me…. Undo the wrappings and whisper you love me…. That's all…" *(bitterly)* But none ever did! I asked for too much! Some felt sorry, so they threw me money and fled like cowards! The others laughed in my face and said they wouldn't dare… "It's against tradition," they said! "Against tradition!"

(excitedly) Suddenly, like magic, my eyes opened! I jumped to my feet! And I laughed and I wept! With joy! It wasn't me after all! There was nothing wrong with me! It wasn't my fault! It was the world… a perversion that made me this way…! I knew then I wasn't going to hide anymore, feeling sorry for myself… I'll parade myself…. Did any one of you see the parade this morning? I marched in that, you know. You should've seen me. The last in line… marching. *(She does so across the stage.)* Left! Right! Left! Right! Left! Right! *(poignantly)* I wish Mme Wu was there with me… marching… on Humiliation Day… the day they took your women away… she would have enjoyed it…

LIAN   All right, that's it! I won't listen any more! How dare you speak like this?! Spitting blood at your traditions! Your people! Have you no shame?! *(to JOHN)* Throw her out!

JOHN rushes forward.

QUEENIE   Are you that brave, John? *(She holds out her foot using the broom as support.)* Then you unbind my feet! *(Startled, JOHN pulls up short.)* Show us how brave you are! Unbind my feet! Make me whole!

> *JOHN lunges at her, grabs hold of her outstretched foot and makes ready to strike her. He hesitates. The air is tense. Finally, he looks away.*

(turning her foot in his direction) How about you, Grandad? No? Then tell us about your rice-cooker!

KUNG   Yes, tell us about your rice-cooker!

QUEENIE   Rice-cooker! What a name to tell your wives!

LIAN   This is an outrage! Look at yourself, woman! The way you carry on! You don't behave like a typical woman! You have no respect! It's not right to question the wisdom of our elders! There are customs! Traditions we must obey to… to keep social order and harmony! Handed down by our ancestors…! What right have you to create ripples in this ancient well?!

KUNG   How dare you use our ancestors to justify yourself? You talk like a feudal lord.

JOHN   Words! Words! Words! Nothing's changed. Tomorrow will be the same as today. The sun will rise and set as usual. And next year there will be another July first and another parade. Nothing's changed!

> *Lengthy pause.*

QUEENIE   He's right, you know. He's right…. Anyway, I've had my say and my drink. *(She picks up her belongings, preparing to leave.)* I must go now…

KUNG   Wait! You can't leave like this! So bitter and angry! I won't let you…!

QUEENIE   I must pay my respects to Mme Wu.

KUNG   *(blurts)* But it wasn't always like this, Queenie. There was a time when you were honoured. When our ancestors honoured you. Grandad is wrong.

QUEENIE   What are you saying?

KUNG   Our ancestors are not ashamed of you! *(then excitedly)* Oh! I'm just a scholar without brains! Why didn't I see this before? They were never ashamed of you!

QUEENIE   What…?

KUNG   Can you read and write?

QUEENIE   Of course!

KUNG   Well then, close your eyes.

QUEENIE   What...?

KUNG   Please. Close your eyes...

QUEENIE   But Kung...

KUNG   Bear with me! And I'll show you what our ancestors really thought of you.... Now then, what is the character for woman?

QUEENIE   Let's not play games... I'm tired of men's games.

KUNG   Queenie, please! It's me, Kung. Well? What is it? Say it?

QUEENIE   Nu...?

KUNG   Again! Slowly...

QUEENIE   Nu...

KUNG   Write that, Asi! On the wall.

   ASI hurriedly does so with a piece of chalk.

 Now, Queenie, what is the character for child? *(brief pause)* What is it? Say it.

QUEENIE   Ji...?

KUNG   Again! Slowly...

QUEENIE   Ji...

KUNG   Write that, Asi.

   ASI does so on the wall.

 Now write them together, Asi. Side by side...

   QUEENIE watches intently as ASI does so.

QUEENIE   Oh, Kung...

KAO   What does it mean?

KUNG   What does it mean, Queenie?

QUEENIE   It means... good...

KAO   Good...?

KUNG   Yes, Kao, the image of woman and child side by side means good.... A long time ago when our ancestors first began to think and write, they took the image of woman and the image of child and honoured them. They put them side by side and said it was good. Whenever we think or speak or write the word good, you are honoured, Queenie. They're not ashamed of you...

   Pause.

QUEENIE   Is that... right? Is it...? Could it be...?

The men react to this in their various ways.

KUNG   They saw the world in such beautiful images... and they made you the good part of it. *(brief pause)* Strange, but I've known this for years but I didn't really know it until today...

    Pause.

KAO   But... I don't understand. What's happened since?

KUNG   I wish I knew.... It's... it's as if we tore the good out of our hearts... and we can no longer see the beauty we once had.... It's as if some darkness fell on us... and we're still paying the price for it... even today...

HUANG   Yes! Yes! And we brought that darkness with us... to the Gold Mountain!

KAO   And it hangs over Chinatown... like mustard gas...

    LIAN reacts to this with a loud moan.

KUNG   You're like the old proverb, Queenie. "It's better to be jade broken than a tile intact." That's the difference between you and me.... I see now I must leave this place... and I thank you for that. Now I must do something for you. *(He hands her the tontine box.)* Take it...

QUEENIE   No...

KUNG   Please...

QUEENIE   You've done enough. I have found my gold in the Gold Mountain, thanks to you.

JOHN   *(uneasy laugh)* Just words! That's all. Typical intellectual. Thinking he can think his way out of everything. Not so, Grandad? *(LIAN turns away.)* Grandad...?

QUEENIE   John, nothing you say now can ever hurt me. Not anymore. You know how I know this? Because I know your ancestors are ashamed of you. You will know it too, whenever you bow before that altar to honour them. Oh yes, you will know it then...

    She moves to the exit.

HUANG   Wait! We must have a funeral for Mme Wu. To show our respects? No one else will...

KAO   Yes, yes, we should. But we have no fake paper money.

KUNG   We'll use real money... the tontine...

JOHN   No!

KAO   You have no say in this!

HUANG hurries forward and clears the table of the mah-jong tiles, sweeping them onto the floor. Then he places MME WU's coffee pot in the middle of the table. HUANG, ASI, KUNG and KAO gather in a circle round the table. They march in a slow, methodical way. ASI tosses money into the air every time they say "Hear!"

As the funeral rites are being performed, LIAN is assailed with mixed feelings. He wants to join in but he hesitates.

HUANG   I weep for Mme Wu... for her tragic fate...

OTHERS   Hear!

QUEENIE   I weep for her sad life... brought on by hate...

OTHERS   Hear!

KUNG   I weep for her... so filled with fear...

OTHERS   Hear!

KAO   We weep! Who else will shed a tear?

OTHERS   Hear!

ASI   I honour her... though I did not know her...

OTHERS   Hear!

QUEENIE   I honour her... a long-lost sister...

OTHERS   Hear!

LIAN appears about to join in the funeral.

KAO   I honour her... for just being a she...

LIAN hesitates then turns away in confusion.

OTHERS   Hear!

HUANG   I honour her... the yin part of me...

OTHERS   Hear!

KUNG   I bury her... and all her sorrows...

OTHERS   Hear!

ASI   I bury all her dark tomorrows...

OTHERS   Hear!

KAO   I envy her... standing at Heaven's Gate...

OTHERS   *(enthusiastically)* Hear! Hear!

QUEENIE   Yes! Yes!

HUANG   I envy her ancestors... as they stand and wait...

OTHERS   Hear! Hear!

QUEENIE   Yes! Yes! *(looking upward to Heaven)* Mme Wu, lucky you! Tell my ancestors to wait a while. Queenie's not yet finished... there's still much to do...

OTHERS   Hear! Hear!

> *They stop. Silence. Short pause.*

QUEENIE   We should burn the money now. *(She glances at JOHN and smiles wickedly.)* No, let's not burn the money.... Thank you, brothers. Just one favour.... Ten years after I'm buried, dig up my bones. Clean them. Mend the breaks and the cracks. Make my feet whole again. So I can stand before my ancestors... the way they meant me to stand, the way they honoured me.... Do that for me... and the slate is clean.... It's all I ask...

> *She moves toward the exit. There is purpose in her stride. She walks erect, her hobble not as pronounced. At the door she turns and smiles.*

Thank you again, brothers... *(She exits.)*

> *Pause. The men look at one another.*

KUNG   Well... *(He gives a final look around at the others and smiles.)* Goodbye... *(He exits.)*

KAO   Wait, Kung. I need to know more... *(He exits.)*

HUANG   Wait for me! *(He stops at the door and turns. He looks at the others.)* So long, Asi. *(He exits.)*

> *GRANDAD looks at JOHN and ASI, then exits upstairs.*

ASI   *(to the audience)* According to legend, the monk Tripitaka went off in search of enlightenment. And the three animal knights-errant, Kung, Kao and Huang, protected him... protected her... on the way...

JOHN   Asi! Get back to work. Pick up the money...

> *ASI looks at JOHN then at the exit, then finally stares out at the audience as the lights come down.*

> *The end.*

MAGGIE'S LAST DANCE

BY MARTY CHAN

ABOUT

MARTY CHAN

Playwright Marty Chan is best known for his play, *Mom, Dad, I'm Living with a White Girl*, which had a successful off-Broadway run in 2004. The play has been produced across Canada, won a Sterling Award for Best New Work and received the ACTS Award from Harvard University. Chan also wrote the Fringe hits *The Bone House* and *Polaroids of Don*. Marty also wrote and performed the *Dim Sum Diaries*, a weekly humour commentary series on CBC radio. He was story editor for the international hit TV series, *Incredible Story Studio*. His kids' book, *The Mystery of the Frozen Brains*, won the 2005 City of Edmonton Book Prize. The sequel, *The Mystery of the Graffiti Ghoul*, was nominated for three readers' choice awards (Willow, Golden Eagle and MYRCA) as well as the Arthur Ellis Award for Juvenile Crime Fiction. Marty's third book, *The Mystery of the Mad Science Teacher*, was released in 2008. He is a regular columnist for the Edmonton Journal. Currently, he's developing *The Forbidden Phoenix*, a fusion of Chinese opera and western theatre, which recounts the plight of the Chinese Bachelor Men. For more information, go to martychan.com.

Maggie's Last Dance was produced at the Edmonton Fringe Festival by Paper Tiger Productions in 1995 with the following company:

JIM	Jeff Haslam
ELLA	Juliana Barclay
CHRISTINE	Marianne Copithorne
DERRICK	John Kirkpatrick
STEPHEN	Jeff Page
HELEN	Davina Stewart

Directed by John Wright
Stage Management by Michelle Chan

CHARACTERS

JIM: Single and hating it, this thirtysomething has passed his milestone and wonders if there's more to life than engraving tombstones.

ELLA: Single, if you don't count her career, she tries to navigate the latter half of her life with a little more care than she had in the first half of her life.

CHRISTINE: Petty as a child, spiteful as an adult, this divorcee can only see the negative side of people but it's a cover for her own insecurities.

DERRICK: He's resistant to change because he fears having to deal with anything new, which may be why he married his high-school sweetheart, Helen.

STEPHEN: Voted most likely to fail in high school and lived up to his reputation, he finds himself between jobs and wives, just trying to make sense of his life.

HELEN: A wife and mother who always wonders, what if she could have done something different with her life and covers her regret with saccharine sweetness.

SETTING

High-school gym complete with hardwood floors and the faded lines for volleyball and basketball courts. A disco ball hangs overhead and metal chairs line either side of the gym. The play jumps back and forth through time, with the actors recreating locations through mime and minimal set pieces.

MAGGIE'S LAST DANCE

ACT ONE

SCENE ONE

A high-school gym decorated for a dance. A glowing disco ball shoots out pinpoints of light and sagging streamers.

Hard metal chairs line either side, separating the boys' side from the girls' side.

In the centre, ELLA Givens (thirty-three) stands.

ELLA   My name is Ella Givens. I'm thirty-three and still single. I've never seen Paris at night. I've never sipped from life's champagne glass. All my dreams have gone unfulfilled. And until I got the invitation to my high-school reunion, I was a happy woman. For me, high school was, in a word, hell.

ELLA puts on makeup.

Sound effect: "Dancing Queen" by ABBA.

HELEN Barbour-Sackett and CHRISTINE McCoy, both thirty-two, join ELLA. They are in their teen years.

HELEN   Ella, you can't be serious. You and Jim Bauer?

CHRISTINE   Helen's right. Jim is the Shaun Cassidy of grade ten. You're just not his type.

ELLA   He wants me. In the hall, he brushed against me twice.

HELEN   Yeah, and if he throws rocks at you, he's in love.

CHRISTINE   But if he throws nickels, it's something else.

ELLA   Shut up.

CHRISTINE   I'm sorry, Ella. It's just that I don't want to see you get hurt. Jim needs a woman and you're a girl. He's a complex man, Ella. One day he struts to the Bee Gees. The next he air guitars "Bohemian Rhapsody." He's deep. I just don't think you could handle him.

HELEN   Yeah, and besides, Christine's got dibs on him.

CHRISTINE   Shut up, Helen.

ELLA   So, you're afraid of a little competition.

CHRISTINE   From you?

> HELEN and CHRISTINE laugh.

ELLA   We'll see who's laughing at the dance.

> HELEN and CHRISTINE exit. ELLA goes out the opposite exit.
>
> DERRICK Sackett (thirty-three) enters. He's the high-school wannabe who never grew up.

DERRICK   Reunions. A chance to relive the times when nothing mattered except the school dance. When the biggest problem for Derrick Sackett was earning enough gas money for the weekend. Hey, remember when we got drunk on tequila? Then we ate that box of wieners in your mom's freezer? I puked all over the back seat of your dad's Pontiac. Man, I miss high school.

> Sound effect: "Walk this Way" by Aerosmith.
>
> STEPHEN Nesbitt (thirty-three) enters with a joint in his mouth and a guitar in his hand. He and DERRICK are sixteen years old.

You feel anything, Stephen?

STEPHEN   Derrick, man, it's like I'm floating. I'm flying through the ceiling. Up. Up. And away. Wow! What do you feel?

DERRICK   I got the munchies.

STEPHEN   Take another hit.

DERRICK   (taking another hit) Oh yeah, now I can feel it. Man, how about some food? I could really go for some pancakes right about now. Let's go to Fuller's.

STEPHEN   Forget it, man. You just want to go to see Helen Barbour.

DERRICK   Is she working tonight?

STEPHEN   Come on, man. You got her schedule memorized. You got the major hots for her.

DERRICK   Do not.

STEPHEN   Derrick, you lie like a sidewalk.

DERRICK   Okay, so I like her. Now can we get something to eat?

STEPHEN   Later, man. Let's fire up another doobie.

> STEPHEN slides a joint out of the guitar and hands it to DERRICK.
>
> There is a knock on the door.

VOICE   (offstage) Stephen, let me in.

STEPHEN   Oh shit man, it's my dad. (to VOICE) Hold on.

DERRICK   What do we do?

STEPHEN   Mellow out, man.

VOICE   (*offstage*) Open the door.

STEPHEN   Give me a minute.

>   *DERRICK tries to hand STEPHEN the joint. STEPHEN won't take it.*

DERRICK   Get rid of it.

STEPHEN   Where?

DERRICK   I don't know. Over—no. Here—no. Eat it.

STEPHEN   What? Are you crazy?

VOICE   (*offstage*) Let me in now.

STEPHEN   I'm coming.

DERRICK   Eat it.

STEPHEN   No way man, this is my last joint.

VOICE   (*offstage*) Now!

STEPHEN   Hold your horses.

>   *STEPHEN slides the joint back into the guitar.*

DERRICK   You're insane man. That joint's as big as a friggin' baseball bat. It'll never fit.

STEPHEN   Relax man. It's under control.

DERRICK   Oh man. We're gonna get caught.

>   *STEPHEN opens the door.*
>
>   *STEPHEN'S DAD (played by JIM) enters.*

STEPHEN'S DAD   What's going on here?

STEPHEN   We weren't doing nothing.

DERRICK   He's right, man. We were just sitting here. Hey man, we were just doing our math homework. We weren't smoking anything. Oh god, please don't tell my dad.

STEPHEN   Shut up, man.

STEPHEN'S DAD   Stephen, I can smell it.

STEPHEN   All I can smell is cheap rye.

STEPHEN'S DAD   Yes, well. Just don't let it happen again.

DERRICK   Yes, Mr. Nesbitt. I won't touch it again. I never wanted to in the first place. Stephen made me do it. Not that your son is a dealer. Trust me, I'm off the stuff today, man. You can count on me. One warning is all I need.

STEPHEN'S DAD   Stephen, there's something we have to talk about.

STEPHEN   So talk.

STEPHEN'S DAD   Do you mind, Derrick?

DERRICK   No man. Go ahead. I'm cool. You can say anything in front of me.

STEPHEN'S DAD   Stephen, your mother is calling our marriage quits. We're getting a divorce.

STEPHEN   What? You can't— What's going to happen to me?

STEPHEN'S DAD   We talked it over. We thought it might be best if you came with me.

STEPHEN   Don't I have a say?

STEPHEN'S DAD   I'm in a better position to take care of you.

STEPHEN   I'm not going with you.

STEPHEN'S DAD   I'll give you some time to think it over. It's for the best. You'll see.

>   *STEPHEN's DAD exits.*

DERRICK   Too bad about the divorce thing, man, but at least we didn't get caught. Hey, I played it pretty cool, didn't I?

STEPHEN   Derrick. Bite me.

>   *STEPHEN pulls out a joint. Lights cross-fade to CHRISTINE at age thirty-two.*

CHRISTINE   High-school reunions. Zits on Christine McCoy's nose. If I ignore them, they'll dry up and go away. But human nature being what it is, I try to pop the zit. But it festers and brings up stuff I never wanted to come up. Sometimes stuff that goes further back than high school.

>   *Sound effect:* Partridge Family *theme.*

>   *CHRISTINE plays seven years old. She has a skipping rope.*

Daddy, Julie buried my doll again.

>   *CHRISTINE'S MOM (played by ELLA) enters.*

Who are you?

CHRISTINE'S MOM   It hasn't been that long, has it? It's me. Your mom.

CHRISTINE   My mommy's dead.

CHRISTINE'S MOM   Is that what your father told you? That scamp. Come here, honey, and give us an Eskimo kiss.

CHRISTINE   I don't think I should talk to you unless Daddy's here.

CHRISTINE'S MOM   Honey, do you know what "visitation rights" means?

CHRISTINE   No.

CHRISTINE'S MOM   Well, you see, it's a special time.

CHRISTINE   Like Christmas?

CHRISTINE'S MOM   Exactly. Santa gives mommies a gift. The chance to see their little children every second weekend.

CHRISTINE   But this is the first time I've seen you.

CHRISTINE'S MOM   Mommy was saving up her special time. Come here, Christine.

CHRISTINE   Mommy?

CHRISTINE hugs her mother.

CHRISTINE'S MOM   Well, well, well. What do you know. You still fit.

CHRISTINE   Come on. I have to show you my room. Daddy let me paint it. I used blue and red and green and purple and, oh yeah, pink.

CHRISTINE'S MOM   Sorry, honey. Mommy can't stay.

CHRISTINE   But you just got here.

CHRISTINE'S MOM   Well, you see honey, there's a thing called "divorce." Do you know what that means?

CHRISTINE   Yes. It's the bitch's way of milking us dry.

CHRISTINE'S MOM   Did your daddy teach you that?

CHRISTINE   Yes.

CHRISTINE'S MOM   Oh, that scamp. No, honey. Divorce is a very long vacation that mommies take from daddies. You like vacations, don't you?

CHRISTINE   Please let me go with you. I won't take up much room.

CHRISTINE'S MOM   Mommy has another family now. Don't worry, honey. I'll still come and visit.

CHRISTINE   Or will you save up your special time?

CHRISTINE's MOM exits. CHRISTINE follows.

HELEN at thirty-two enters.

HELEN   High-school reunions. The do-overs of your life. One shot at making things right for Helen Barbour. One chance to correct high-school mistakes.

Sound effect: "Rich Girl" by Hall and Oates.

CHRISTINE enters. She mingles with HELEN as if they were at a dance. They both play sixteen.

Isn't he gorgeous?

CHRISTINE   If you're into big hair. I can't figure out what you see in Stephen Nesbitt. He's a head.

HELEN   I like to walk on the wild side. He's so intense. It's like he can explode at any minute. There's something dangerous about him. And I just know he'd drive Daddy up the wall.

CHRISTINE   Me, I'll stick with Jim Bauer.

HELEN   That's if Ella doesn't get him first.

CHRISTINE   Doubt's Ralph.

HELEN   You never know. Jim hasn't returned any of your notes. Maybe he's not interested in you. Maybe he's into the girl next door.

CHRISTINE   Maybe I'll just have to try harder.

STEPHEN enters.

STEPHEN   Hey ladies, who wants a piece of Stephen Nesbitt?

CHRISTINE   I don't handle damaged goods.

HELEN   I might be interested.

STEPHEN   *(to CHRISTINE)* Feisty. I like a woman who plays hard to get.

CHRISTINE   You'll love me then.

STEPHEN   Dance floor's waiting for us.

CHRISTINE   Let it.

STEPHEN   Come on.

CHRISTINE   I'm tired.

STEPHEN   But you just got here.

CHRISTINE   Maybe someone else would like to dance.

HELEN   I feel perky.

STEPHEN   Yeah, good idea. There's Ella. Thanks. See ya.

STEPHEN exits.

HELEN   What a jerk.

CHRISTINE   Yeah, I can't believe that scab snubbed you like that.

HELEN   Do you think he was playing hard to get?

CHRISTINE   I'm sure he was.

DERRICK comes over to HELEN.

DERRICK   Cool dance, huh? Too bad Mr. Henderson is chaperone. He's going to check the equipment room every five minutes. Not that I'd go there. Not unless it was with someone like—I mean—that is—hey, I really liked your speech on the Canadian Constitution. It moved me. Too bad about the volleyball team missing the finals, huh? I hate sports. Do you want to dance?

HELEN   What could it hurt?

Lights cross-fade to JIM Bauer (thirty-two). He's the boy next door all grown up.

JIM   Regrets rise up at reunions like so many fish in the North Saskatchewan. What if you studied harder? What if you didn't lip off the principal? What if you asked that certain girl to dance?

Sound effect: "Stayin' Alive" by the Bee Gees.

JIM at sixteen struts across the stage.

Francis Langley High School. First dance of the year. And Jim Bauer's got Saturday-night fever. I'm hot. Even the grade-eleven babes are checking me out. Well, they've got a lot to look at. Shirt: one-hundred percent velour. V-necked. Opened just enough to reveal my two neatly groomed chest hairs. Pants: bell-bottoms. Shoes: standard two-inch platforms. Clothes by Woolco. Attitude by Foreigner. Cold as ice. Keep playing it cool. Only nerds dance this early.

DERRICK and HELEN come out and dance. They are sixteen.

Sound effect: "Three Times a Lady" by the Commodores.

Later in the dance, while Derrick Sackett and Helen Barbour are slow dancing, Derrick's hand slides down to Helen's butt. She slides it up. His other hand drops. Helen shoves it back. He tries again and again. It's like watching a perpetual drinking bird.

ELLA and CHRISTINE (sixteen) enter.

They distract me so much that I almost miss her arrival. The hottest girl in grade ten. Ella Givens. She's everything Joanie Cunningham is and more. If only I could be her Chachi. I've had this thing for her since we were seven. She scans the gym. I see her head flick in my general direction. Cool, she wants me. Got to make my move soon. Next song, I promise.

Sound effect: "You Make Me Feel Like Dancing" by Leo Sayer.

Leo Sayer's "You Make Me Feel Like Dancing." A cool song. A danceable song. A song where couples are made. The other guys sense this. They launch from the safety of the bleachers. They want to glide like Tony Manero, but they shuffle like Tim Conway. Still, they move closer to the promised land. If I wait, someone else might ask her. I have to make my move now.

I join the race everyone wants to win but no one wants to lead. I make it past the chaperone. Past groping couples. Past the volleyball line. Midpoint. No turning back. I smell the sweet aroma of Pert wafting from her hair.

Breath gets short. Legs shaky. My zits on high beam. Velour shirt suddenly feels very heavy. She looks at me. I make a right-angle turn and head to the punch bowl. I slug back two glasses of orange punch. Liquid courage. Okay, I'm going to do it now. I spin around to see… Christine McCoy. She flashes me a smile. The disco light bounces off her braces and blinds me. I look to the dancing couples.

> *ELLA dances with STEPHEN.*

Oh man, she's dancing with Stephen Nesbitt. Mr. Hockey-Basketball-Volleyball-Highest-Marks-in-Grade-Ten-Drives-his-Own-Car. What's he got that I don't? He tells her a joke. She laughs. He leans in. She lets him. She touches his arm. If they slow dance, I'm done for. Next song—slow dancin'.

> *Sound effect: "Swayin' to the Music" by Johnny Rivers.*

> *STEPHEN clinches ELLA.*

Fifty glasses of punch later, the punch bowl is a mound of wet sugar. On the floor, old and new couples clinch. And in the middle, Stephen clings to her. Francis Langley High School. First dance of the year. I'm alone and my bladder hurts.

> *He exits.*

> *As he does, ELLA separates from the groping STEPHEN.*

ELLA No, Stephen.

STEPHEN What's wrong, Ella?

ELLA I'm sorry. I can't. I don't like you that way.

STEPHEN But I'm wearing Hi Karate.

ELLA It's not you. It's me. I like someone else. You understand, don't you?

STEPHEN No problem. It's cool. My dad says rejection builds character. I'm building a lot of character tonight.

ELLA Stephen, you're a cool guy. You'll find someone.

STEPHEN Yeah, I hear some junior-high girls crashed the dance.

ELLA Stephen, if it weren't for this other guy, I'd love to be with you. But this guy, he's different. When we're together, I feel weak. I feel dizzy. I feel like I want to throw up.

STEPHEN Sounds serious.

ELLA   Stephen, can we be friends?

STEPHEN   Always. Hey, if I ever make you want to throw up, you'd tell me, right?

ELLA   Of course.

She exits. STEPHEN transforms into an adult.

STEPHEN   Reunions. Havens for the desperate and the dysfunctional. A place to remember what a jerk you were in high school. A time to realize how little you've changed.

Lights down.

SCENE TWO

Lights up. Everyone sits around the circle. Present age.

DERRICK   Isn't this great? The old gang's back together. It's like we never left. Helen was worried you guys wouldn't come. But I knew you guys wouldn't let me down.

CHRISTINE   This and my root canal are the only two things I've been looking forward to.

DERRICK   Christine, you haven't changed a bit.

CHRISTINE   Derrick, you really know how to hurt a girl.

STEPHEN   Don't worry, Christine. You look more haggard than I remembered.

CHRISTINE   Stephen, lost the Epstein look. Good choice.

ELLA   Don't pay attention to her. You look great.

HELEN   Does anyone want to know what I've been doing since high school?

JIM   Can't we just forget this stupid comparison contest?

STEPHEN   But Jim. This is why everyone came. Coming to a reunion is like driving past a freeway accident. You slow down, get a good look and thank God it's not you laying in the twisted carnage.

JIM   You're morbid.

HELEN   Let's get to it.

JIM   Pass.

ELLA   I have an idea. What if we just give our job and our marital status? We just state the facts and get it over with.

DERRICK   That's a great idea, Ella.

HELEN   Just let me go first.

JIM   Whatever.

STEPHEN   Anything to shut Derrick up.

CHRISTINE   Time to whip out and compare.

ELLA   Who wants to start?

HELEN   If no one else minds. I'm into real estate. I made the top-ten list every month this year. I make enough to afford a trip to Disneyland every fall, a new fur coat every winter and a new BMW every summer. I make close to six figures a year. I can't get any more specific. That would be crass. I also sit on the council for—

DERRICK   You're forgetting an important detail, honey.

HELEN   Oh yeah. I'm married to him.

DERRICK   And Helen and I have two wonderful girls. It's like I never left high school. I teach here now. Isn't that a gas? Me, a teacher?

CHRISTINE   Yeah, you're a regular *Welcome Back Kotter*. My turn.

HELEN   But I'm not finished.

CHRISTINE   Yes, you are. I'm divorced and I sell babies on the black market.

DERRICK   You're doing it wrong, Christine.

CHRISTINE   What are you going to do? Give me detention?

ELLA   Jim, do you want to go next?

JIM   Pick someone else.

STEPHEN   I'll let you off the hook. I've sunk the lowest since high school. I'm between jobs and between wives. All my dreams lay shattered someplace between here and my last pink slip.

HELEN   I'd never let you go.

DERRICK   Let the man finish, honey.

STEPHEN   You want more? Okay. I'm considering panhandling as a full-time career. How's that?

ELLA   Jim, it's your turn.

JIM   I'm single and I'm an artist.

HELEN   Pfff. Not much money in that.

ELLA   That's great. I knew your art would take you places.

STEPHEN   What do you do? Painting? Sculptures?

JIM   I engrave tombstones.

CHRISTINE   At least we know where to find your work.

ELLA   Jim's doing what he loves. That's what's important.

DERRICK   What about you, Ella?

ELLA   I'm single. I used to work for the government. Then the cutbacks hit. I figured other people needed their jobs more, so I bowed out. Now I work at a travel agency. Pretty ironic, considering—

HELEN   Yeah, yeah, yeah. Things didn't work out the way you hoped. The tragic story of your life. Now can we get back to me?

ELLA   You're the luckiest woman here, Helen. The rest of us, we're still piecing our lives together. And look at you. A husband. Two kids. A career. You've got everything.

HELEN   Of course. I have no regrets.

    Sound effect: "Car Wash" by Rose Royce.

    Lights change.

    Everyone tosses paper at each other. A typical class in high school. Everyone is in their teen years.

JIM   Make way for the Fonz.

DERRICK   Ayyyy.

STEPHEN   Way to go, man.

DERRICK   She was a little cold at first, but I wore her down.

JIM   How far did you get?

STEPHEN   Second base?

DERRICK   Home run.

HELEN   *(to CHRISTINE)* No way, man. The creep kept trying to feel me up. I wouldn't let him go any further.

CHRISTINE   But you kept dancing. You should have ditched him after the first song.

HELEN   I wanted to know why Stephen wouldn't ask me to dance.

CHRISTINE   *(looks at ELLA)* You needed Derrick to tell you that?

ELLA   Hey, Stephen and I are just friends.

HELEN   *(to CHRISTINE)* Tell Ella I don't talk to sluts.

ELLA   I have no interest in Stephen.

CHRISTINE   Get real. You two were locked up like wrestlers.

JIM   *(to STEPHEN)* Yeah, man. You two were pretty chummy.

DERRICK   No way, man. She shot him down like one of Pappy's Black Sheep gunning down a Zero, man.

>   *He makes a machine-gun noise followed by plane dive and crash.*

STEPHEN   Bite me, Derrick.

JIM   So she ditched you?

STEPHEN   She's not really my type. She's more Jim's speed.

JIM   Get out. No way, man.

DERRICK   Maybe Christine's more your speed, man.

ELLA   *(to CHRISTINE)* Oh yeah, I didn't see you hanging around Jim too much.

HELEN   That's 'cause he left early.

CHRISTINE   We both left early.

HELEN   You didn't. Did you?

JIM   *(to STEPHEN)* Are you crazy? I wouldn't touch Christine with a ten-foot pole.

STEPHEN   I heard it was a different kind of pole.

DERRICK   Yeah, man.

JIM   Who's been spreading rumours?

HELEN   Christine, you bag.

CHRISTINE   In name only.

ELLA   You won't get away with it.

CHRISTINE   What are you going to do about it?

ELLA   Watch.

>   *ELLA crosses to JIM.*

  Hey Jim. It's time to teach you a few things you don't know.

JIM   Already?

ELLA   Don't think you can handle it?

JIM   I'm ready if you are.

ELLA   I'm always ready. Let's go.

JIM   Okay.

>   *They exit.*

DERRICK   That scab.

CHRISTINE   Did you see what she did?

STEPHEN   That dog. He better treat her right.

HELEN   That slut.

CHRISTINE   What does Ella see in him?

HELEN   *(to CHRISTINE)* It's probably a pity date.

DERRICK   *(to STEPHEN)* Hey man, you want to blow this class?

STEPHEN   Derrick, you dope. This is spare.

Lights down.

SCENE THREE

Lights up on STEPHEN and HELEN sharing a silver flask. They are adults.

HELEN   Two unruly brats.

STEPHEN   One ugly divorce.

HELEN   A self-righteous husband.

STEPHEN   A malicious wife who's taken everything.

HELEN   I sell blue-ribbon homes but I live in a rundown shack. All because my husband thinks it has charm.

STEPHEN   I share my sagging motel bed with cockroaches.

HELEN   I'd be a millionaire now if it weren't for Derrick.

STEPHEN   Seven failed careers. Even Amway fired me.

HELEN   You win. Your life sucks more than mine.

STEPHEN   I'd like to thank my parents for this award…

HELEN   Partners in misery. It'd be perfect if we were married.

STEPHEN   You couldn't cover my alimony.

HELEN   You never know. If I sell an extra bungalow here and there…

STEPHEN   Thanks for the offer, but I'll suffer alone. Besides, you got Derrick.

HELEN   There's always divorce.

STEPHEN   They're overrated.

HELEN   I'm a very good seller, Stephen. I could cover your alimony.

STEPHEN   People change, Helen.

HELEN   I can move three houses a month. Four if I have to.

STEPHEN   You'd be miserable.

HELEN   Let me show you how well I can sell.

STEPHEN   I'll take your word for it.

HELEN   Prime location. Close to schools and malls. Ten minute drive to downtown. Look at the view. Five percent down. Amortized over twenty years at only six and a quarter percent. An affordable mortgage. A steal—

She kisses him hard. STEPHEN pushes her away.

What's wrong?

STEPHEN   Your kids deserve better.

STEPHEN exits.

Lights cross-fade to JIM and ELLA in teen years.

Sound effect: "ABC" by the Jackson Five.

ELLA   You seem kind of nervous, Jim.

JIM   It's my first time.

ELLA   Don't worry. I'll be gentle.

JIM   Don't take it easy just because of me. Treat me like everyone else you've been with.

ELLA   Are you sure? It can get pretty rough.

JIM   I can handle it.

ELLA   Okay. Who is the prime minister of Canada?

JIM   Pierre Trudeau. He owns the dry-cleaning chain. And his wife slept with every one of the Rolling Stones.

ELLA   Good, Jim. Everything before the dry-cleaning stuff was right. Now, what is the ruling party of Canada?

JIM   It's the… you know. They're in Ottawa. Trudeau's in charge. It's the… I don't know.

ELLA   That's okay. Let's try another one. Why do the people of Quebec want to separate?

JIM   Ella, no one cares about this except a bunch of frogs.

ELLA   Jim. It's the seventies. We don't call them that anymore. They're Quebecers. Now why does Quebec want to separate?

JIM   Who cares? I mean, in a couple of years this whole thing's going to be ancient history.

ELLA   Jim, concentrate. Tell me why Quebec wants to separate.

JIM   I give up. Social Studies sucks, man.

ELLA   It's important, Jim. You need to know what's happening out there. It'll help you get a job.

JIM   Yeah, maybe in government.

ELLA   Don't knock it. I hear if you get in there, you're set for life.

JIM   Dream on, Ella. Social Studies is useless, and besides, Rendall's got it in for me.

ELLA   She's an old bat.

JIM   Hey, guess who I am? *(whiny voice)* Class. Class. Come to order, please. Now listen up, people. I know there's a big dance this weekend. I expect you all to act like young ladies and gentlemen. Some of you will want to follow your eager hormones into the equipment room. I want you all to know that Mr. Henderson and I will be there to ensure each and every tongue stays in its own mouth. That means you, Miss Givens.

ELLA   Ha ha, good one. Hey, I missed you at the dance.

JIM   I didn't feel well. Had to go home early.

ELLA   Christine said she spent the night with you.

JIM   I barely saw her. Did you have a good time with Stephen?

ELLA   He's nice… as a friend. But he's not my type.

JIM   What is your type?

ELLA   Maybe we should keep studying.

JIM   Come on. Tell me.

ELLA   Only if you tell me what your type is.

JIM   Quebec wants to separate because Canada doesn't recognize their right to language.

ELLA   Good answer. See? You get this stuff.

JIM   Can I ask you a question?

ELLA   Sure.

JIM   Why would Quebec want to separate if Canada wants her to stay?

ELLA   I'm not sure.

JIM   I mean, Canada has a lot to offer.

ELLA   Maybe Quebec doesn't know that.

JIM   What if Canada wanted to tell Quebec but didn't know how?

ELLA.   All Canada has to do is ask.

JIM   What if Quebec laughs in Canada's face?

ELLA   What if Quebec doesn't?

JIM   Ella, do you want to go to the dance with me?

> Sound effect: "Raindrops Keep Fallin' on My Head" by B.J. Thomas.

(*as a seven-year-old*) I can get popcorn. I have some money. My mom gave me three dollars.

ELLA   (*starts to sob*) I can't. I can't.

> Music out.

JIM   (*at sixteen*) What's wrong?

ELLA   I can't go. I'm sorry.

> ELLA exits, crying.

> Lights cross-fade to CHRISTINE and DERRICK as adults.

DERRICK   Hey, remember when we took your dad's car to the lake? I left it in drive and it went into the water. Boy, was your dad pissed when we brought it back. How long did he ground you? Three months, wasn't it?

CHRISTINE   I can always count on you to dredge up these Hallmark moments.

DERRICK   Remember the day Henderson caught you cheating on the math exam?

CHRISTINE   Hey, Derrick, how are your kids?

DERRICK   Perfect angels. The spitting image of their mother. Hey, do you remember when you and Helen dressed up as Laverne and Shirley for frosh? That was a hoot.

CHRISTINE   I'd love to catch up, Derrick, but—

DERRICK   Hey, remember when the whole gang went to Helen's cabin?

CHRISTINE   Haven't got a clue.

DERRICK   Hear me out. Helen disappeared with Stephen for an hour. I almost didn't notice because you kept yakking at me. Babbling about how Henderson was an awful teacher. You wouldn't let me go. Do you remember?

CHRISTINE   Not really.

DERRICK   Funny. I didn't either, until I saw Helen with Stephen tonight. I was mopping up a spill when I saw them in the hall. They were so close I felt like

I was intruding on a private moment. Then the memory just popped into my head. Strange how the mind works.

CHRISTINE   I'm a dental hygienist, not a psychologist.

DERRICK   You two were best friends. You'd do anything for each other.

CHRISTINE   There are some lines I won't cross.

DERRICK   You know what happened.

CHRISTINE   Ask her yourself.

DERRICK   She won't talk to me.

CHRISTINE   Who cares what happened in the past?

DERRICK   It was always Helen and me. That's the way I remember us. You have to tell me if I'm wrong.

CHRISTINE   It's nice to get new memories when your old ones get worn out.

Lights cross-fade to ELLA and JIM.

JIM   Not much has changed since we left, eh?

ELLA   Not even the people. Hey, you know who I haven't seen? Mr. Henderson. I wonder where he is.

JIM   Edward Henderson. Loving husband. Dedicated teacher. 1932–1993.

ELLA   Oh. I guess you would know. You know what's strange? Look around. Everyone's still the same. Sure, we update our fashion sense, but we're all the same people we were in the seventies.

JIM   Yeah, it's like the notes in our yearbooks are curses. Stay just the way you are.

ELLA   "Always, Ella." That's how I signed mine.

JIM   Mine was "Just Jim."

ELLA   I got a half-page essay from a girl I barely knew. She went on about how she wanted to stay the best of friends after graduation. I felt so bad because all I wrote in hers was "Hang loose."

JIM   Yeah, I know what you mean. Someone signed mine: "Forever your friend."

ELLA   Who wrote that?

JIM   I can't remember.

ELLA   Guess that's what reunions are for.

JIM   Among other things. Still single, eh?

ELLA   Just like you.

JIM   You know, it's amazing that Helen and Derrick are the only couple from high school that have stayed together.

ELLA   Yeah, considering we're a disposable society these days. Pre-nuptial agreements. Quickie divorces. It's like marriage has become the Pampers of the nineties. And in all that, Helen and Derrick found a way to make it.

JIM   I think they were too scared to find someone else.

ELLA   I see you're still single.

JIM   That's another story. You ever wonder about the couples that never got together in high school?

ELLA   All the time.

        Sound effect: "Raindrops Keep Fallin' on My Head."

JIM   *(as a seven-year-old)* I can get popcorn. I got three dollars. My mom gave it to me.

        Music out.

ELLA   But sometimes things weren't meant to be.

JIM   *(at present age)* And sometimes they're fated.

ELLA   My mom believed in fate. She said that's how she ended up with my dad. Except he found his soulmate a few years later. Blond from the neck up. Plastic from the neck down. I'll pass on love.

JIM   So it didn't work out for your mom. Love works for lots of other people.

ELLA   Like the people in high school? Face it, Jim, love doesn't just happen. You have to work at it.

JIM   Love will punch you in the stomach when you're not looking.

ELLA   You're a hopeless romantic.

JIM   Why are you so scared?

ELLA   I'm not scared. I just don't want to be naive.

JIM   You're running away from your feelings.

ELLA   And you're living in some kind of fantasy world.

JIM   At least I'm living.

ELLA   Couldn't tell from the company you keep.

JIM   You'd fit right in.

ELLA   Go chisel an ode.

        ELLA exits.

Lights change.

Sound effect: "Kung Fu Fighting" by Carl Douglas.

JIM takes a fighting stance. STEPHEN enters. HELEN, CHRISTINE and DERRICK cram around the two. They are in their teen years.

DERRICK, CHRISTINE & HELEN   Fight, fight, fight.

DERRICK   Take him, man.

CHRISTINE   Bash his head in.

HELEN   Don't hit him in the face.

STEPHEN   You had this coming, man. I saw what you did to Ella.

JIM   I didn't do nothing.

STEPHEN   Then why was she crying?

JIM   Ask her.

STEPHEN   Man, your ass is grass and I'm the lawnmower.

JIM   Yeah, yeah. Try it and I'll kick your ass till your nose bleeds.

STEPHEN   You won't touch me. You little scab. You couldn't punch your way out of a wet paper bag.

JIM   I'm gonna rearrange your ugly little face.

STEPHEN   Come on, man. I'm waiting.

JIM   Make your move.

DERRICK   Come on. Stop talking and start fighting.

HELEN   Take him, Stephen.

CHRISTINE   Shut up, Helen.

JIM and STEPHEN push each other but never fight.

HELEN   What? You think Jim's gonna take Stephen?

CHRISTINE   Yeah, he's gonna bash him around like a pinball until he scores a bonus game.

HELEN   Get real. Stephen's gonna mop the floor with Jim.

CHRISTINE   Stephen's got the hair for mopping.

HELEN   Get off his hair.

CHRISTINE   It's like a Chia Pet exploded on his neck.

HELEN   Shut up, bitch.

CHRISTINE   Make me.

HELEN and CHRISTINE go at it.

DERRICK, JIM & STEPHEN   Fight, fight, fight. Skrag fight. Skrag fight.

JIM and STEPHEN break off their fight.

HELEN   Slut.

CHRISTINE   Skank.

HELEN   Let go!

CHRISTINE   Ouch.

DERRICK   Cool it, man. Henderson's coming.

HELEN   You die at lunch.

CHRISTINE   In the quad.

HELEN   Any time.

Everyone splits.

Lights down.

SCENE FOUR

Lights up on DERRICK and HELEN as adults.

DERRICK   Looks like my reunion is a success.

HELEN   It's okay.

DERRICK   You know, there's nothing like a reunion to stoke up old flames.

HELEN   I was just talking to him.

DERRICK   Did you see how everyone was checking me out?

HELEN   Who?

DERRICK   Not everyone, but I saw a few hungry looks. I've still got the flowing hair of a teenager, you know.

HELEN   Of course you do. It's just ingrown.

DERRICK   Don't laugh, Helen. I was a hot dude in high school. Guess I still am.

HELEN   Yeah, right. Before you met me, you were sucking your neck with a vacuum cleaner so people wouldn't think you were alone on the weekends.

DERRICK   It didn't happen before we met. Hey, it was the seventies. It doesn't bother you, does it?

HELEN   Not at all. You know, the seventies were a crazy time for both of us.

DERRICK   Yeah, I guess we both have secrets.

HELEN   It's in the past now. Why don't you point her out?

DERRICK   A gentlemen has his secrets. Does it bug you?

HELEN   Honey, I'm just curious.

DERRICK   Helen, I wouldn't do anything now. I respect you too much to betray your trust.

HELEN   Is she still pretty?

DERRICK   It's not bothering you, is it?

HELEN   Not at all. So, when did you two get together?

DERRICK   At the cabin. I can't remember if you were there or not. Oh yeah, you stepped out for awhile. I felt the urge. She was there. You understand, don't you?

HELEN   Hey, it was the seventies. Derrick, be a dear and get a mop. I'm afraid it might get messy later.

Lights cross-fade to JIM and ELLA in teen years.

Sound effect: "If I Can't Have You" by Yvonne Ellimon.

ELLA   I heard about the fight.

JIM   You're full of surprises. I could see Christine pulling a stunt like this, but not you.

ELLA   What are you talking about?

JIM   You were just using me to get to Stephen.

ELLA   We're just friends.

JIM   Seemed more than that when he tried to take my head off. Man, all the time we were studying, you were just using me.

ELLA   Jim, I'm not interested in Stephen at all.

JIM   Then why are you hanging around with me?

ELLA   I think you've got a lot of talent. You're an artist. I've seen the doodles on your book. They're art, man. Pure art. The Henderson sucks. The stairway to Heaven.

JIM   You noticed my binder?

ELLA   Yeah. There's something I'd like to show you.

ELLA opens her binder and takes out a piece of paper.

This is my essay for Social Studies. I'm supposed to read it next week. I wanted your feedback. It talks about Margaret Trudeau leaving the prime minister.

JIM   She's a skrag. You don't just up and leave three kids like that.

ELLA   There's two sides to every story.

JIM   *Maggie's Last Dance.* The title's cool.

ELLA   Yeah, it's about the last night Pierre and Margaret had together. It's kind of like an analogy for the Quebec separation thing. It would mean a lot to me if you read it.

JIM   Maybe I'm not the best person to read this.

ELLA   I think you are.

JIM   Do you want Quebec to stay or go?

ELLA   I want Quebec to do what it feels is right.

JIM   I think Quebec is confused right now.

ELLA   Read the essay. It'll clear things up. Maybe we can talk about it at the dance.

> *Lights down.*

SCENE FIVE

> *Sound effect: "We Are Family" by Sister Sledge.*

> *Lights up on STEPHEN in his teen years. He sucks back a shot from his flask. Then he picks up his guitar and does a very good job of "Smoke on the Water" by Deep Purple.*

> *STEPHEN's DAD enters. He's pissed (emotionally and chemically).*

STEPHEN'S DAD   Christ, Stephen. How many goddamn times do I have to tell you? Don't play that thing in the house.

STEPHEN   Hey, man. It's my dream. I'm going to be the next Gene Simmons. Look at how long my tongue can go out.

STEPHEN'S DAD   Cut the crap. Your coach called. He says you're off the team.

STEPHEN   Good, now I can work on my music.

STEPHEN'S DAD   What happened?

STEPHEN   Just wasn't into it anymore.

STEPHEN'S DAD   So you gave up on it like you gave up on everything else. When's it going to stop, Stephen?

STEPHEN   It's just starting, Dad. This cherry Fender is going to take me places. I'm going to be a heavy-metal king. A genius ahead of my time. My drummers are all going to die hideous deaths involving their own vomit while I crash and burn in a plane accident. I'll be the biggest of the death stars. Bigger than Jim Morrison. Jimi Hendrix. Even Lynyrd Skynyrd. Man, that would be sweet.

STEPHEN'S DAD I'll never know why your mother bought that goddamn thing.

STEPHEN Hey man, she cared.

STEPHEN'S DAD She pampered you. That's why you're so soft now. You're nothing more than a loser. You can't stick with anything. You're a quitter, and it's all that woman's fault.

STEPHEN She treated me better than you ever did.

STEPHEN'S DAD All you do is sit there like a bump on a log. You're nothing. You're nobody. You're not going to amount to anything.

STEPHEN Yeah, I'm exactly like you.

STEPHEN'S DAD Put that damn thing away. You're going to give up on it just like the basketball. Just like the volleyball. Just like the hockey. Just like everything else you've failed at.

> *STEPHEN's DAD exits.*
>
> *STEPHEN takes a last look at his guitar, then puts it away. He slides the case offstage. He sucks back a shot from his flask.*
>
> *Lights change.*
>
> *STEPHEN at reunion age. ELLA storms through. He grabs her.*

STEPHEN Whoa! You look like a woman with a purpose.

ELLA You ever been in love?

STEPHEN Once or twi—

ELLA Then you find out the person you think you're in love with is a complete and utter jerk.

STEPHEN Looks like you got more than you bargained for at this reunion.

ELLA Get this. He still believes in love at first sight. Isn't that the most ridiculous thing you ever heard?

STEPHEN You think he's a jerk because he believes in spontaneous love?

ELLA Of all people, I thought you would understand.

STEPHEN Hey, Ella. The minute you're born your parents start loving you, unconditionally. It's only after they get to know you that the conditions start in.

ELLA Love at first sight leads to tragedy.

STEPHEN Sometimes you got to take a chance. Jump in with both feet first and who knows what might happen.

ELLA   Sound advice from Mr. Divorce.

STEPHEN   I didn't say it works all the time.

> *Lights change.*
>
> *STEPHEN and ELLA exit.*
>
> *Sound effect: "Barracuda" by Heart.*
>
> *Enter CHRISTINE and JIM as teens.*

CHRISTINE   Whatcha doing, Jimbo?

JIM   I'm reading.

CHRISTINE   But it's spare.

JIM   It's not for school.

CHRISTINE   Oo, maybe it's a love letter.

JIM   Do you mind?

CHRISTINE   *Maggie's Last Dance.* Sounds boring.

JIM   It's Ella's essay, if you must know.

CHRISTINE   Why would the smartest girl in grade ten want you to look over her homework? I mean, like, are you an expert on dancing or something? I think she likes you.

JIM   Christine, I'm trying to read.

CHRISTINE   Bet you like her too. I mean, what's not to like? She's smart and she's sort of good-looking.

JIM   In a Joanie Cunningham sort of way.

CHRISTINE   Be careful, Jim. She's trouble. I've seen her kind before. Shy and intelligent on the outside. A cruel animal on the inside. Once she gets her hooks into you, she won't let go.

JIM   Ella's not like that.

CHRISTINE   Think about it, Jimbo. You tell her what you like about the essay and she'll smile politely and nod. The minute you start criticizing it, she'll tear into you like a rabid badger. She'll pull your still-beating heart out and chew it while you watch. Face it, Jim. You're blue collar and she's starched collar. The two don't go together.

JIM   It worked for Margaret and Pierre Trudeau… for a while anyway.

CHRISTINE   Then the next thing you know she's measuring Mick Jagger's lips with her tongue.

JIM   Why did she give me this essay then?

CHRISTINE   Work it through, Jim. The essay is about two people who weren't meant to be. Get it?

JIM   Yeah. I think I'm getting the picture.

CHRISTINE   If it were me, I'd take the direct approach. You know, if I liked a guy, I'd tell him to his face. You know, first I'd make eye contact.

JIM   She said it would make things clear.

CHRISTINE   Then I'd get close. Face to face.

JIM   But I didn't think it would mean this.

CHRISTINE   Take his hands in mine.

JIM   She should have just said it right out.

CHRISTINE   Push my lips against his.

> *JIM walks away. CHRISTINE kisses air.*

JIM   Man, am I that blind?

CHRISTINE   I'm starting to think so.

JIM   She's not going to get away with this.

CHRISTINE   Don't get mad, get even.

JIM   But how?

CHRISTINE   I've got a few ideas.

JIM   What?

> *She kisses JIM.*

I didn't know you were French.

CHRISTINE   That's just the start of your world tour.

> *CHRISTINE grabs JIM and necks with him. While doing so, she takes the essay.*
>
> *Lights down.*

ACT TWO

SCENE ONE

Sound effect: "The Hustle" by Van McCoy.

One by one the characters get on stage. They sway to the music. Once they are all on they dance the hustle.

ELLA *(to JIM)* Are you finished with my essay, Jim?

JIM Uh… I'm a slow reader. I'll get it to you soon.

ELLA No rush. I'm just anxious to hear what you think.

JIM So far it looks pretty good.

DERRICK *(to HELEN)* Come on, Helen. What's wrong? Aren't you having a good time?

HELEN Leave me alone.

DERRICK What did I do?

HELEN Everything.

STEPHEN *(to CHRISTINE)* Wanna score some hash?

CHRISTINE Get lost.

STEPHEN Thought you might want to loosen up. All that sneaking around has to put stress on a person.

CHRISTINE I don't know what you're talking about.

ELLA *(to JIM)* I haven't seen you around the last couple of days.

JIM Hey man, I've been busy.

ELLA Mellow out. I was just asking.

JIM Sorry. I got a lot on my mind.

HELEN *(to DERRICK)* You ever wonder what's going to happen to us after high school?

DERRICK Never gave it much thought. Figure we'd both get into university. Maybe stay in the same dorm. Coed. That would be cool.

HELEN What if you couldn't go? What if you had to stay here?

DERRICK Oh man, I'd go nuts. This place is so boring. Why do you ask?

HELEN I hate you.

STEPHEN   *(to CHRISTINE)* Hang loose, Christine. I won't tell Ella a thing.

CHRISTINE   You better not.

STEPHEN   It's none of my business.

CHRISTINE   And it better stay that way.

STEPHEN   Just think you should be more up front about it.

CHRISTINE   I won't have to sneak around after tonight.

ELLA   *(to JIM)* What's bugging you, Jim?

JIM   I'm just thinking about stuff.

ELLA   Can I help?

JIM   Yeah, tell me what the essay means.

ELLA   What do you think?

JIM   Does it mean Quebec should separate?

ELLA   No. It means it should stay.

JIM   But in the essay, Maggie leaves. I'm really confused.

ELLA   Read it again. We can go over it together after you're done.

JIM   I have to think about it.

ELLA   Okay. Sure. Take your time.

They dance until the music ends. Everyone exits.

ELLA at her present age remains on stage.

Francis Langley High School Reunion. There he is. Jim Bauer. My Hardy Boy all grown up. I see him after fifteen years and the queasy feeling in my stomach comes back. I want to throw up. It must be love. Tonight, I had the chance to make things right. So what do I do? Get in a fight. Smooth move, Ex-Lax.

I don't know why I got in the fight. I guess you can never escape the past. Jim and I had a dark history. And here she comes.

CHRISTINE enters and goes to JIM, who enters from the opposite side.

Christine McCoy chats with him by the bleachers. If I don't go over there soon, she's going to rekindle the old spark. He tells a story. I don't know if it's funny. She doesn't care. She laughs and touches him on the arm. He smiles and moves closer.

I have to go now. I cross the dance floor. My legs feel like wet blubber. I'm Jamie Summers. Moving in slow motion. My pulsing heart rings like bionics in action. I have no idea what I'm going to do when I get there, but I know I have to move faster.

I walk over the faded volleyball line. I stretch past the faint footprints of a thousand teenagers. I step on decades of scraped knees, on sneaker dirt, on the dashed hopes of teenaged lovers at countless school dances.

Christine sees me. She smiles and turns back to Jim. They laugh. She takes his arm and whispers in his ear. Suddenly my bionics short-circuit. I'm sixteen again. I'm the geek who plays Yahtzee against her cat. Christine McCoy is stealing away the only boy who made me want to throw up. I opened my heart to him when I should have opened my blouse.

Francis Langley High School Reunion. I'm alone and my stomach hurts. I'm letting him get away. No.

>ELLA crosses to JIM and CHRISTINE.

JIM *(to CHRISTINE)* Can't you get over it?

CHRISTINE Screw you.

ELLA Jim? Can we talk?

CHRISTINE Do you mind? We're busy.

JIM *(to ELLA)* I'll catch you later.

ELLA We have to talk now. I know I should have done this in high school.

CHRISTINE High school? Ella, you sure this can't wait another fifteen years?

ELLA Jim, you were right about love, but you forgot one detail.

JIM What?

ELLA It's spontaneous.

>She pulls him away from CHRISTINE and kisses him.
>
>Sound effect: "Raindrops Keep Fallin' on My Head."
>
>ELLA pushes away from JIM as the music swells.

This is wrong. I'm sorry.

CHRISTINE You always went for sluts.

JIM I dated you, didn't I?

>She exits.
>
>Lights cross-fade to DERRICK and HELEN as teens.
>
>Sound effect: "You're Having My Baby" by Paul Anka and Odia Coates.

DERRICK Oh man, oh man, oh man. This is so ace.

HELEN It's been two months and nothing.

DERRICK   Oh man. We've got to make plans. Two months. We'll get married right after grad. This is so ace.

HELEN   But I have other plans. I wanted to backpack across Europe.

DERRICK   That's frivolous. What do you think you are? A teenager?

HELEN   Yes.

DERRICK   Not anymore. You're a mother. And I'm a father. Daddy. Man, I can't wait to hear that.

HELEN   What about university?

DERRICK   I'll still go.

HELEN   I meant me.

DERRICK   You'll have to take care of our little baby. Did you hear what I said? Our baby.

HELEN   Forget it. We're both taking care of it.

DERRICK   Imagine if it's a boy. No baseball or football. No, my son's going to learn how to appreciate fine wine, beautiful music, the classics of literature. He's going to grow up to be a great scholar. A leader among academics. The only thing that can stop him is a stupid piece of rubber that breaks in the middle of sex. Then he'll be burdened with a kid of his own. One that he'll have to give up everything to raise. Oh man, why did we keep going? Why didn't you stop me?

HELEN   I told you to stop.

DERRICK   But you should have meant it.

HELEN   There's nothing we can do about it now.

DERRICK   There is one way.

HELEN   No way, man. I don't believe in that. We're keeping the baby.

DERRICK   Just a thought. I didn't want to press you. It's just something to consider. You know, with both our lives hanging in the balance.

HELEN   I said no and this time I mean it.

DERRICK   Then what are we going to do?

HELEN   First, you put on your hockey gear. Then we go tell my dad.

DERRICK   Oh man. I'm dead.

    Lights down.

SCENE TWO

Lights up on STEPHEN and CHRISTINE.

CHRISTINE   Made your rounds?

STEPHEN   Yeah, by now everyone knows how screwed up my life is. So they're all feeling pretty up about their lives.

CHRISTINE   Could be worse. You could be an alcoholic.

STEPHEN   Yeah, that would be a real kick in the pants.

CHRISTINE   Nothing like a reunion to put reality into perspective, eh?

STEPHEN   Too much perspective can kill you.

CHRISTINE   Why did you come here, Stephen?

STEPHEN   Wanted to purge some demons.

CHRISTINE   Damn. Here I thought it was my charming personality.

STEPHEN   What about you? You don't strike me as wanting to keep up with the Helen Barbours of the world.

CHRISTINE   It's kind of stupid, really.

STEPHEN   Come on, Christine. I saw you with an Afro and bell-bottoms. After that, nothing is stupid anymore.

CHRISTINE   It's kind of like home. You guys are the only family I ever had. I know that because I hated all of you.

STEPHEN   Sounds like family to me.

CHRISTINE   But after high school, I missed you all.

STEPHEN   And how is your homecoming?

CHRISTINE   You remember Fuller's? I used to order the quiche all the time. Best-tasting thing on the menu. I used to drool just thinking about it. First thing I did when I pulled into town was go to the Fuller's. Except it was gone. There was a breakfast-joint there. I went in all the same. Figured one diner was like the next. I ordered the quiche. It smelled the same. Looked the same. I took one bite and spewed. I guess it's true what they say. You never can go back.

STEPHEN   Yeah. Look at the crowd. The start of the night, they were all divided into the same groups as they were in high school. Jocks with jocks. Nerds with nerds. Now look at everyone. Parents with parents. Singles with singles. It's a different mix. If you try to stick with the old gangs, you'll end up alone. If you leave the past behind, you get to talk about dirty diapers.

CHRISTINE   No diapers for me.

STEPHEN   No kids?

CHRISTINE   Couldn't hang on to a husband long enough to get one. Can't seem to hang on to anyone these days.

STEPHEN   Get a cat.

CHRISTINE   I'm serious. What's wrong with us? Why can't we be more like Derrick and Helen?

STEPHEN   For one thing, we grew up.

CHRISTINE   We haven't changed at all. We never will.

STEPHEN   Speak for yourself. I started as the high-school all-star and look at me now. No job. No future. Nothing. I've come a long way, baby.

CHRISTINE   I guess if you put your mind to it, you can fuck up any life.

STEPHEN   But if you face your past, you can put it where it belongs. Behind you. Standard AA spiel.

CHRISTINE   You?

STEPHEN   I'm a part-time member. Fell off the wagon about the same time I got my invitation.

CHRISTINE   And you still came?

STEPHEN   Hey, I'm facing my past. Ounce by ounce. Care to join me?

CHRISTINE   You've had enough. Give me the mickey.

STEPHEN   I've grown attached to it. It keeps me warm at night. It never nags. And it'll never leave me. Say hello to my fourth wife.

CHRISTINE   Go ahead. I don't care what you do.

STEPHEN   It's nice to see you haven't changed.

CHRISTINE   I know I'm not going to end up like you.

STEPHEN   You're already there. You just don't know it.

Lights cross-fade to JIM and ELLA at reunion age.

JIM   You have to stop being afraid at some point.

ELLA   I'm sorry. It didn't happen the way I wanted it to. You make me want to throw up. In a good way.

JIM   Then take a chance.

They move closer.

ELLA   Oh God, here we go again. Is this love?

JIM   Only one way to find out.

ELLA and JIM kiss. ELLA stiffens. The moment is definitely awkward for her.

I missed you.

Lights down.

SCENE THREE

Lights up.

Sound effect: "Welcome Back" by John Sebastian.

CHRISTINE, STEPHEN, JIM, ELLA and DERRICK at sixteen file into the room and set up a classroom setting.

Everyone sits as MRS. RENDALL (played by HELEN) enters.

MRS. RENDALL   Class. Class. Settle people. Settle. Mr. Nesbitt, feet off the desk. Miss McCoy, so kind of you to join us today. Sit down. Every minute you waste, we stay after class. I don't care what the other teachers say. Now settle people. Thank you. Today we're continuing our essays on Canadian politics. I believe Christine is next.

CHRISTINE gets up with her essay.

CHRISTINE   This is an essay I wrote in honour of the Trudeau's recent separation. I call it *Maggie's Last Dance*.

ELLA   That's my essay. Jim, you—

JIM   I didn't know. I swear.

MRS. RENDALL   Miss Givens. Mr. Bauer. I'm sure what you have to say is relevant, but save it until the end of class. Please continue, Ms. McCoy.

CHRISTINE   Thank you. Margaret Trudeau took her ultimate freedom trip on March 27, 1977. She packed her camera and a pair of blue jeans and left. Who was this mother who could leave her three children? Who was this wife who could leave her husband? Who was this stateswoman who could leave the prime minister of Canada? Some say she was a flower child, never ready to settle down. To others she was a gold digger. I saw her simply as Maggie. She did only what she knew how to do. Be herself.

I remember the first time I heard of Maggie. CBC Radio announced that she had disgraced Canada. What was her crime? Did she try to assassinate a president? Did she declare war on China? No, she sang. In Venezuela she serenaded Madame Perez with an aria. Maggie must have really sang off-key. However, everyone will remember the one disgrace she will always be known for. That is, her rendezvous with the Rolling Stones on her sixth wedding anniversary.

No one cared that she and Mr. Trudeau had decided to separate. They just saw a woman who should have been at her husband's side. People wanted her to be a good prime-minister's wife and say all the right things. To serve guests. To obey protocol. She once said protocol is learning all the things that you have to do no matter how much you find them unnatural and trying. I wonder. How long can someone do that before they crack?

Maggie's answer was not long. After six years, she left. The people hated her for it. But no one hates the husbands who abandon their wives. No one expects fathers to be around to raise children. Why, then, did they pick on Maggie? Did anyone stop to think that she and Mr. Trudeau agreed to separate? I don't think so.

I wonder what their last night together was. Sometimes, I imagine they had one last dance. Just like a dance starts your marriage, they had one to end theirs. I can see Mr. Trudeau tenderly embracing his wife for what he knew would be the last time. Maggie pressed her cheek to Pierre's. For the last time, she kissed him. Then whispered goodbye. Other times, I saw them dance at arm's length. A formal waltz. Kept apart because protocol dictated it and shaped their relationship. But in reality, I knew there was no last dance. He sat in his study trying to figure out a way to keep Canada together while she packed her camera and a pair of blue jeans and left. The end.

MRS. RENDALL   Excellent. A truly moving essay, Miss McCoy. You've outdone yourself. A remarkable improvement over your last essay.

> *ELLA crosses downstage. JIM follows her. Lights cross-fade to her their position.*

> *Everyone else exits.*

JIM   Ella, wait. Let me explain.

ELLA   You jerk. I can't believe I trusted you with my essay.

JIM   I don't know how she got it.

ELLA   You gave it to her. You took my most private thoughts and you passed them around like cheap gossip.

JIM   Hey, man. Don't freak on me. You could have found a nicer way to put me down.

ELLA   You missed the point.

JIM   Maggie's last dance. Two people drifting apart. She leaves him. Au revoir, Quebec.

ELLA   I was talking about the pain they suffered. That's how I felt when my dad left. I was telling you something no one else knew about me.

JIM   Man, are you for real? The essay didn't say anything about that.

ELLA   Remember when I wrote about how Maggie and Pierre agreed to go their own way? How I pictured the last dance?

JIM   But you said they never had one.

ELLA   If they did, they might never have broken up. You know, maybe if she felt his arms around her or if he felt her head against his shoulder, things might have been different. They might have had a chance. But they never had that last dance, so we'll never know what could have happened.

JIM   You talking about Maggie and Pierre or your mom and dad?

ELLA   I always wanted them to have a last dance.

JIM   I never saw that, Ella. I'm sorry.

ELLA   Everyone else in Rendall's class did.

JIM   I swear, Ella. I didn't give the essay to Christine. She must have stolen it. I'll tell Rendall everything.

ELLA   Don't.

JIM   Don't you want credit for it?

ELLA   I don't want everyone knowing how I feel. Just you. What did you think?

JIM   It was ace. A great essay.

ELLA   I hope it clears things up.

JIM   Yeah. You know, this whole Quebec separation thing would be cleared up if everyone put their cards on the table. I mean, Quebecers think Canada thinks one thing, when Canada is thinking another.

ELLA   Politics don't work like that. There are always hidden agendas.

JIM   Not if I was in charge. I'd be up front about everything. No secrets. I'd go up to Quebec and say I want you to stay. Let's do what it takes to make it work.

ELLA   I think Quebec would go for that.

    They move in for a kiss.

    Sound effect: "Raindrops Keep Fallin' on My Head."

JIM   *(at age seven)* I can get popcorn. I got three dollars. My mom gave it to me.

    Music out.

    ELLA backs away.

ELLA   Let's take it slow, okay?

JIM   *(at age sixteen)* Sure.

    Lights down.

SCENE FOUR

Lights up on HELEN, CHRISTINE and ELLA as adults.

HELEN   It's so nice that just we girls get to chat. Just like the old days.

ELLA   You never talked to me.

HELEN   I know, but I want to make up for it now. I thought we could play a little game of confessions.

CHRISTINE   Oh Helen, there's that Catholic side of you creeping out again.

HELEN   Don't you want to play?

ELLA   I'm game.

CHRISTINE   Sure.

HELEN   Let's start with an easy one. Did you ever steal anything?

CHRISTINE   Yeah.

ELLA   Maybe.

HELEN   What did you steal, Christine?

CHRISTINE   A Bic pen from Dryden's Drug Store.

ELLA   I tried to steal twenty dollars from my mom's purse. She caught me. Never tried to steal again. What about you, Helen?

HELEN   I'd never steal. How could anyone steal, knowing how much it would hurt other people?

CHRISTINE   And the game's off to a rocking start.

HELEN   I'm sorry. Let's try a better confession. Who was your first lover?

CHRISTINE   This isn't fair. We all know who yours is.

HELEN   My game. My rules.

ELLA   Was it good?

HELEN   I think the foreplay lasted longer than the actual act.

CHRISTINE   You had foreplay? Keep that man.

HELEN   I don't have any reference point. I think Derrick's a good lover. He's my only one. I came close with someone else once, but I chickened out.

ELLA   Anyone we know?

HELEN   No one important. What about you? Who was your first?

ELLA   Mine came after high school. It was a guy I met at a club during my university days. Greg. We were watching *The Dukes of Hazzard* at his place.

One thing led to another and the next thing I know, we're on the carpet. Shag is not the most romantic of carpets, let me tell you. My ass was chafed for a week. Anyway, he's into the whole thing, but I'm feeling kind of, you know. I didn't know what to do. I mean, he seemed to know where he was going. So I just looked at the TV. After that, whenever Greg wanted to do it, all I could picture was Uncle Jesse. It made me feel too weird. We broke up a couple of weeks later.

CHRISTINE   Could have been worse. It could have been Enos.

HELEN   What about you, Christine?

CHRISTINE   I can't remember. All I know is that it hurt. It was short. And unlike Chinese food, I wasn't hungry for more in an hour.

HELEN   But was he?

CHRISTINE   Of course. He's a guy.

ELLA   Could he?

CHRISTINE   Of course not. He's a guy.

HELEN   It was someone in our class, wasn't it?

CHRISTINE   No. Not really.

ELLA   It was. Who?

CHRISTINE   No one important.

HELEN   You slept with Derrick, didn't you?

CHRISTINE   What? No way.

HELEN   Don't lie to me. He told me everything.

CHRISTINE   You're crazy. I never slept with him.

HELEN   Slut.

CHRISTINE   I covered for you.

HELEN   And you took Derrick for yourself.

CHRISTINE   It was Jim. I slept with Jim. Okay? I would never touch Derrick.

HELEN   Why not?

CHRISTINE   No offense, but he's repulsive.

HELEN   Why didn't you just say it was Jim in the first place?

CHRISTINE   Because of Ella.

ELLA   I knew you two were dating. So what?

CHRISTINE   It was a matter of timing.

ELLA   When did you two?

CHRISTINE   It doesn't really matter.

ELLA   Yes, it does. When?

> *Lights change.*
>
> *Sound effect: "Go Your Own Way" by Fleetwood Mac.*
>
> *HELEN exits. CHRISTINE and ELLA take opposite ends of the stage. JIM steps into the middle.*

ELLA & CHRISTINE   *(at sixteen)* Happy anniversary, Jim.

JIM   *(at sixteen)* Man, it's been two weeks already?

ELLA   Yes. Look, I made you a Pukka Shell necklace.

CHRISTINE   I bought you a rubber.

JIM   Thanks. That's cool. Great. Just great.

ELLA   I had to go to five different stores to find just the right shells. It took me seven hours to string them on.

CHRISTINE   One drugstore. Two minutes.

JIM   I'm impressed.

ELLA & CHRISTINE   Thanks.

JIM   I'm sorry. I didn't get you anything.

ELLA   That's okay. Knowing you're happy is present enough for me.

CHRISTINE   You promised you were going to dump her.

JIM   *(to CHRISTINE)* She gave me her essay. I don't want her to feel like I betrayed her. Give me time.

ELLA   This feels so right, Jim.

CHRISTINE   If you don't do it now I'm taking my present back.

JIM   Ella, it's not you. It's me.

ELLA   What are you saying?

JIM   I like someone else. I wanted to tell you now before things got out of hand. I didn't want to sneak around on you. Man, it wouldn't be fair to either of us.

ELLA   Who is it?

JIM   Christine.

ELLA   I see.

JIM   I'm sorry. I like you as a friend, but that's all. There's, like, no spark.

ELLA   I can change. Give me a chance.

CHRISTINE   I wonder what French tickler means.

JIM   *(to ELLA)* Man, I don't think you can. You said it in the essay. You're afraid of being hurt, so you don't reach out. I couldn't even get you to hold hands at the movie last week.

ELLA   Give me time.

JIM   Uh...

CHRISTINE   I guess we'll find out together.

JIM   Sorry. I can't wait. Can we still be friends?

ELLA   Please don't go. I'll change. Give me your hand now. I know we can work this out. Just give me another chance.

> *JIM exits.*

CHRISTINE   *(as an adult)* Get over it. It's in the past.

ELLA   *(as an adult)* You don't understand. Everything we've done affects what we are today. Look at you. You're just like your mother.

CHRISTINE   She's got nothing to do with this.

ELLA   Ever since she left, you've never had a stable relationship.

CHRISTINE   At least I have relationships.

ELLA   You jump from man to man. You dump them before they can hurt you.

CHRISTINE   You won't even let a man get close to you. If I didn't tell you about this, you'd find another excuse to run away from Jim.

ELLA   I'm not running from him.

CHRISTINE   Yeah right. You're just like Maggie Trudeau, the slut.

ELLA   She wasn't a slut.

CHRISTINE   You knew what it's like to lose a parent. And you still wrote about that slut like she was some kind of saint.

ELLA   They agreed to separate.

CHRISTINE   She ran out on him. Left him without a word. Abandoned her children. She doesn't deserve to be praised. She deserves to be shot.

ELLA   She's not your mother.

CHRISTINE   She didn't care about anyone but herself.

ELLA   Just like you. I feel sorry for you, Christine.

CHRISTINE   Remember this, Ella. Your past is nothing but my hand-me-downs.

ELLA exits.

Lights cross-fade to STEPHEN and DERRICK as adults.

DERRICK   Hey, remember when Helen and I won king and queen of the grad? Pity vote. We brought our kid. Remember when you guys went to the after-grad party, but Helen and I had to go home because our kid started throwing up.

STEPHEN   That's pretty much what happened at the party.

DERRICK   Helen says it's my fault we're stuck here. Says I'm an ostrich with his head in the past.

STEPHEN   She's right. You're stuck like a record. Remember when. Remember when. You're pathetic.

DERRICK   You're one to talk. You and that mickey. Like father, like son.

STEPHEN   What about you? You organize this stupid reunion so you can relive your old glory? What's the point?

DERRICK   You remember when I said I taught at Langley? I don't. Never went to university. I'm the janitor here. Helen made me tell everyone I'm a teacher. Said it would look better. That's my greatest glory. Getting to lie about a job I never had. But at least I don't need to pop breath mints before I kiss my kids good night.

STEPHEN   That was my dad. Not me.

DERRICK   And what's the difference between you two?

STEPHEN   I don't need you to preach to me.

DERRICK   No, you need my wife to screw. Just like you did in high school.

STEPHEN   You got problems with your wife, that's between you two. Don't drag me into it.

DERRICK   Go crawl inside your mickey.

STEPHEN   You want to step outside?

DERRICK   You're not worth it.

STEPHEN   Come on, let's go. Come on.

STEPHEN takes a wild swing. DERRICK dodges it.

DERRICK   Grow up, Stephen.

STEPHEN   You bastard.

STEPHEN takes another swing and falls on his ass.

DERRICK   Stephen, this isn't high school anymore.

STEPHEN   *(laughing)* First time I heard you admit that.

DERRICK Give me the booze, Stephen.

STEPHEN It's the only thing I'm good at.

DERRICK You don't have to do this.

STEPHEN Hey, remember the first time we got stoned. You were scared shitless when my dad came in. You promised never to touch the stuff again.

DERRICK I kept my promise. I keep all my promises.

STEPHEN How did you do it? What's your secret?

DERRICK No secret, Stephen.

STEPHEN I never touched Helen.

DERRICK It's behind us. Now give me the mickey.

STEPHEN I'm not a quitter.

DERRICK You never were.

> STEPHEN hands DERRICK the mickey.
>
> Lights cross-fade to CHRISTINE and JIM in their teen years.
>
> Sound effect: "Tuesday's Gone" by Lynyrd Skynyrd.

CHRISTINE But we've been together for only a month.

JIM It's not you. It's me.

CHRISTINE You scab. Don't you dare pull that line on me.

JIM I thought I cared about you. But you don't make me feel the same way Ella did.

CHRISTINE It's too late for you two, you know that.

JIM I fucked up royally.

CHRISTINE So what's the point of giving up on us?

JIM It's not right. With us, it's just sex. That's not enough.

CHRISTINE I love you, Jim.

JIM I'm sorry, Christine. I love Ella.

CHRISTINE You'll never get her back.

JIM We'll see.

> Lights down.

SCENE FIVE

Sound effect: "School's Out" by Alice Cooper.

Lights up on everyone sitting around in a circle. They are in their teen years. They are passing two yearbooks around.

JIM has one. HELEN has the other.

STEPHEN   Come on, Jim. Hurry up and sign Ella's yearbook.

JIM   I'm working on it. Just sign mine and pass it around.

STEPHEN   Hang loose and have a great summer. Stephen.

DERRICK   Math class was a blast. Let's get kicked out again. Have an ace summer, dude. I know I am.

CHRISTINE   Hope you get herpes. Love Christine.

ELLA   I'll never forget you, Jim. Have a totally awesome summer. Forever your friend.

HELEN   I wish I could say I'm going to have a great summer. But after the end-of-the-year dance, I have to go shopping with my mom for a waitress uniform that will fit my bloated body so that I can earn enough money to clothe and feed my unborn child. That's because my deadbeat boyfriend won't take responsibility for his baby. While this scab is whooping it up at some summer cabin, I will be sweltering in polyester, serving coffee to truckers. All because he won't help with the raising of his own child. My life sucks. I wish I were dead. Have a great summer. Helen.

CHRISTINE   Is this a yearbook message or a cry for help?

DERRICK   Man, what's taking you so long, Jim?

JIM   There. I'm done.

STEPHEN   Ace. You drew KISS.

ELLA   Cool. It looks just like them.

HELEN   Right arm.

DERRICK   Awesome.

CHRISTINE   It's okay.

ELLA   Thanks Jim. This is the coolest. I love it.

DERRICK   KISS is so cool.

STEPHEN   They're going to be bigger than The Beatles.

HELEN   They're going to be around forever.

CHRISTINE   They're just a flash in the pan.

STEPHEN   Don't mind her. She's on the rag 'cause she can't get a date for the dance.

CHRISTINE   Bite me, Stephen.

DERRICK   Hey man, you're all going to the dance, right?

JIM   Wouldn't miss it.

HELEN   I have to talk to my dad. I can't go out that much anymore.

CHRISTINE   Screw your dad, Helen. It's the end-of-the-school-year dance. The biggest bash. I'm sneaking some vodka.

DERRICK   She can't drink. It's not good for the baby.

HELEN   What do you care?

STEPHEN   Come on, guys. Are we all going or what?

EVERYONE   Yeah.

JIM   It's going to be an awesome party. Who wants to go for a booze run?

DERRICK   I'm in.

HELEN   Wait for me.

ELLA   Me too.

> *Everyone moves into pairs. CHRISTINE with STEPHEN. HELEN with DERRICK. JIM with ELLA.*

> *Lights change.*

> *CHRISTINE and STEPHEN are at the reunion age.*

STEPHEN   You can't leave the reunion now. The traditional last dance is coming up.

CHRISTINE   I don't feel like sticking around to see a bunch of nerds groping on the dance floor.

STEPHEN   What's wrong?

CHRISTINE   Had enough old times for one night.

> *JIM and ELLA at their reunion age.*

JIM   I'm sorry I never told you. I didn't think you needed to know.

ELLA   I think it would be a valuable piece of information. "By the way, Ella, I slept with Christine behind your back."

JIM   We didn't do it until after you and I broke up.

ELLA   That makes me feel so much more secure.

JIM   Why are you dredging this up now?

HELEN and DERRICK as adults.

DERRICK   There was no her.

HELEN   I know.

DERRICK   I wanted to see if you still cared.

HELEN   It would make things a lot easier if there was one.

JIM and ELLA.

JIM   I was a kid. I didn't know any better.

ELLA   You did it once, you'll do it again.

JIM   It happened fifteen years ago. I regretted it ever since. Don't punish me again for it.

ELLA   You're all alike. You expect me to forget it, like it's a little glitch in my memory. It doesn't work that way, Jim. I can't forget what you did.

STEPHEN and CHRISTINE.

CHRISTINE   You can't just let your past go. It comes after you like bloodthirsty hounds.

STEPHEN   If you can't hide from the past, face it.

CHRISTINE   Ounce by ounce?

STEPHEN   See it for what it really is. Memories. They're harmless.

Sound effect: Partridge Family *theme.*

CHRISTINE is seven.

CHRISTINE   Mommy. You can use your special time whenever you want. I'll be here.

Sound effect: "Tuesday's Gone."

STEPHEN is seventeen.

STEPHEN   I'm a loser just like you, Dad. No rock-and-roll dreams. No plane crashes. Just two pathetic quitters.

Sound effect: "You're Having My Baby" by Paul Anka.

DERRICK and HELEN as teens.

DERRICK   I'll take responsibility for my baby. But promise you'll never hold this decision against me.

HELEN   You know I won't.

DERRICK   I got big plans for you, little one. Just you wait and see.

Sound effect: "Raindrops Keep Fallin' on My Head."

ELLA and JIM are seven.

JIM   Uh, you want some popcorn? I can get popcorn. I got three dollars. My mom gave me it.

ELLA   Daddy says I can't eat anything before supper.

JIM   Okay. We can just watch the movie.

ELLA   Who do you like better? Butch or Sundance?

JIM   I guess Butch. He's great. He kicked that guy in the nuts. Who do you like?

ELLA   Yeah, I like him too. He's funny.

JIM   Heh, heh, heh…. Um, do you want some popcorn? I could get some. I have three dollars. My mom gave it to me. I promise I won't tell your dad. He's down front. He can't see us anyway.

ELLA   Okay.

JIM   I'll get some. Hey, it looks like your mom came.

ELLA   But she's working today.

JIM   Look. She's kissing your dad.

ELLA   That's not my mom.

JIM   Oh. Um. I—You—Uh…. Maybe we should… um. Do you still want popcorn?

ELLA   I want to throw up.

Music swells.

Lights change as the music goes out.

JIM and ELLA as adults.

You're all alike.

JIM   I'm not your dad.

DERRICK   It's not you. It's me.

STEPHEN   You can change.

CHRISTINE   No, I can't.

HELEN   Then it's over.

JIM   Why does it have to be like this?

ELLA   I look at you and all I can see is my father.

DERRICK   Then there's only one thing left to do.

STEPHEN   Let go of your bad memories. Keep the good ones.

HELEN   What about the kids?

CHRISTINE   They're all fucked. My mother ruined them all.

DERRICK   I'll take care of them.

JIM   Don't do that to yourself. Don't let him wreck your entire life.

HELEN   I'm in a better position to do that.

STEPHEN   So you're going to let her ruin the rest of your life too?

ELLA   You have no idea what I've been through. Your parents never had a divorce. You've got a normal life. You've got normal memories.

DERRICK   And I want them.

CHRISTINE   I don't have to listen to you.

JIM   And look where that's gotten me.

STEPHEN   At least try, Christine.

JIM   I care about you, Ella.

DERRICK   Give me this at least.

HELEN   You can have them.

CHRISTINE   Not my style.

JIM takes ELLA's hand.

ELLA   You were there. When my dad was with her.

JIM   Yes.

ELLA   You never left me.

Sound effect: "Last Dance" by Donna Summer.

What happens next is a moving tableau of the essay, Maggie's Last Dance.

STEPHEN   Last chance for romance.

CHRISTINE   Been there. Done that. See ya.

She exits. He goes out another exit.

DERRICK   Last dance for old-time's sake?

HELEN   What good will it do?

DERRICK   Think of it as a "remember when" that I'll never talk about.

HELEN and DERRICK dance formally. Then they break apart and walk out opposite exits.

JIM and ELLA at the centre of the dance floor.

JIM   I'll always be here for you, Ella.

ELLA   I still feel sick about it all.

JIM   Give it time, Ella.

ELLA   I'll try, but I can't make any promises.

JIM   Kind of reminds me of Quebec and Canada. All they can do is try.

ELLA   Do you think Quebec will ever separate?

JIM   I think Canada cares too much to let Quebec go.

ELLA   Yeah, there's always hope.

ELLA moves to hold JIM.

Lights down.

The end.

MOTHER TONGUE

BY BETTY QUAN

ABOUT

BETTY QUAN

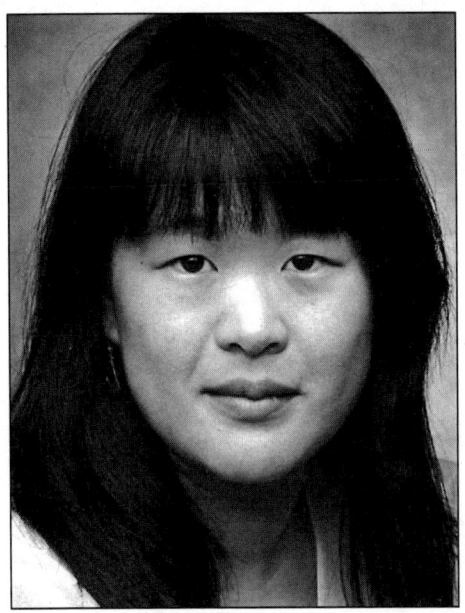

Betty Quan writes for the stage, radio and television. Her other theatre credits include the touring production of *Naomi's Road* (adapted from the book by Joy Kogawa) and *The Dragon's Pearl*, as well as the Dora-nominated *Ghost Train* (adapted from the book by Paul Yee) and the Jessie award-winning *Fault Lines*. *Mother Tongue* was previously shortlisted for the Governor General's Literary Award for drama.

BLINDNESS CUTS PEOPLE OFF FROM THINGS.
DEAFNESS CUTS PEOPLE OFF FROM PEOPLE.

—HELEN KELLER

Mother Tongue premiered at the Firehall Arts Centre, Vancouver, in February 1995, with the following company:

MOTHER	Allanah Ong
MIMI	Laara Ong
STEVE	Kameron Louangxay
FATHER	Michael Hirano

Directed by Donna Spencer
Costume Design by James Glen
Set Design by Neil Fleming
Lighting Design by Neil Fleming and James Proudfoot
Sound & Music Design by Ted Hamilton
Movement Consultation by Lee Su-Feh
American Sign Language Consultation by Astrid Evensen-Flanjak
Assistant Direction by Michael Hirano
Stage Management by Damon Fultz and Amadea Edwards

CHARACTERS

MOTHER fifty-three, widowed parent of Steve and Mimi; has a Chinese accent (but not pidgin English); also speaks Chinese (Cantonese).

STEVE sixteen, no Chinese accent (at age eleven lost his hearing so is fluent in American Sign Language).

MIMI twenty-two, Steve's sister, no Chinese accent; speaks some Cantonese and when speaking with Steve occasionally mixes in signed words.

FATHER thirties, has a Chinese accent. (Father can be a physical presence on stage but always in shadow; alternatively, his dialogue may be done as voice-over.)

SETTING

The Chan family home in Vancouver, BC.

NOTES

When parentheses appear, (E) means the next line is in English. (C) means the next line is in Chinese/Cantonese. (ASL) refers to the text being signed, not spoken.

Steve's signed dialogue attempts to follow the linguistic principles of American Sign Language. It is recommended that a member of the deaf community or a certified sign-language interpreter be consulted.

In the moments when Mother speaks Chinese, I have not provided a translation from the English to Chinese; rather I have written her dialogue/monologues in English. This is to allow the actress playing the part flexibility with the character and how much Chinese she wants to, or is able to, use.

MOTHER TONGUE

SCENE ONE

Voice-over montage like a sea of voices ebbing and flowing, reverberating, cutting and inter-cutting. The stage remains dark.

MOTHER   A long time ago.

STEVE   Listen.

MIMI   A story.

MOTHER   Like a bird in your hand, I was, until you set me free—

STEVE   —across the sky—

MIMI   —across the ocean.

MOTHER   The wave became a blanket. And the little girl died.

MIMI   *(C)* Father? Come back! Come back!

STEVE   Did I stop hearing her?

MOTHER   It was my favourite story.

MIMI   Our favourite story. He would tell it to me.

STEVE   All my senses were swimming inside a seashell.

MIMI   Sometimes when I dream, I dream in Chinese.

STEVE   The ghost of your voice is inside me.

MOTHER   He called you his little Jingwei.

STEVE   Listen to my hands as I speak to you.

MIMI   Sign.

STEVE   Sign.

MIMI   Speak.

STEVE   Speak.

MIMI   Hear.

STEVE   Listen to me. Please.

MOTHER   I am my language. I speak Chinese. Your voices. Your words. You drown me out.

STEVE   Silence. Silence.

      Suddenly, the voices are cut off.

SCENE TWO

      Lights up. MIMI and STEVE are doing homework. MOTHER prepares dinner. STEVE signs to MIMI.

STEVE   *(ASL)* University go you? Ontario. Letter I see room your.

MIMI   Again, please. You what?! Steve! You read my letter. *(She looks over her shoulder to make sure MOTHER doesn't hear.)* Don't.

STEVE   *(ASL)* Don't understand she.

MIMI   She can so understand. Even a little bit is enough. Snoop. What's the sign for snoop? *(ASL finger-spells)* S-N-O-O-P. *(resumes)* Yes, you. What were you doing going through my stuff?

MOTHER   *(C)* Mimi, come help me with dinner.

MIMI   Okay, wait a minute. Well?

STEVE   *(ASL)* Pencil search I.

MIMI   You were looking for a pencil…. That doesn't excuse the fact that you opened my letter.

STEVE   *(ASL)* Go?

MIMI   I don't know. Queen's is a good university and they have one of the best architecture departments…

STEVE   *(ASL)* Money, find where you? Expensive!

MIMI   It's a scholarship. You know Mother can't afford to send me. She thinks a bachelor's degree is enough. And you still have a couple more years left at the deaf institute.

STEVE   *(ASL)* Up-to-now you not-yet out Vancouver you. This will first time.

MIMI   I know it'll be my first time out of Vancouver alone.

STEVE   *(ASL, trying to scare her)* Jails. Many have. K-I-N-G-S-T-O-N.

MIMI   Finger-spell that again, please.

STEVE   *(ASL, finger-spells)* J-A-I-L-S. K-I-N-G-S-T-O-N.

MIMI   *(reads out spelling)* J-A-… jails. K-I-… Kingston. Oh, stop it about the jails, will you?

STEVE   *(ASL)* Five.

MIMI   Really, there's five in Kingston? How do you know?

STEVE   *(ASL)* Decide finish you?

MIMI   I still have time to decide. And I have to talk to her.

> *STEVE becomes agitated.*

STEVE   *(ASL)* Letter hide you. Not right.

MIMI   Wait, Steve! I'm the one who should be mad. I was going to tell you. Honest! I would never let you down. Never.

STEVE   *(ASL)* Liar. Remember?

MIMI   You won't let me forget that, will you?

MOTHER   *(C)* Mimi! Help set the table!

MIMI   Coming!

> *MIMI makes her exit. As her back turns, STEVE reaches out to her and speaks as a deaf person would. It is barely understood and the way the words are modulated indicate he has not spoken for some time. MIMI hears him, but exits still.*

STEVE   Don't go, Mimi. Come back. Come back. Don't go. Don't leave me all alone.

> *STEVE becomes bathed in a blue light. He turns to the audience. At first he tells his story silently, only mouthing the words. It is as if the audience has become deaf. STEVE then places his hand against his throat and speaks.*

It's like liquid. Drowning. When I would go swimming, I would do the backstroke. I'd immerse my head in the water and listen to the swirling, swirling echo. It was a game I used to play—no one can hear under water, can they? But now, it's not a game. Not anymore. There: the waves of air… circulating. It's like that inside my head. Air floats inside me. The sound of ether rising. *(places hands over his ears)* I feel my voice coming from inside my body. The thought becomes articulation, the movement of the throat, the exhalation of air as it forms into sounds as it forms into words. Air forming into sounds I can't hear. Into words I can't speak. Into sentences no one will listen to.

SCENE THREE

> *They are eating their dinner in front of the TV.*

MOTHER   *(C)* Good?

MIMI   Yes.

MOTHER   *(C)* Some more?

MIMI   *(E then repeat in C)* I'm full.

MOTHER   *(C)* Maybe Steve wants more. You ask him.

MIMI   He's right there.

MOTHER   *(C)* Ask him. Mimi.

MIMI   One day you'll have to learn how to sign.

MOTHER   *(E)* I have to learn English. *(C)* Too late now.

MIMI   It's never too late to start. Who knows, I might not always be here. I mean, I know there's a Chinese sign language but Steve and I learned American Sign, so maybe, I mean, I can write stuff down…

MOTHER   *(C)* I don't understand what you're talking about.

> *MOTHER gestures toward STEVE again, wanting MIMI to ask him if he wants more dinner.*

MIMI   You have to learn English one day.

MOTHER   *(C)* Ask Steve.

> *MIMI touches STEVE to get his attention.*

MIMI   *(ASL)* Food more want you?

STEVE   *(ASL)* Finish. Enough.

MIMI   No—you tell her. She's right there. Go on.

> *STEVE and MOTHER look at each other. STEVE shakes his head. A moment of silence. MIMI tries to conciliate, as usual.*

Mother, remember when you would tell us stories?

MOTHER   *(C)* I remember.

MIMI   We were young.

MOTHER ·   *(E then repeat in C)* Before all the trouble.

> *STEVE's inner voice is not heard by the others.*

STEVE   I remember your voice, Mother. This, this is the sign for mother.

> *MIMI looks at STEVE and sees the meaning of his signing.*

(He signs as he speaks it.) A thumb on the chin with the fingers extending out. I've showed it to you before. Look, Mother. Please.

MOTHER   *(C)* What? What? I don't understand. Mimi?

MIMI   He's saying…

STEVE   (*inner voice spoken aloud*) Tell us a story, and I will read your lips. English or Chinese. I don't care. Just look at me when you talk. (*ASL*) Look-at-me. Look-at-me.

> *MIMI understands but does not translate the full message.*

MIMI   Steve says the same thing: tell us a story. Like you used to.

MOTHER   (*C*) I know a good one. A favourite. (*E*) My father used to tell it to me when I was a little girl. (*C*) You'll remember this one, Mimi.

MIMI   *The Emperor and his Daughter.*

MOTHER   (*C*) Yes, that's right. (*E*) Your father used to tell it too.

MIMI   Why don't you sit here, Steve, so you can see better? Oh, wait—

> *MIMI goes to the kitchen, returning with sliced up oranges. During her absence, silence; it is obvious that STEVE and MOTHER are uneasy with each other.*

MOTHER   (*C*) Not from the fridge?

MIMI   I know you don't like them cold.

MOTHER   (*C*) So sweet. (*E*) Soon, we eat the oranges from bi sin. (*beat, then C*) A long time ago—

MIMI   (*ASL*) Long-time-ago.

MOTHER (*C*) What does that mean?

MIMI   A long time ago.

STEVE   (*ASL*) Long-time-ago. Story. Yes. Understand.

> *MOTHER begins the motion of the hand sign, but stops and stares ahead.*

MOTHER   (*C*) A long time ago there was an emperor who had a young daughter. They loved each other very much. But although his power could touch all corners of the land, the emperor could see only as far as the shoreline that divided his kingdom with the sea. Beyond that shoreline, his vision was limited, like a kite held high in a strong breeze—he could see the shape, but not the colours.

> *FATHER's voice is heard only by MIMI. His voice blends into MOTHER's and when he stops, MIMI takes over. The effect is like a chorus.*

FATHER   A long time ago...

MIMI   (*C*) Father?

FATHER   There was an emperor who had a young daughter. They loved each other very much. Tell it, Mimi, my Jingwei. A long time ago.

MOTHER & MIMI   (*They talk in unison, but with MOTHER speaking C and MIMI speaking E. MIMI's voice takes over the story until only she speaks it.*) A long time ago. It was my favourite. A story.

MIMI   About the Jingwei bird and why she is always dropping sticks and stones in the ocean. When I was small, I used to pretend I was that little bird. I would soar through our garden with arms for wings. Father. Tell me about the Jingwei. Yes, like you used to do when I was small. Like a bird in your hand, I was, until you set me free across the sky, across the ocean. Such a long time ago, yet so close I can still see it unfolding before me. Father? Tell me a story. Like you used to do.

FATHER   A long time ago.

STEVE   (*ASL*) Long-time-ago.

FATHER   A long time ago there was an emperor who had a young daughter. They loved each other very much.

MIMI   But although his power could touch all corners of the land, the emperor could see only as far as the shoreline that divided his kingdom with the sea.

FATHER   Beyond that shoreline, his vision was limited, like a kite held high in a strong breeze—he could see the shape, but not the colours.

MIMI   (*as Jingwei*) Father, look at the waves, so tall they must be hiding something behind them. I will take my boat for a ride.

FATHER   (*as Emperor*) Not so far, not so far.

MIMI   (*as Jingwei*) Don't worry, Father. I'll be careful.

FATHER   (*as Emperor*) Why don't you wait a while? I'll join you. We can journey to the horizon together, where the sea meets the sun.

MIMI   (*as Jingwei*) When? When can we do this? (*laughs*) You're always promising such things, Father! I'll go out on my own first. On my own adventure. Then I'll show you what I've seen.

STEVE   (*ASL*) Come, when you?

FATHER   (*as Emperor, laughs*) When?

STEVE   (*ASL*) When?

MIMI   (*as Jingwei*) What does that matter? We have all the time in the world.

MOTHER   (*C*) The sun was warm upon the little girl's face—

FATHER   —and the salty breeze off the water tempted the little girl to travel farther and farther. To see what hid behind the tall waves of the sea.

MIMI   Far, far, far away she went, when suddenly—

FATHER   (*as Sea God*) Who dares come this far upon the ocean of my reign?

MOTHER   *(C)* The Sea God's bad temper came upon the little girl.

STEVE   *(ASL)* Drown. Water. Waves.

FATHER   The water became a blanket that covered her. And the little girl died.

MIMI   *(gets onto her knees)* Died? I don't remember her dying. Is that right? I thought the water changed her into a bird. Like magic.

FATHER   I would tell you that when you were small. When you didn't understand death.

MIMI   Like I do now.

   A dreamlike light surrounds MIMI.

Sometimes when I dream, I dream in Chinese. Not the pidgin Chinese I've developed, but the fluent, flowing language my father used to coo as he walked with me, hand in hand. There is this one dream. I am walking with my father in the alleyway behind our house. I am seven years old. This is just before my father… before…. My father and I are holding hands and in perfect Cantonese talk about the snow peas in the garden that are ready for picking. Father doesn't know it, but for the past week I've been hiding amongst the staked vines, in the green light, gorging on the snow peas until there can't be any more left. I'm about to tell him this—air my confession—when we come across a large kitchen table propped against the side of the garage. "A race, my little Jingwei!" my father says. "I'll go through the tunnel and we'll see which way is faster. One, two, three, GO!" We run; him in the tunnel, me on the gravel. I finish first and wait, expecting to meet him and rejoin hands. But he doesn't come out of the shadows. My extended hand is empty. I wait and wait and wait. I start screaming, *(C)* "Father! Father! Come back! Please come back! Father!" *(E)* And then I wake up.

   Moment returns to the real. MIMI is visibly upset.

MOTHER   *(continuing the story, C)* A wave came over the little girl and her boat, and the ocean pulled her down. Down to where the Sea God lived. And that day, she died.

MIMI   *(repeating, simultaneously signing to STEVE)* A wave came over the little girl and her boat, and the ocean pulled her down. Down to where the Sea God lived. And that day, she died. *(to MOTHER)* When *(C)* Father *(E)* told that story, I don't remember him saying that the little girl died.

   MIMI turns away from STEVE.

I thought everything had to have a happy ending.

MOTHER   *(starts to clear up some of the dishes, E)* Story not over.

STEVE   *(ASL)* Crying, why?

MOTHER   *(C)* Mimi, my little Jingwei, why are you crying?

MIMI   Please don't call me that.

MOTHER   *(C)* What, Jingwei? But I don't mean anything by it. *(E)* It's a pretty name. *(C)* My father used to tell the Jingwei story to me when I was a little girl. Before I came here. *(E)* It's a good story. It was my favourite story. Just like you.

STEVE   *(ASL)* Mother tell her?

MIMI   *(signs and speaks)* Not now. Later.

MOTHER   *(C)* What are you talking about?

STEVE   *(ASL)* When? When?

MIMI   *(ASL)* Stop. When ready I.

STEVE   *(ASL)* Wrong.

MIMI   *(ASL)* My problem.

> *STEVE exits.*

MOTHER   *(C)* Why does he leave like that, without a word? Always he does that!

MIMI   *(lying)* He said he was going upstairs.

MOTHER   *(C)* When? I didn't hear him.

MIMI   *(used to this conversation, but nevertheless lying)* He signed it.

MOTHER   *(C)* He doesn't talk anymore, Mimi. Never.

> *Offstage sound effect: water running in the bathtub.*

MIMI   It embarrasses him. You should understand that by now. Steve can't hear what he's saying. He thinks he might sound stupid. I've got an essay due tomorrow. Do you want me to help with the dishes?

> *MOTHER shakes her head. MIMI exits. MOTHER cleans up. Her inner voice speaks. MOTHER is awash in light like smoking red incense.*

MOTHER   *(C then repeat in E)* A long time ago. I was eighteen, I left China for Canada. Alone. We were rich. Capitalists. *(E)* But the war had brought the Japanese, followed by Mao's government. Every night, we turned off the lights, closed the curtains and we waited. Waited for the knock at the door, for someone to come and in the name of the Red Army take away everything we had… everything I had. I arrived in Vancouver in 1959, without a word of English, wearing my hairspray and makeup and high heels, eager and excited. But I didn't fool anyone. Only myself. More than twenty years gone and I sometimes wonder why I ever came at all. My husband dead and me alone. None of my own family here to comfort me. No. There are my children. But I often feel as if I bore strangers who have my eyes, my skin, my hair, but whose souls have been stolen by invisible spirits. I wonder, when I am dead, if my children will remember to honour me on Chingming. Will they follow tradition? Clean my grave, bring flowers, burn incense? Will they pay me tribute as I have done to ancestors they do not know? Yes, there are my children.

MOTHER moves out from her inner voice. She calls.

Mimi? Steve? *(as if talking to herself)* Is anyone home? Or is it just me?

SCENE FOUR

MIMI does homework. She drifts into sleep. MIMI's own dreamscape light fades up as she begins to dream.

MIMI   For years I've been sorry. Make a fist and circle it on my chest. Sorry.

MOTHER   *(C)* Don't forget, Mimi. I have to work late. *(E)* Overtime pays good! Take Steve to the doctor.

MIMI   He's eleven years old! *(to MOTHER)* He can go to the doctor himself.

MOTHER   *(C)* He's too sick to go by himself.

STEVE   Yeah Mimi. I'm too sick to go by myself.

MOTHER   *(C)* Such a high fever!

STEVE   If my temperature gets any higher, I'll burn up! I'll spontaneously combust. *(He makes exploding noises.)*

MIMI   But there's a game. At the school. You know I've never been to one.

STEVE   Boys will be playing.

MIMI   Shut up, Steve. *(to MOTHER)* Why can't you go?

MOTHER   *(C)* I have to work overtime!

MIMI   But all my friends will be there.

STEVE   Boys.

MOTHER   *(C then repeat in E)* Mimi, you're too young for a boyfriend.

STEVE   I'll go to the doctor by myself.

MIMI   You're really not that sick, Steve.

STEVE   Forget it. Your friends are more important than me.

MIMI   Don't be such a baby. Okay! I'll take you to the doctor.

MOTHER   *(C)* Don't forget.

STEVE   She'll forget.

Simultaneously.

(ASL) Tell her.

MOTHER   *(C)* Tell him.

> *STEVE and MOTHER repeat their separate languages as MIMI is driven under the weight of their words.*

SCENE FIVE

> *MOTHER pays tribute to an ancestral shrine.*

MOTHER   *(C then repeat in E)* Husband, father-in-law, mother-in-law. Three cups for you each to drink from. Fragrance of incense and smoky tea. Chingming, the end of the second moon. Take care of my family. I'm burning money for you to spend in heaven.

> *MOTHER burns spirit money then sets out an offering of oranges. STEVE watches, trying to gather courage to move closer. Because her back is turned to him, MOTHER is unaware of his presence and STEVE cannot see what she is saying.*

(C then repeat in E) Obey and serve one's parents when they are alive. Bury them with honour when they are dead. Respect them always. If family does not pay tribute to the dead, they will bring evil upon those still living.

> *STEVE exits.*

(E) Five years ago, I didn't burn enough spirit money. Cups were full. Incense burned. But not enough spirit money for you to buy more time in heaven. I gave you all I had—but it wasn't enough. Since then, you have made me remember. Every day, I see the evil you brought upon my son. The oranges here are sweet. Eat them and fill them with your luck.

I will give them to my children.

SCENE SIX

> *STEVE in a blue light.*

STEVE   It's nice. The water. Six months after... after I lost my hearing, I wasn't allowed to swim. Or take a plane ride; not that I'd be going anywhere. Not that any of us are going anywhere. Except for Mimi. *(beat)* I missed the water. Being in the water. Mother was probably glad though. She hated it when I went swimming. Thought I would catch a fever, leaving the pool without drying my hair. Maybe, maybe she was right. I remember when I was a baby. Even before I was born. Floating—rotating around and around in my mother's stomach like the earth around the sun. I could hear her voice too. I remember hearing my mother laughing and singing. But not anymore. Did she stop being happy? Or did I stop hearing her?

> *STEVE steps out of his light briefly.*

(ASL) M-I-M-I stay. Please.

> *STEVE repeats the sign for "please" as the lights fade down on him.*

SCENE SEVEN

> *MOTHER is in the living room sewing. MIMI enters, back from school.*

MIMI   Is anybody home?

MOTHER   *(C)* Here, Mimi. I got some *(E)* piecework *(C)* from the factory. *(E)* Pockets. *(C)* All day I've been sewing pockets. You'll have to mark for UIC.

MIMI   I'll work on the UIC statement tonight. Is Steve home yet?

MOTHER   *(C)* I don't know.

MIMI   Have you seen him?

MOTHER   *(C)* In his room.

MIMI   Then why didn't you say… *(sighs)*

> *MOTHER gestures at the burning incense.*

MOTHER   *(C)* The incense is very fragrant, isn't it?

MIMI   Moon festival?

MOTHER   *Chingming. (C)* Have you forgotten already?

MIMI   No, I remember. I just get all of them confused, that's all.

> *MOTHER explains the festival; it's a lecture MIMI knows.*

MOTHER   *Chingming. (E)* Not same as Moon Festival. *Chingming.* Time to remember all our dead family. *(C)* We'll go to the cemetery and bring your father flowers.

MIMI   What day do you want to go to the cemetery?

MOTHER   *(C)* Why? Are you busy? Too busy to visit your father's grave?

MIMI   It's not that. I just thought that if we went Sunday we could go *(C)* drink tea.

MOTHER   *(C)* Drink tea! But we don't have enough money. *(E)* Next time. *(C)* We'll go next time.

MIMI   When?

MOTHER   *(E)* Next time. *(C)* Remember how your father loved to go drink tea? Every Sunday, early in the morning, we'd take the bus to Chinatown?

MIMI   Father loved the shrimp dumplings.

MOTHER   *(C)* Shrimp dumplings. Pork dumplings. Sticky rice.

MIMI   *(E then repeat in C)* Pork with black bean sauce.

> *Together, in Chinese, MIMI and MOTHER imitate FATHER.*

MIMI & MOTHER   Hurry! Eat while it's still hot.

> *They laugh. MOTHER looks at her watch and realizes it's time to make dinner.*

MOTHER   *(E)* I remember when your father died, you were just seven, and Steve, Steve was just two. *(C)* Still a baby. He doesn't remember your father, does he?

MIMI   He remembers him a bit; I don't know.

MOTHER   *(C)* Sometimes during the night you'd wake up screaming. You had terrible nightmares. Do you remember?

MIMI   Yes.

MOTHER   *(C)* Nightmares about your father. Do you still have them? Mimi?

MIMI   *(lying)* It doesn't matter. I don't have nightmares about him anymore.

MOTHER   *(C)* Your father holding his chest. And me holding the two of you. *(E)* Too young to have a heart attack.

MIMI   Lucky the doctor was Chinese.

MOTHER   *(C)* I was so scared. I didn't know what was happening.

MIMI   It was the same for Steve, Mother. Remember? When he got sick? We were all scared. We all didn't know what was happening.

MOTHER   *(E)* I didn't understand Steve's doctor. Lucky I have you, Mimi.

> *MOTHER begins chopping vegetables.*

(E) For Chingming we can't eat meat. *(C)* We'll eat *jai*.

MIMI   Buddha's Feast.

MOTHER   *(C)* Good: you remember the tradition. One day—you'll make *jai* for me.

> *STEVE enters the room to grab a snack. He looks at MIMI then exits.*

MIMI   I'll cook *jai* for you. One day. *(beat)* I've got some good news. Mother—stop for a moment; I have to talk to you. You know I'll be getting my bachelor's degree soon. That's why we should go *(C)* drink tea. *(E)* Celebrate.

MOTHER   *(C)* Now you can get good job. Make lots of money. *(E)* Good daughter—take care of your mother and brother. *(E then repeat in C)* No more pockets to sew.

MIMI   I was thinking about going into post-graduate studies. Study architecture. Go to school for a few more years.

MOTHER   *(C)* Too expensive.

MIMI   I got offered a scholarship. They'll pay. For everything.

MOTHER   *(C)* Mimi! That's so good!

MIMI   My professor says that only two students got it.

MOTHER   *(C)* I'm so proud of you! Such a smart girl!

MIMI   It's at Queen's University.

> *MOTHER doesn't understand most of what MIMI is saying, but MIMI looks happy, so MOTHER is happy for her.*

MOTHER   *(C)* Good. Good.

MIMI   They say it's one of the best universities in the country. They have an excellent architecture program. I'll design things, Mother. I'll make buildings like Arthur Erickson, the man who designed the courthouse over at Robson Street, or the American, Frank Lloyd Wright.

MOTHER   *(C)* Good.

MIMI   They have a beautiful campus. Lots of very old buildings. Tall and wide and open.

MOTHER   *(C)* Such a smart girl.

MIMI   Queen's is in Ontario.

MOTHER   *(C)* But that's so far away.

MIMI   It's only a three-hour difference. *(mumbles)* By phone.

MOTHER   *(C)* Three hours. Are you trying to fool me?

MIMI   You know I can't write Chinese, but we can talk on the phone.

MOTHER   *(E)* Long distance. *(C)* No money for that. Piecework can't pay!
UI can't pay!

MIMI   There'll be one less mouth to feed without me around—

MOTHER   —Mimi—

MIMI   —plus the scholarship will pay for my room and board at Queen's. I won't really need any money except for my textbooks. Maybe I'll take a part-time job. I'll pay for the telephone calls, then you—

MOTHER   *(C)* UI forms, who'll take care of those?

MIMI   I've showed Steve how to do them.

MOTHER   *(C)* He won't know how to do it!

MIMI   He's been doing them already. You just haven't noticed because I've been coming to you for the signatures.

MOTHER   *(C)* And when the UI runs out we'll be on *(E)* welfare. *(beat, C)* What if there's trouble?

MIMI   What kind of trouble?

MOTHER   *(E)* People phone, they come to the door. *(C)* I never understand what they're talking about!

MIMI   Steve can take care of that too.

MOTHER   *(C)* He can't hear them.

MIMI   He doesn't need to hear them. They can phone on the TTY line. They can write down what they want.

MOTHER   *(C)* Someone breaks into the house, he can't hear them.

MIMI   Mother, you're worrying too much.

MOTHER   *(C then repeat in E)* You're too young to leave home, Mimi. Young women should only leave home to get married.

MIMI   You were eighteen when you came to Canada all by yourself.

MOTHER   *(C)* But that was different.

MIMI   How? How was it different? You came here. I want to go to Ontario.

MOTHER   *(E)* I didn't want to come here! *(C)* Inflation because of all the trouble with Mao Zedong. *(E)* My father only had enough money to send me. A cousin—someone from my father's family—met me at the airport. *(C and repeat in E)* My first day, no sightseeing, nothing. My first day I started working.

> *MOTHER holds out her hands.*

(C) Look at my hands, Mimi. I've been working since I was eighteen years old. *(E)* I worked hard. Saved enough to sponsor my mother and father. *(C and repeat in E)* I was too late.

MIMI   I'm twenty-two. I'll go to Queen's, study hard. And when I finish, I'll become a great architect and buy you a new house. I'll build you and Steve a new house. In Shaughnessy!

MOTHER   *(C)* No, you get scholarship here.

MIMI   The scholarship is not for here.

MOTHER   *(C)* What about Steve?

MIMI   He's deaf, not retarded. If you would only just listen…

MOTHER   *(C)* No. You listen. I am the mother!

MIMI   Then act like one!

> *MIMI is surprised by her words; MOTHER reacts as if she's been slapped in the face.*

MOTHER   *(C)* Who works hard, day and night? I put food on the table; you're going to an expensive university and Steve needs special things. *(E)* Where do you think the money comes from? *(C)* Ever since your father died!

MIMI   I know, Mother! I know! But look at us. Look at you. When Father died…. And Steve…. What are you afraid of?

MOTHER   *(She mimes the action of her words, of her fear. C.)* In China, every night we would turn out the lights, draw the curtains. We waited for the knock at the door. It could be a friend, a neighbour—wearing a Red Army badge, ready to take everything away from us. To take everything away from me.

MIMI   You're not in China anymore. The Red Army won't be knocking at the door. I'm here, Steve's here—

MOTHER   *(C)* Taking everything away from me. *(E)* And now they're taking you away from me too!

MIMI   I loved him too. But I can't be him, Mother. I can't always protect you. Mother.

MOTHER   *(C)* He called you his Jingwei bird.   ·

MIMI   Don't call me that! *(C)* Mother. *(E)* You came all the way across the Pacific Ocean. All by yourself. That's farther than I have to go.

MOTHER   *(C)* I had no choice!

MIMI   Then let me choose what I want to do!

MOTHER   *(C then repeat in E)* My family never came to Canada, your father died young, and Steve… now you. *(C)* You're going to leave me too.

MIMI   I'm not leaving you! I just want—

MOTHER   *(C) Bi sin*, Mimi. Go, pay tribute to your paternal grandfather and grandmother. *Bi sin*. You should've done that when you first came in. *(E)* Bow to your family.

MIMI   *(C)* Mother.

MOTHER   *Chingming.*

> *MIMI exits. MOTHER resumes food preparation.*

(to herself, C) Eat jai. Bean sprouts. Bean thread noodles. *(E)* Ginger, garlic, onions. Tofu to remember how Buddha did not eat meat. Rice wine, mushrooms, onions. Onions. Onions.

> *MOTHER stops. She begins to silently cry.*

SCENE EIGHT

> *STEVE is doing homework. MIMI enters, fresh from her argument with MOTHER.*

STEVE   *(ASL)* Know now, Mother, she?

> *MIMI nods.*

(ASL) University, can't?

MIMI   I'm going. I don't care what she says.

STEVE   *(ASL)* Not fair.

MIMI   *(ASL)* Don't. Please.

STEVE   *(speaks as a deaf person would)* Can't go. Not fair.

MIMI   I'm going to come back! I promise!

STEVE   *(speaks as a deaf person would)* Forget it. Don't bother!

> *STEVE gestures at his ears, doing the signs for listen and for deaf. He then points at MIMI accusingly. MIMI exits. STEVE faces the audience as if facing a mirror. He practises enunciating words. He speaks as if a deaf person would who is unused to speaking.*

My name is Steve Chan. *(He is getting angry.)* My name is Steve Chan. I cannot hear you. My sister, sister, sister. *(The deaf have particular difficulty with sibilant words. This frustrates STEVE.)* Sister! Sister!

> *STEVE puts his hand over his throat. We move into his inner voice.*

I remember the last voice I heard. It was my mother, screaming my name. Steve! Steve! And she was crying. I was eleven. I remember that because we were reading *White Fang* in school and I decided I wanted to have a wolf-dog. I was making up a speech inside my head, about getting a dog, and how I could convince my mother that I should have one for my birthday. I'm always making up speeches inside my head. It was cold outside, and I already had a cold. I was supposed to wait for Mimi. She was supposed to take me to the doctor. She never showed up.

I went home with a temperature. By evening my fever shot up. Everything was moving in slow motion. My mother with the cold, wet cloth, trying to keep me cool, Mimi asking the paramedic questions and translating as best she could to my mother. Sixteen and already my sister was a mother. I fainted, and when I finally woke up, all my senses were swimming inside a seashell. Liquid had filled up my mouth and my ears.

I lay back, trying to breathe. I thought I would drown in all that liquid. But there was nothing there, no water, no blood. Just a hole. A hole.

> *Each character moves into his/her individual lights, e.g., STEVE's blue light, MOTHER's red, MIMI's dream light. Their inner voices speak to one another but they are physically unaware of each other. The overall effect is like that of Scene One.*

MOTHER   Chinese.

MIMI   English.

STEVE   *(ASL)* Sign language.

MIMI   The little girl drowned.

MOTHER   Not understand.

STEVE   I cannot hear you.

MIMI   I can't do this. Not anymore.

MOTHER   Bow to your family.

MIMI   Inside me, it's been asleep for so long. What does it feel like to wake up from inside?

MOTHER   That is the way it works. In Chinese.

MIMI   Let me open the windows. Just a crack.

STEVE   *(ASL)* Please. Please.

MIMI   Let me pull back the curtains. Can I?

STEVE   I... can... not—

MOTHER   *(C)* Cannot.

STEVE   *(ASL)* Can't.

MIMI   Let me see what's outside.

STEVE   *(ASL)* Sign. Speak. Hear. Listen. Silence.

MIMI moves into the centre, her hand outstretched to STEVE who has moved to one side while MOTHER stands at the opposite side. For a moment, MIMI's hands touch both MOTHER and STEVE's hands. She fails to join all hands. STEVE and MOTHER recede into the darkness. MIMI's dream light fades up.

FATHER   The little girl's soul became a small bird called Jingwei. Continue. *(beat)* Mimi.

MIMI   Angry was the spirit in that bird, angry at the sea it was for taking her away from her beloved father. And every day the Jingwei would carry in her beak stones and twigs from the mountains of the east and ahead, flying west, she would drop her small stones and twigs into the sea. Finally, the Sea God noticed what the Jingwei was trying to do.

She expects to hear FATHER's voice again, but is greeted by silence.

(C) Father? *(E)* How do I finish the story? Where are you? Are you here with me? Did you come back across the ocean to find me? Did you fly away like a kite in the breeze? So high up you can see the shape, but not the colours? Can you see me? You're so far away but all I have to do is pull you home. Father. Father. When I finish building a bridge, will you cross it? Even if the stones are loose and the twigs are breaking. Will they cross it? Father? Will they cross it? Don't let me do this alone. Please. *(beat, C)* Father? *(E)* How big is the ocean?

SCENE NINE

MIMI and STEVE say goodbye to one another. Off, MOTHER watches them.

MIMI   *(ASL and E)* All the bills have been paid. The chequebook's in the desk. Mother's supervisor at the factory said there might be some work next week. I gave her our TTY number. Once you get the dates, tell Mother… *(STEVE looks questioningly.)* Call me collect then if she doesn't understand and I'll—

MIMI becomes overwhelmed. STEVE puts his fingers against his lips: shhh. MIMI understands. Her mouth moves but makes no sound. STEVE presses his fingertips against MIMI's throat.

(ASL and E) And the Sea God said, "Silly Jingwei, my sea is wider and deeper than your limited imagination. You can never fill me up in a million years." To that the Jingwei replied, "But I can. Every day for a million years I will do this. Every day until one day. Until one day… *(begins to fade down)* until one day… until one day…"

STEVE   (*speaking as a deaf person would*) And the small bird flew back to land, only to return with another small stone or twig to drop into the sea.

> *MIMI smiles and gently pulls STEVE's hand from her neck. MIMI turns and moves into the shadows where she picks up a suitcase. She doesn't turn around. MOTHER moves forward, as if trying to reach MIMI. MOTHER also moves into the shadows. STEVE is alone. Lights fade down on him.*

SCENE TEN

> *STEVE and MOTHER are at the kitchen table. They are bent over their food, avoiding eye contact. MOTHER speaks as she gets other dishes out. With STEVE's face bent down, he cannot see that MOTHER is speaking to him.*

MOTHER   (*C then repeated E*) Can you understand me? When I try to speak English to you, can you understand me? In this ocean I am swimming and I am underwater and I cannot speak. What? I can't hear you. I am my language; I speak Chinese. Your language is not Chinese. Your voices, your words. I cannot understand. You drown me out.

> *MOTHER is seated with her head bent down. When STEVE does his monologue in English, he speaks from his inner voice. The ASL, however, is directed at MOTHER.*

STEVE   (*E then repeat in ASL*) Move your lips. Look at me. I can remember the sound. Say my name. I can hear the memory of how you used to say my name. Inside me. Look at me. Just because I can't hear anymore doesn't mean I've forgotten how to listen. If only you would just speak to me. The ghost of your voice is inside me. My mind hears you. It hears you, Mother.

> *During the ASL repeat, STEVE gets more angry. He tries to get MOTHER's attention, almost throwing his signs at her. MOTHER's head remains bent. He dares her to look at him.*

(*speaking as a deaf person would*) Mother. (*C*) Mother.

> *MOTHER looks up at him finally. She looks back down. STEVE exits to another space. His inner voice speaks.*

Can you see the words as they float in the air? My hands release them—out, out to be heard. Can you see the wind? The branches bending, the wind's fingers drumming against the window. There—thunder. The vibration crosses my spine. I can hear it. Yes, there's lightning. Music, music touches the floorboards, rises through my feet. My body hears all these sounds. Listen to my hands as I speak to you. Listen to me. Please.

SCENE ELEVEN

MOTHER goes to the shrine.

MOTHER   *(C then repeat in E)* I was born in 1940: the Chinese year of the dragon, the highest sign. *(E)* Steve was also born in the year of the dragon: 1976. It is considered a great honour to be born a dragon. We have tempers like fire and generosity like liquid, which pours from our mouths and fingertips. Dragon: *loong.* That is the Chinese word. The Chinese also call someone who cannot hear *loong.* I do not know why. When Chinese people pray to the dragon, for rain, for good luck, for happiness, they throw birds into the water. The dragon feeds on the meat of swallows and sparrows. Birds who make sweet sounds. Birds who have sweet flesh. Birds are sacrificed to our dragons, the *loong.* Are you that little bird, Mimi, my Jingwei? *(to herself)* Loong.

MOTHER takes one of the oranges from the shrine.

SCENE TWELVE

STEVE is huddled in his room, alone. MOTHER enters.

STEVE   *(ASL and speaks simultaneously)* Brother none. Sister one. Father dead. Mother have. Family my.

> *STEVE looks up. Sees MOTHER. She holds one of the oranges from the shrine.*

MOTHER   *(C)* Her soul became a small bird called Jingwei. Angry was the spirit in that bird, angry at the sea she was. And every day that bird would pick up pebbles and twigs in her beak and drop them into the water.

MIMI   *(Her voice flows with that of MOTHER, but an echoing translation.)* Her soul became a small bird called Jingwei. Angry was the spirit in that bird, angry at the sea she was. And every day that bird would pick up pebbles and twigs in her beak and drop them into the water.

STEVE   *(ASL and speaks simultaneously)* Together. Separate. Hearing person. Deaf person. Sign. Speak. See. Hear.

> *MIMI appears in spotlight, which recedes toward the end of her speech. She holds a bird cage, opens it. Sound effect of a bird in flight.*

MIMI   And the Sea God said, "Silly creature, you can never fill me up in a million years." "But I can," said the Jingwei. "Every day for a million years I will do this. Every day until one day there will be no more water between me and my family. I will build a bridge, a bridge that they can walk across. That my family can walk across." And the small bird flew back to the land, only to return with another pebble or twig to drop into the sea.

Lights fade down on MIMI. STEVE signs "sister." He huddles and cries silently. He signs "mother." He signs again. MOTHER enters STEVE's light. STEVE is finishing the motion of the sign for "mother" with his fingers stretched out to her. MOTHER moves forward. Her hand holds out the orange. STEVE is hesitant to take it. MOTHER reaches out again, this time using her other hand to force STEVE to face her.

Lights out.

The end.

NORAN BANG: THE YELLOW ROOM

BY M.J. KANG

ABOUT

M.J. KANG

M.J. (Myung-Jin) Kang started writing plays at seventeen years old, placing second in a playwriting competition for high-schoolers. *Noran Bang: The Yellow Room*, her first full-length play, was produced when she was eighteen years old at Toronto's prestigious Theatre Passe Muraille with Cahoots Theatre Projects. It was later remounted at Factory Studio Theatre in association with Cahoots Theatre Projects in 1998 and nominated for a DORA Mavor Moore Award, Toronto's professional theatre award for best new play. At the age of twenty-one, she was the youngest to be produced on Tarragon Theatre's main stage—Canada's mecca for new plays, with *Blessings*, an auto-biographical, full-length, three-character journey of her first visit to Korea since her immigration at the age of two. She has had a total of seven plays produced. As an actor, she was a series regular on CBC's *Riverdale*. She has also been featured in *Owning Mahoney*, opposite Philip Seymour Hoffman, *The Book of Eve*, opposite Claire Bloom, A&E's *Nero Wolf*, opposite Timothy Hutton, as well as many other roles on television, film and theatre. Currently, she is staying at home and raising her daughter, Mia. She lives in Santa Monica, California.

DEDICATED TO THE MEMORY OF

LANCE KOYATA

PLAYWRIGHT'S NOTES

Noran Bang: The Yellow Room was written through partial memories and dreams and what I imagined it might have been like for my family to be in Canada during the early years. Before I started writing *Noran Bang: The Yellow Room*, I went on long walks. During one of these walks, an image of my mother sitting by a kitchen table crying came into my head. She had just found out her mother passed away.

I have chosen to have the same actor play multiple roles because I believe each character the actor plays is an extension of her main character. For example, the actor who plays Umma also plays White Dog. Umma is an explosion waiting to go off. She has a lot of conflicting emotions that are mixed with a great need for justice and righteousness. White Dog, an older character, has seen much in his lifetime and provides a wonderful counterbalance to the Umma character. He doesn't have to prove anything, though he is willing to do anything for love.

Please feel free to cast according to your own vision of the play. The play contains Korean words and phrases followed by their English translation in square brackets. As a child, I grew up with both Korean and English, and in many ways believed they were one language. Many people may not feel the same way, so do substitute the English translation if necessary.

Noran Bang: The Yellow Room was developed with the assistance of the Banff Playwrights Colony and the Toronto Arts Council, under the guidance of Kim McCaw and with the assistance of the Ontario Arts Council during my playwright-in-residency at Cahoots Theatre Projects, under the patient and kind guidance of Marion de Vries.

A great deal of thank yous are extended to Marion de Vries, Woo-Suk Kang, Chun-Ja Kang, Jin-Kyung Kang, Yun-Suk Kang, Tony Rauchberger, David Rubinoff, Dilara Ally, Lynda Hill, Jane Luk, Jacoba Knaapen, Stephania Joy, Dave Carley, Jean Yoon and the board of Cahoots Theatre Projects.

Noran Bang: The Yellow Room was first produced in 1993 by Cahoots Theatre Projects, in association with Theatre Passe Muraille, as part of the 3-D Festival: Three Daring New Works by Writers of Diverse Cultures presented at Theatre Passe Muraille's Backspace, Toronto, with the following company:

MEE-GYUNG   Shelly Hong
KYUNG-MEI
HALMONEE

HARABOGEE   M.J. Kang
GYUNG-JUNE
KYUNG-MA (age twelve)

KOREAN DRUMMER   Mrs. Kim

APBA (SUNG HEE-GYU)   Lance Koyata
HYUCK-DONG
EDWARD
MAN
PARK CHUNG HEE
NORTH KOREAN SOLDIER
SOUTH KOREAN SOLDIER

UMMA (KYUNG-MA)   Jean Yoon
WHITE DOG
KIM JAE KYU

Directed by Marion de Vries
Set and Lighting Design by An Ge Zhang
Costume Design by Jocelyn Hublau
Prop Design by Timothy Hill
Choreography by Xing Bang Fu
Produced by Lynda Hill and Jean Yoon
Production Management by Andrea Lundy
Production Stage Management by Cheryl Francis
Stage Management by Ellen Flowers
Carpentry by Will Sutton

An altered version of *Noran Bang: The Yellow Room* was produced in 1998 by Cahoots Theatre Projects at the Factory Studio Cafe, Toronto, with the following company:

MEE-GYUNG   Shelly Hong
KYUNG-MEI
HALMONEE

HARABOGEE   Marjorie Chan
GYUNG-JUNE
KYUNG-MA (age twelve)

KOREAN DRUMMER   Charles Hong

APBA (SUNG HEE-GYU)   Denis Akiyama
HYUCK-DONG
EDWARD
MAN
NORTH KOREAN SOLDIER
SOUTH KOREAN SOLDIER

UMMA (KYUNG-MA)   Jean Yoon
WHITE DOG

Directed by David Oiye
Set Design by Kelly Wolf
Lighting Design by Jeff Logue
Costumes Designed by Cecile Belec
Choreography by Jamie Baik
Produced by Maria Costa
Production Management by David James
Stage Management by Marla Friedman
Assistant Stage Management by Alexa Carroll
Painting by Joanne Thompson
Carpentry by Matt Farrell, Sandra Janzen and Doug Morum

Noran Bang: The Yellow Room was nominated for a Dora Mavor Moore Award in 1998 for Outstanding New Play in the independent theatre category.

Excerpts from *Noran Bang:The Yellow Room* were previously published in *Fireweed Magazine* (Spring 1994, no. 43) and the Playwrights Canada Press collections *Beyond the Pale* (1996) and *Taking the Stage* (1994).

CHARACTERS

Kyung-Ma, who is called **UMMA** ("Mother")
Sung Hee-Gyu, who is called **APBA** ("Father")
GYUNG-JUNE and **MEE-GYUNG**, their daughters
HYUCK-DONG, a cousin in Korea
EDWARD, a Canadian boy
WHITE DOG, Gyung-June's dog in Korea
HALMONEE ("Grandmother"), Umma's mother in Korea
HARABOGEE ("Grandfather"), Umma's father in Korea
KYUNG-MA (Umma), as a twelve-year-old girl in Korea
KYUNG-MEI, Umma's younger brother in Korea
SOUTH KOREAN SOLDIER
NORTH KOREAN SOLDIER
MAN

SETTING

The play is set in Toronto in the seventies and Korea in the past.

NORAN BANG: THE YELLOW ROOM

ACT ONE

SCENE ONE

A slide collage is projected onto the stage, depicting the family together in Korea and Canada, as UMMA (the mother), GYUNG-JUNE and MEE-GYUNG (the daughters) perform a Korean folk dance on stage. APBA (the father) plays the Korean hourglass drum and another drummer plays offstage. As the dance reaches its climax, a slide of HALMONEE (the grandmother) appears on stage.

SCENE TWO

UMMA is alone on stage, crying.

UMMA   Ahh-u! Ahh-u!

Her daughter, MEE-GYUNG, enters hesitantly.

MEE-GYUNG   Umma? Umma, I'm sorry. Umma?

MEE-GYUNG also starts crying.

UMMA   Halmonee. Halmonee dor-ah-cah-soh-yoh! Halmonee dor-ah-cah-soh-yoh! *[Grandmother has died! Grandmother has died!]*

Her other daughter, GYUNG-JUNE, enters as if in a trance.

GYUNG-JUNE   Umma. I had a dream. Grandmother is dead. We were in a battlefield and she gave me a red flower. Everything else was black and white. She kissed me with a blood flower and told me to be strong. Then she walked along a line—a white line on the ground—to a farm. The farm was on the line. Her hair shed to the ground and her clothes became full of bullets. I couldn't kiss her. I was holding onto her, but I couldn't touch her. She flew me a rose—a white rose—and told me to love this country. She wants to hold me, Umma. She can't die unless I hold her.

UMMA   Moo-seun mal-ee-yah! *[What are you saying?]*

MEE-GYUNG   Grandmother's dead? Where is she?

GYUNG-JUNE   In Korea.

MEE-GYUNG   Korea?

APBA (*offstage*) Yo bau. *[Darling.]*

UMMA Your father.

GYUNG-JUNE I want to go back to Korea.

> *UMMA's husband, APBA, enters.*

APBA Yo bau! *[Darling!]*

GYUNG-JUNE I need to go back to Korea.

UMMA (*referring to APBA*) He tells me we have no money to see Mother buried. No money to go anywhere.

APBA Yo bau, come here now!

GYUNG-JUNE I'm going back on my own!

> *UMMA slaps GYUNG-JUNE.*

UMMA Selfish child!

> *UMMA exits.*

MEE-GYUNG Cah *[sister]*, why'd she hit you?

> *Pause.*

GYUNG-JUNE Grandmother is dead.

SCENE THREE

> *UMMA and APBA in their bedroom.*

APBA Stop crying. Crying doesn't help. (*passing her a roll of toilet paper*) Here.

UMMA Am I supposed to shit my tears?

APBA Come back to bed.

UMMA Why won't you let me go?

APBA It's late. Time to sleep.

UMMA You made me come here. You made me pack my bags and travel to this— this place!

APBA Shee-guh-ruh-wuhoo! *[Better be quiet!]*

> *UMMA lies down beside him, with her back to him.*

Sleep well.

SCENE FOUR

MEE-GYUNG and GYUNG-JUNE's bedroom. GYUNG-JUNE is crying and MEE-GYUNG is staring at the ceiling.

MEE-GYUNG   Cah, what happened tonight?

GYUNG-JUNE   Halmonee promised to be with me. Always.

MEE-GYUNG   Oh.

GYUNG-JUNE   Why were you crying?

MEE-GYUNG   Umma was crying.

GYUNG-JUNE   Do you even remember Halmonee?

MEE-GYUNG   No. Am I bad for not remembering?

GYUNG-JUNE   No. You were young when we left. Only four years old. Everyone loved you because you were so quiet. Not as loud as our cousin. Do you remember Hyuck-Dong?

Flashback to Korea: Their cousin, HYUCK-DONG, is in the yard of a small house, giving commands to WHITE DOG.

HYUCK-DONG   Sit down. I said "Sit!" Listen to me!

GYUNG-JUNE   He annoyed everyone and kept on trying to hurt my dog.

HYUCK-DONG prods WHITE DOG with a stick.

HYUCK-DONG   I'll poke you until you sit. Do you like being poked?

WHITE DOG   I hate you, you jerk!

GYUNG-JUNE   Remember the dog I had?

MEE-GYUNG   The big white one?

GYUNG-JUNE   Yes. White Dog.

HYUCK-DONG whacks the ground with the stick.

HYUCK-DONG   I'm not scared by you!

WHITE DOG   I haven't shown you my teeth yet!

He shows HYUCK-DONG his teeth. GYUNG-JUNE exits from the house.

GYUNG-JUNE   Hyuck-Dong! Leave my dog alone!

WHITE DOG   *(to GYUNG-JUNE)* Let me bite him. Right on his bum.

HYUCK-DONG   Hey, what's he saying?

WHITE DOG   One little bite. Right there. Left cheek. Bull's eye!

GYUNG-JUNE   *(to WHITE DOG)* No. I'll get in trouble.

HYUCK-DONG   *(to GYUNG-JUNE)* Your dog is stupid!

GYUNG-JUNE   *(to HYUCK-DONG)* You're stupid!

HYUCK-DONG   You're stupid! And that dog is stu-pi-dest! He can't respect that I am the smar-test!

> *HALMONEE enters the stage without being noticed.*

GYUNG-JUNE   My dog is smarter than you. My dog is smarter because he knows you are a bad person, a bad person he won't play with—he's not allowed to play with!

HYUCK-DONG   What do you mean—"Not allowed to play with"?

GYUNG-JUNE   'Cause I said so.

WHITE DOG   Uh oh.

HYUCK-DONG   Your mother said I can play with him whenever I want. Your mother said he's my dog too! You mother said I get everything of yours because we're cousins!

GYUNG-JUNE   He's my dog!

HALMONEE   Shee-guh-ruh! *[Too noisy!]*

GYUNG-JUNE   Halmonee, Hyuck-Dong tried to kill my dog!

HALMONEE   Gyung-June-na, everything is okay. Come inside and have yummy ducc gouk *[rice-cake soup]*.

GYUNG-JUNE   You put some mandu *[pork dumplings]* too?

HALMONEE   Yes, my special dumplings for my only Gyung-June. Hyuck-Dong, you may join us after you finish tying up the dog and take a bath. Nem-say-nah! *[You smell bad!]*

WHITE DOG   Hey! Steal some mandu for me too—okay, Gyung-June?

> *HYUCK-DONG drags poor WHITE DOG to be tied up.*

GYUNG-JUNE   *(to MEE-GYUNG)* That's how Grandmother was. Even when I wasn't the saint, she took my side.

MEE-GYUNG   Halmonee liked me too, right?

GYUNG-JUNE   Yes, but I was her favourite.

MEE-GYUNG   White Dog liked me best though.

GYUNG-JUNE   He was my dog!

MEE-GYUNG   I liked him. He was my friend too. Cah, how come they're in Korea and we're in Canada?

GYUNG-JUNE   Because of you. You screwed everything up.

MEE-GYUNG   Really?

GYUNG-JUNE   We just came here and they stayed there.

MEE-GYUNG   I miss White Dog.

They both fall asleep.

SCENE FIVE

Flashback to Korea: UMMA and APBA perform a courtship dance. APBA exits and UMMA is left sitting alone, drinking coffee in a café, waiting. APBA rushes in.

APBA   Kyung-Ma?

UMMA   Sung Hee-Gyu?

APBA   Yes. Your picture—it doesn't do you justice. You're much prettier in person.

UMMA   Thanks. You're late.

APBA   Sorry. Would you like anything?

UMMA   Look, I only came here because my mother and my oldest sister told me I should.

APBA   *(sitting down)* Well… why don't you tell me something about yourself?

UMMA   I work as an assistant calculus professor. It's part of my doctorate. I plan to finish my Ph.D. in the next couple of years and start working full time. I am the youngest of six children—three boys and three girls. My oldest sister and my mother think you would be a good match for me, but I am not planning to date until I finish my Ph.D. Your turn.

APBA   I studied theology in university, but because of my parents' financial situation, I switched my major to business. I work at the Bank of Korea, as a manager. I recently got promoted. I am the youngest as well. Of five. One girl and four boys. All live in Seoul, except my oldest brother who lives in Canada and my second-oldest brother who lives in North Korea. They both chose to live in the different countries after the war. *(beat)* Do you have a problem with my brother living in North Korea?

UMMA   It was his choice. Why would it bother me?

APBA   Do you see it as being shameful? Do you pity me?

UMMA   No. I am ashamed of what happened during and after the war. What was the point of the Korean War? Death? Further separation? Devastation everywhere?

Who won the war? Russia and the United States. Who lost the war? Koreans. Who do I pity? Anyone who believes one regime is better than the other. North Korea has Kim Il Song. South Korea has Park Chung Hee. We both have dictators as our government head. How can anyone say one is better?

APBA   Boy, you're really passionate about politics.

UMMA   People have to take responsibility for their government, for who they elect or who leads them. No one is powerless. *(checks her watch)* Sorry, I have to go.

        She gets up to leave.

APBA   We sat and talked. We know a little bit about each other. Now we can leave. It was nice meeting you. *(also gets up to leave, then stops)* Look, I find you attractive, interesting and you're obviously intelligent... so...?

UMMA   So...?

APBA   So why don't you give me a chance?

        Pause.

UMMA   What took you so long?

APBA   Why was I late today?

UMMA   The picture. My sister gave your sister-in-law the picture of me to give to you a month ago. It took you a month to decide if I was worth dating?

APBA   When I was first given your picture, I wanted to call you right away, but then I thought I should wait until I got my promotion. So I could impress you. I guess I don't impress you.

UMMA   It would have been good if you were on time. Today.

APBA   I was figuring out what to wear. Do I look good?

        Pause.

UMMA   Do you like movies?

APBA   Yes.

UMMA   Well?

APBA   Well what?

UMMA   Ask me to go to a movie.

APBA   Would you like to go to a movie?

UMMA   Next week? Saturday? Evening show? You'll pick me up at my place at six so we can walk to the theatre. And talk some more?

APBA   How would you like to go to a movie... next week, Saturday? And I could even pick you up at your place around... six... if that's all right with you.

UMMA   It was nice meeting you. I'm sorry but I do have to rush off. I made an appointment to tutor someone. I didn't think we would be long.

APBA   Your appointment—is it far from here?

UMMA   A few blocks.

APBA   Would you mind if I walked you?

UMMA   No, not at all.

> They start to walk off stage.

APBA   Just a question—how many children would you like to have… one day… with whomever you marry?

UMMA   Two. One boy and one girl. How many would you like?

APBA   Two is a nice number.

SCENE SIX

> Flashback to Korea: The home of HALMONEE and HARABOGEE, UMMA's parents.

HARABOGEE   I understand you want to ask me something.

APBA   Yes.

HARABOGEE   Go on then.

APBA   I would like—I would like—

HALMONEE   This is so wonderful.

APBA   I would like your daughter's hand in marriage… if you please.

HARABOGEE   My daughter is stubborn.

UMMA   (to her father) Apba.

HARABOGEE   And pigheaded.

UMMA   Apba.

HARABOGEE   She does what she wishes. She took after her mother.

HALMONEE   Yo bau! [Darling!]

HARABOGEE   Do you think you can handle a lifetime of this?

APBA   I would love to.

HARABOGEE   Well then… congratulations on your engagement. It would be best to wait before you have children.

SCENE SEVEN

In a schoolyard during lunch time. GYUNG-JUNE is sitting by herself, quietly singing "Ah Ree Rang." HALMONEE is standing above her, humming along, and GYUNG-JUNE's singing underscores HALMONEE's words. ["Ah-Ree-Rang" loosely translates as: "I'll always be with you no matter how far the walk, or even if my feet hurt."]

HALMONEE   When you sing these words, remember the times we've shared in Korea. Don't forget where you're from. Don't forget me, Gyung-June-na.

HALMONEE exits as GYUNG-JUNE finishes the song. EDWARD enters with his lunch.

EDWARD   Gi-ung… June? Am I saying it right?

GYUNG-JUNE   Edward, everyone calls me June. Okay!

EDWARD   Sorry. So, June, what do you have for lunch?

GYUNG-JUNE   What do you have for your lunch?

EDWARD   Tuna fish. Every day—tuna fish. My mom thinks I love tuna fish. I can't stand tuna fish.

GYUNG-JUNE   What do you do with it?

EDWARD   The tuna fish? Eat it. I get hungry. C'mon, tell me what you have for lunch.

GYUNG-JUNE   You really want to know?

EDWARD   I'm curious about you.

GYUNG-JUNE   My mom packs me bap *[rice]* and kimchi *[pickled cabbage]* with other pan-chan *[side dishes]*.

EDWARD   Huh?

GYUNG-JUNE   In English they call it rice. "Bap" is rice. "Kimchi" is—it's smelly food, so I don't like eating it around other people.

EDWARD   Is that why you sit alone at lunch?

GYUNG-JUNE   So?

EDWARD   It's just that I want to sit with you.

GYUNG-JUNE   Really?

EDWARD   Gi-ung-June—June—I like your real name.

GYUNG-JUNE   You do? How come?

EDWARD   It's beautiful. Like you.

GYUNG-JUNE   I'm beautiful?

EDWARD   Sure, why not?

GYUNG-JUNE   I like you, Edward.

EDWARD   Gi-ung-June, can I call you Gi-ung-June?

GYUNG-JUNE   Sure.

EDWARD   Gi-ung-June, I came to ask you a favour. I… um… well, my friend likes this person, but he doesn't know if she likes him. What do I do? I mean, how does my friend find out if she likes him?

GYUNG-JUNE   Well, first you must tell me who your friend likes.

EDWARD   Patty.

GYUNG-JUNE   Patty?

EDWARD   She's cute.

GYUNG-JUNE   Patty and I are friends.

EDWARD   She's really cute.

GYUNG-JUNE   Edward, did you really mean it when you said I'm beautiful?

EDWARD   Sure. Do you know if she likes me?

GYUNG-JUNE   Many people like you, Edward.

EDWARD   Thanks. You're great, Gi-ung-June.

> *MEE-GYUNG enters.*

MEE-GYUNG   Cah, can I eat lunch with you? I'm mad at Michelle.

GYUNG-JUNE   No!

MEE-GYUNG   She told me I can't be her friend.

GYUNG-JUNE   Leave me alone!

EDWARD   Is this your little sister?

GYUNG-JUNE   No. Yeah. My bratty sister.

> *EDWARD stands up to greet MEE-GYUNG.*

EDWARD   Nice to meet you, little sister of Gi-ung-June.

> *MEE-GYUNG starts laughing, pointing at EDWARD's crotch. His zipper is open.*

GYUNG-JUNE   Mee-Gyung!

EDWARD   Excuse me. *(He urns around and fixes his zipper.)* Your sister looks at interesting body parts.

GYUNG-JUNE   She can't help it. It's where her eye level is.

EDWARD   *(to MEE-GYUNG)* You think that's funny, huh? You think that's funny?

MEE-GYUNG   Yeah! Very funny!

EDWARD   Let's see if you think this is funny! *(He starts tickling MEE-GYUNG.)* Hey, want a piggyback ride?

MEE-GYUNG   Sure!

EDWARD   C'mon, hop on! It'll be my way to thank you for telling me I was flying low.

> *MEE-GYUNG hops on his back and they exit as if he is an airplane and she is his passenger.*

MEE-GYUNG   Vroom, vroom. Zoooommmmm!

GYUNG-JUNE   *(with adolescent sexual angst)* I noticed his fly was open too.

SCENE EIGHT

> *MEE-GYUNG is sitting in her room, playing with her truck, half-heartedly. APBA enters.*

APBA   There you are. Usually when I come home for dinner, you're running to my side, ready to lie down on my stomach. Aren't you going to ask if I have any cho-co-late?

MEE-GYUNG   Apba, I'm not going back to school. Ever.

APBA   You know education is very important. Now, guess what's in this bag.

MEE-GYUNG   Apba, I can't go to school anymore.

APBA   What is happening in Mee-Gyung's life?

MEE-GYUNG   I'm in trouble. You can't tell Umma, okay? I hit someone at school today. *(APBA laughs.)* Why are you laughing?

APBA   You are always hitting someone.

MEE-GYUNG   Stop laughing! Listen, okay. I'm telling you a secret.

> *APBA puts his finger to his mouth as a promise of silence.*

Michelle told me I had a rip in my pants, right where my gung-deong-ee is. *(gestures to her bum)* Not only that, but she told everyone in class. And they asked to see my hole. Then, when the teacher asked what was going on, I farted. Michelle said coloured gas came out of my bum. The teacher yelled at me to go to the office. Only me. So I hit Michelle.

MEE-GYUNG takes an envelope from her pocket.

Now I have to get this signed, and there's a meeting with the principal you have to go to.

APBA *(laughing)* You are the son I never had.

MEE-GYUNG You're weird.

SCENE NINE

UMMA is alone on stage, sleeping, and has a dream.

GYUNG-JUNE *(offstage)* Kyung-Ma, tell me a story.

GYUNG-JUNE enters.

UMMA Gyung-June-na, let me tell you a story.

GYUNG-JUNE About Halmonee?

UMMA No. Once upon a time, there was a younger brother—Kyung-Mei. *(MEE-GYUNG comes on stage as KYUNG-MEI.)* And an older sister by three years—Kyung-Ma.

KYUNG-MEI gives GYUNG-JUNE a shirt and GYUNG-JUNE becomes KYUNG-MA.

This was Kyung-Mei's favourite story.

KYUNG-MA Once upon a time, the family owned an enchanted farm. The farm was enchanted because it was built on land given to one of our ancestors by the king of Korea, back when Korea was governed by monarchy. This ancestor of ours built this farm so future generations of his family could grow and prosper. Do you know why the king gave land to our ancestors?

KYUNG-MEI Because this ancestor was the king's court jester, who in reality was the best-trained assassin in Korea. Kyung-Ma, tell me how the court jester killed the king's enemies. Tell me about the man who ate all the kimchi.

KYUNG-MA Kyung-Mei, are you sure you want to hear that story again?

KYUNG-MEI Yes. Massive quantities of kimchi…

KYUNG-MA Massive quantities of kimchi were disappearing from all round the country. Everyone became worried. With no kimchi, who could eat their rice? One month of investigations went by. And still no one found the kimchi. Two months of investigations went by and it still remained a mystery. All around the country people were fainting because there was no kimchi! Finally, the king asked his dear court jester—our ancestor—to please use his smarts to find the kimchi. During investigations, our ancestor found out who the abductor was. Normally a person of such menace would be hanged, but the court jester asked the king to invite this low-life for some entertainment. At first the king refused.

KYUNG-MEI   Such a man would taint the great tradition of torture.

KYUNG-MA   But the court jester ensured the king that this was the only way to get the kimchi back. So, as the low-life sat laughing at the entertainment provided by the court jester, he noticed his stomach growing—

KYUNG-MEI   Until it exploded, popping his belly and exposing all the kimchi he had eaten!

KYUNG-MA   And everybody lived happily ever after because they had kimchi to go with their rice.

KYUNG-MEI   And to reward the court jester, the king gave him land.

KYUNG-MA   With that land, the court jester built a farm and lived happily ever after.

KYUNG-MEI   What happened to the farm? You've never told me that part.

KYUNG-MA   What is there to tell? When you were inside Umma's belly, the family was forced to leave the farm.

KYUNG-MEI   Why?

KYUNG-MA   Some people don't believe in having homes, so they take them away from others out of jealousy. That's why soldiers wear green.

KYUNG-MEI   Huh?

KYUNG-MA   Our home was on a line. A stupid parallel where no man can live. The D.M.Z. It doesn't make sense to me either.

KYUNG-MEI   We have to get the farm back.

KYUNG-MA   It is the most beautiful farm. Ever. When we get to it, you have to close your eyes. I want it to be a surprise.

> They close their eyes. A SOUTH KOREAN SOLDIER enters.

SOLDIER   (grabbing KYUNG-MA's arm) Hey, what are you doing here? This is no place for children. Go home.

KYUNG-MA   We're going home.

SOLDIER   Here? What home?

> KYUNG-MA slowly becomes GYUNG-JUNE again.

KYUNG-MEI   Our home. The king gave the land to the court jester.

SOLDIER   This is the D.M.Z. The demilitarized zone. No man's land.

KYUNG-MEI   But the war is over.

SOLDIER   It will never be over. Go home, your parents will worry.

UMMA   And so, Gyung-June-na—Kyung-Ma and Kyung-Mei went home to their parents, but promised to return to their real home. One day.

GYUNG-JUNE   Umma, I don't want to hear your stories.

> *GYUNG-JUNE exits. KYUNG-MEI sees a stick, picks it up and pretends it is a gun. UMMA sees this and slowly walks away.*

SCENE TEN

> *Early morning in APBA and UMMA's bedroom. APBA is about to leave for work. He sits on the bed, stroking UMMA's hair as she sleeps.*

APBA   Sleep. What are you dreaming about? Dreaming of a time when everything went well? We have two beautiful children. We don't live in shambles. It's only been five years. Time is all we need. Remember when you passed your English course and you said to me, "I am a true Canadian. I can read and write the word 'maple leaf.'" I remember your smile, your laughter, your willingness to begin anew. Where did it go? Where is the lady who enchanted me by her determination? I miss her. She has become empty. You gave up. Left me to hold the family. I'm trying. But it's hard when you have no support. Bank manager turns waiter as he crosses the ocean into the new world. *(snaps his fingers, imitating a restaurant customer)* "Mr. Chinaman! Mr. Chinaman!" That is what they call me at work: "Mr. Chinaman." And I nod and smile, pretending I do not hear. It is better that way. Is that what you do when I talk to you? Because you never seem to listen.

SCENE ELEVEN

> *Flashback to Korea: APBA and UMMA's home. UMMA is alone as APBA enters.*

APBA   I am home!

UMMA   Shhhh. Mee-Gyung is finally asleep. She was crying a lot today. I think she's teething. How was your day?

APBA   Good. I stopped by somewhere on my way home. Would you like to know where I stopped by?

UMMA   You stopped by the grocery store and picked up what I asked you to pick up. For dinner?

APBA   I forgot.

UMMA	Hope you don't mind ramen then.
APBA	Stop. Relax. Close your eyes. Stick out your hand.

As UMMA does so, APBA takes a jewellery box from his pocket. As he opens the box, she opens her eyes and sees a pearl necklace.

UMMA	It's very beautiful.
APBA	Put it on.
UMMA	Why?
APBA	Because I bought it for you to put on!
UMMA	Why the gift?
APBA	Can't I give my wife presents? Here. Let me put it on for you.

He takes the necklace from the box and puts it on her.

Turn around. You are so beautiful. Look in the mirror. How was your day today?

UMMA	Busy.
APBA	How was your meeting?
UMMA	Like any other meeting.
APBA	What did you talk about at the meeting?
UMMA	The new budget—where we are going to allot the funds. Fairly boring discussion.
APBA	Tell me, why is it that every time you have "a meeting with the faculty," I hear from other people that you were at a protest. At all the protests against the government? How long has this been going on?
UMMA	Why don't you tell me?
APBA	Yo bau, I don't want to fight. Why don't you tell me these things?
UMMA	You know what the government is doing to the Korean people—all under the guise of democracy. And you don't care.
APBA	I care about my family. About my wife. I care about—Yo bau, I've been thinking. Korea isn't safe for us anymore. And demonstrating against the government doesn't help that much either, does it?
UMMA	It helps more than doing nothing.
APBA	Do you really believe that?
UMMA	Isn't it our duty as Koreans to fight for what we believe? Park Chung Hee is a totalitarian. How can we tolerate such a leader?

APBA   My duty is for the safety and prosperity of my family. I don't know if it's possible to grow here. There are too many political rules and regulations. And it won't change. Not for a long time. They want to promote me. The bank wants to promote me to vice president of international operations.

UMMA   That's wonderful.

APBA   There is a condition. Not a condition—a normal procedural practise. To go through my family lineage to make sure I am of good blood. They will find out about my brother. My brother in North Korea. When they find out, I will be fired.

UMMA   But it's not your fault…

   Pause.

What are you going to do?

APBA   I've been talking to my father, and he thinks the best thing for us to do is to move away, move away to another country. My eldest brother in Toronto is willing to sponsor us. We can start over. Canada is a country full of opportunities. What is going to happen when either Gyung-June or Mee-Gyung are up for promotion, and they will be fired because their uncle lives in North Korea? Can you live with the knowledge that we limited their lives? And what about your involvement with the student committee? Don't you realize you are only putting your family in jeopardy?

UMMA   Things are going to change.

APBA   They haven't changed for over twenty-five years.

UMMA   I don't want to leave here.

APBA   And once we're there, we can sponsor some of our relatives. They can start their lives over too. A whole new world of possibilities. Your mother and father can come live with us. In our new home. We can have our own Korea in Canada. It will be best for us. Always do what's best for you.

UMMA   Thank you for the necklace. I don't want to leave.

SCENE TWELVE

The family kitchen. MEE-GYUNG and GYUNG-JUNE are playing "Scissors-paper-stone." UMMA is cooking.

GIRLS   Ga-ooee ba-ooee bo! *[Scissors, paper, stone!]*

MEE-GYUNG   Paper covers stone. I win.

GYUNG-JUNE   No! No! It's best four out of five. You've only won three, you still have to win one more.

GIRLS   Ga-ooee ba-ooee bo!

MEE-GYUNG   Stone crushes scissor. My fourth win.

GYUNG-JUNE   That one doesn't count. I wasn't ready.

MEE-GYUNG   I won. You lost. I get to lie on Apba's stomach when he gets home.

GYUNG-JUNE   No. You cheated.

MEE-GYUNG   I did not.

GYUNG-JUNE   Chinks always cheat.

MEE-GYUNG   Umma, cah called me a Chink.

UMMA   (*not knowing what "Chink" means*) Don't call her a Chink, Gyung-June.

MEE-GYUNG   (*in a whisper*) What's a Chink?

GYUNG-JUNE   You are. We are. Funny-looking people are.

MEE-GYUNG   Why are we funny looking?

GYUNG-JUNE   We're ugly.

MEE-GYUNG   I'm not ugly. I'm going to be… I'm going to be pret-ty.

GYUNG-JUNE   No Chinks are pretty!

MEE-GYUNG   I'll be the first.

GYUNG-JUNE   Not only are you a Chink, but a Chink from a black witch's family. Umma and Apba saw you being thrown out of a gypsy's van, so they took you home because they felt sorry for you. You were so ugly, you were giving the gypsies warts!

MEE-GYUNG   That's not true. Then how come I don't give Mommy and Daddy warts?

GYUNG-JUNE   They took some of my beauty and gave it to you. That's why I'm a Chink too.

MEE-GYUNG   You must have been pret-ty.

GYUNG-JUNE   I was very pret-ty.

MEE-GYUNG   'Cause I'm more pret-tier than you. They gave me too much! Right, Umma?

UMMA   You both are my darlings. Now, no more fighting before dinner.

MEE-GYUNG   Mommy loves me more. 'Cause I'm pret-tier.

GYUNG-JUNE   'Cause you give her the most pain.

MEE-GYUNG   I don't get it.

GYUNG-JUNE   She pretends she loves you more so you'll stop bugging her. Bugger! *(She laughs at MEE-GYUNG and points at her eyes.)* You have bug eyes! With no eyelids. Bug eyes! Bug eyes!

MEE-GYUNG   So do you!

GYUNG-JUNE   And you have a flat nose. A flat nose like you bang yourself into walls as a daily sport. And you have thick, coarse, bone-straight hair. Black as the black witches you're from!

MEE-GYUNG   Umma, cah's scaring me!

GYUNG-JUNE   Stop calling me "cah"! That's not my name.

MEE-GYUNG   But I have to. It's respect.

GYUNG-JUNE   It's "Kun-uhn-nee"—"Big Sister," not "cah," like "caca."

MEE-GYUNG   But I always call you "cah."

GYUNG-JUNE   You're not a baby anymore. You can say "Kun-uhn-nee." Before it was fine, before you were cute, but now you're a Chink. A Chink from black witches!

MEE-GYUNG   I don't like how you talk. You're from black witches too. You! And your lies!

GYUNG-JUNE   Go back to where you belong!

> *Pause.*

MEE-GYUNG   Do you want to play another game?

GYUNG-JUNE   No. I have homework.

MEE-GYUNG   Cah, how come people are so mean? I was walking from the store today, not doing anything—I promise. But a man came up to me and—

> *Flashback: A MAN enters.*

MAN   Hey, do you live here?

MEE-GYUNG   Uhhh… *(shaking her head)* Uh uh.

MAN   What are you doing here?

MEE-GYUNG   Walking to the store.

MAN   How come your feet ain't bound?

MEE-GYUNG   Huh?

MAN   Don't all Chinese girls have their feet bound?

MEE-GYUNG   I'm not Chinese.

MAN   Then what are you?

MEE-GYUNG   None of your business!

MAN   Go back to where you came from!

>   *As the MAN starts to walk away, MEE-GYUNG punches him on the back.*

MEE-GYUNG   This is my home!

>   *The MAN grabs her, but MEE-GYUNG kicks him and runs back to GYUNG-JUNE.*

GYUNG-JUNE   Were you with anyone?

MEE-GYUNG   My friend Michelle. No, I was by myself.

GYUNG-JUNE   What were you doing by yourself?

MEE-GYUNG   I found a quarter and wanted candy.

GYUNG-JUNE   You don't talk to strangers. Okay!

MEE-GYUNG   Yes.

GYUNG-JUNE   And you don't hit strangers. Okay!

MEE-GYUNG   I got angry. How come I hit him? I didn't mean to. It was just… what do you call it?

GYUNG-JUNE   Reflexes?

MEE-GYUNG   Yes. Re-flec-sives-sives. My arm. It has re-flec-sives-sives.

GYUNG-JUNE   The man was stupid. Next time, ask me to go to the store. Okay? *(MEE-GYUNG nods her head.)* Little sister, let's play "Thumb War."

MEE-GYUNG   I hit him hard.

GYUNG-JUNE   Good.

>   *APBA enters as MEE-GYUNG and GYUNG-JUNE start to play.*

MEE-GYUNG   One, two, three, four, I declare a thumb war. Bow and kiss. You have to bow and kiss! Bow and kiss.

UMMA   *(to APBA)* Park Chung Hee was on the Korean radio again. Spewing about the good he has done for "Democratic Korea," the good he has done for the people of his nation. When is that man ever going to shut up and die? *(APBA laughs.)* Why are you laughing?

APBA   It's good to see that passion. Hello.

UMMA   Hello to you too.

>   *They sit together.*

APBA   I made some very good tips today. To put into our savings. One day we will have everything we've ever dreamt about.

UMMA   One day. In this country.

APBA   In our country. One day, when we are rich. *(pause)* How was your day?

UMMA   Good.

APBA   How are you feeling?

UMMA   Better.

APBA   What did you do today to make yourself feel better?

UMMA   I had a nice talk with my sister.

APBA   Your sister?

UMMA   Yes, I called her.

APBA   You called her? You called her long distance?

UMMA   It was short.

APBA   When?

UMMA   What?

APBA   When did you call her?

UMMA   Today. Sometime during the day.

APBA   What time?

UMMA   I don't know. Around three. Maybe three—three o'clock.

APBA   No discount! No discount!

UMMA   She said the family will pay half if I want to visit my mother's grave.

APBA   With what money? They paid for the funeral and the burial costs. Now you want to take money from them so you can visit a block of cement? No more long distance.

UMMA   The kids are waiting for you.

APBA   No more long distance.

UMMA   I heard!

    APBA enters the living-room area.

APBA   Mee-Gyung-a, Gyung-June-na?

MEE-GYUNG   Apba, I found a quarter today.

GYUNG-JUNE   And she hit a man on her way to the store.

MEE-GYUNG   Cah.

GYUNG-JUNE   He was calling her names and told her she didn't belong here—so she hit him.

APBA   Is that true?

MEE-GYUNG   Is that good or bad, Apba?

APBA   You don't hit people. It is not good to hit.

MEE-GYUNG   But Umma hit cah.

GYUNG-JUNE   Don't tell him that. I deserved it.

APBA   *(to UMMA)* Is this true, yo bau? True that you hit our eldest?

UMMA   It was after our fight. I was upset, Gyung-June was being disrespectful.

APBA   *(to GYUNG-JUNE)* Don't give your mother trouble. *(pause)* I learned a Canadian song. Want to hear it?

MEE-GYUNG   Yes. Please. But Apba, do you have anything for us? Cho-co-late? Cho-co-lates?

APBA   Let me look at your teeth. *(with a look of displeasure)* Eshh! Smelly! Have you been brushing them after treats?

MEE-GYUNG   Sometimes. No.

APBA   Why not?

MEE-GYUNG   Cahhh.

GYUNG-JUNE   Because she's too busy playing with her truck… or doing homework.

APBA   Playing with your truck. Hmmm. Wouldn't you rather play with a doll?

MEE-GYUNG   Why? They're ugly. I like trucks.

APBA   Close your eyes. *(He takes out a doll.)* Open them.

MEE-GYUNG   It's a doll.

APBA   Do you like it?

MEE-GYUNG   A doll with blond hair and blue eyes. Apba, I can't have it. It can't be part of our family.

APBA   What do you mean?

MEE-GYUNG   It doesn't look like us.

APBA   Who said that?

MEE-GYUNG   Michelle.

APBA   Don't tell her. Leave it at home. Your own secret toy.

MEE-GYUNG   Thank you. Go-mahb-seun-nee-da. *[Thank you very much.]*

>   *MEE-GYUNG bows and holds the doll limply.*

GYUNG-JUNE   Do you have something for me?

APBA   For you, a book. A book about Canada: *Anne of Green Gables.*

GYUNG-JUNE   Go-mahb-seun-nee-da, abogee. *[Thank you very much, Father.]*

>   *GYUNG-JUNE flips through the book.*

APBA   What? You don't like it?

GYUNG-JUNE   Abpa, it's just—next time, can I get a book about Korea?

APBA   I thought you would like *Anne of Green Gables.* The saleslady said all the Canadian school kids read that book.

GYUNG-JUNE   But I'm not Canadian.

APBA   You are now. You will enjoy being Canadian. Now the song. A man I work with sang it today. I said to him, "What a nice song." So he taught me. It has a catchy tune. The man said him and his family sing this song all the time. Okay, listen carefully. *(begins to sing slowly)* "Row, row, row your boat—"

MEE-GYUNG   "—gently down the stream. Merrily, merrily, merrily—"

APBA   Oh, you know it.

MEE-GYUNG   My teacher taught us that one a long time ago.

GYUNG-JUNE   Sing it for us. Please, Apba.

MEE-GYUNG   But you have to lie down on your back first. I won. I get to lie on your stomach.

GYUNG-JUNE   She cheated.

APBA   Cheated—is that true?

GYUNG-JUNE   No. I lost, so I lie on your leg.

>   *APBA lies down on his back. MEE-GYUNG lies down and puts her head on his stomach. GYUNG-JUNE lies down and puts her head on his right leg. They all sing "Row, Row, Row Your Boat."*

That's my favourite song.

MEE-GYUNG   Me too.

>   *Lights go down, except on UMMA, who stands alone, looking pensive. "Ah-Ree-Rang" is drummed lightly offstage, as lights fade to black.*
>
>   *End of Act One.*

ACT TWO

SCENE ONE

Early in the morning in UMMA and APBA's bedroom. APBA is getting ready to go to work. UMMA comes into the bedroom with breakfast.

UMMA   Man-nee jab-soo-sae-yo. *[Please eat a lot.]*

APBA   They feed me at work.

UMMA   Junk food.

APBA   Good food. People pay good money for—

UMMA   Junk. They feed you junk. You work so hard, you should eat a proper meal before you go.

APBA   You want something from me.

UMMA pauses as she lays out food.

UMMA   I've been thinking…. Why are you never home?

APBA   I work. You know how hard I work. I have to pay the bills.

UMMA   We never spend time together. You spend one hour with the children. And children grow up so fast. They miss you.

APBA   We need the money.

UMMA   What if I start to work?

APBA   Who is going to hire you? What kind of job will you get? Your diploma is useless. You can hardly speak the language.

UMMA   I saw a job posting. It's a job at a school—janitorial engineer. Speaking English is not necessary and they don't care about your education.

APBA   You think you can just apply and they'll hire you? It's not so easy.

UMMA   I want to help. I don't want to stay home all the time. The kids have school during the day. Yo bau, I am so lonely. Please.

APBA   Do what you want to do. Do what's best for yourself.

UMMA   Com-oh-way-oh. *[Thanks.]*

She bows and exits.

APBA   But know that children need a mother more than they need a father. Especially two girls.

SCENE TWO

MEE-GYUNG and GYUNG-JUNE in their bedroom.

MEE-GYUNG Cah? Cah, can I talk with you?

GYUNG-JUNE I'm busy. I'm reading *Anne of Green Gables*. What do you want?

MEE-GYUNG I don't know. Just to talk.

GYUNG-JUNE What do you want to talk about?

MEE-GYUNG I don't know. What do you want to talk about?

GYUNG-JUNE Do you miss anything about Korea?

MEE-GYUNG Should I?

GYUNG-JUNE You don't care about anyone but yourself. You don't realize how I had to give up everything because of you. If it weren't for you, I would have been able to stay in Korea with Halmonee. You're a brat, and I have to take care of you. Because of you, Halmonee died.

GYUNG-JUNE exits.

SCENE THREE

WHITE DOG enters the children's bedroom.

WHITE DOG Meeeeeee-Gyung.

MEE-GYUNG White Dog? What are you doing in Canada?

WHITE DOG It got lonely in Korea. It got boring biting Hyuck-Dong, day in and day out.

MEE-GYUNG Everyone is acting strange. Halmonee died and everyone is sad about it. But I'm not. Should I be?

WHITE DOG Death is a funny thing. Do you want to be sad?

MEE-GYUNG Nope.

WHITE DOG Then don't be.

MEE-GYUNG I got a new truck. I took it from school. And Apba gave me an ugly doll. Want to see them?

WHITE DOG Yeah!

MEE-GYUNG rushes off stage, then rushes back on with the doll and a big red truck.

MEE-GYUNG   Vroom, vroom, vroom.

MEE-GYUNG moves the truck forward, throws the doll in front of the truck, then runs it over. MEE-GYUNG looks to WHITE DOG to see if what she did was okay.

WHITE DOG   Do it again!

She backs the truck up and runs the doll over again and again. Then she picks the doll up again.

MEE-GYUNG   *(as the doll)* Help me! Help me! *(backs the truck up and runs the doll over several more times)* Help me! Help me!

MEE-GYUNG finally kicks the doll offstage.

WHITE DOG   Good work!

MEE-GYUNG pushes the truck and follows it off stage with the doll.

SCENE FOUR

GYUNG-JUNE has a nightmare/fantasy.

HALMONEE   See the colour. What is it? The colour of your face.

EDWARD   Is it light or dark?

GYUNG-JUNE   Light.

HALMONEE   And your eyes.

GYUNG-JUNE   Dark.

HALMONEE   Black. Black almond eyes.

EDWARD   No eyelids. Like a slimy snake's.

HALMONEE   Smooth eyelids to blink back wetness. Salty wetness. I miss you too.

EDWARD   Your eyebrows are in the middle of your forehead.

HALMONEE   They hover over your lashes.

EDWARD   Almost to your hairline.

HALMONEE   Your hair. Black. Straight. Thick.

EDWARD   Coarse.

GYUNG-JUNE   I can't help how I look!

EDWARD   Change your looks to what you want to be.

HALMONEE   Darling child, you can be anything you want to be.

GYUNG-JUNE   Change so Edward will like me?

HALMONEE   If that is so important.

GYUNG-JUNE   Make me look like Patty.

HALMONEE   What does Patty look like?

GYUNG-JUNE   My hair—

EDWARD   Yeah.

GYUNG-JUNE   Take the colour out. Make it pale.

EDWARD   Cool.

GYUNG-JUNE   Push my face out. It's so flat. My nose.

EDWARD   It's puffy and flat.

GYUNG-JUNE   Make it look like a button. A button to kiss every night before bed. This wide face.

HALMONEE   As round as the moon.

EDWARD   Big with everything spaced out.

GYUNG-JUNE   Condense it. Bleach it. Lighten it so my hair will match my face. I want bigger eyes. Wide, beautiful blue eyes like the lapis.

HALMONEE   You are colder. Your hair is ice, your eyes stone. Your face a block of marble.

EDWARD   Tough.

HALMONEE   Less penetrable.

GYUNG-JUNE   Beautiful.

HALMONEE   A matter of perspective.

SCENE FIVE

The phone rings. MEE-GYUNG answers it and mocks the person on the other end with nonsense words.

MEE-GYUNG   Chi-chi-nee-whoa-fong-nee-too. Me no speakie no dirty Chinese. You have the wrong number.

MEE-GYUNG hangs up. The phone rings again and she answers it in the same way.

You Chinese people are smelly. Tee-tee-now-sing-fong-fong-tee-too. You Chinese people leave me alone!

> *She hangs up, and when the phone rings again she just looks at it.*
> *UMMA rushes into the room to answer it.*

UMMA   Yuh-bo-sae-yo? *[Hello?]* Uhn-nee! *[Sister!]* Ahn-yung-ha-sae-yo. *[Hello.]*

> *Pause.*

Woos-gee-ji-ma-sae-yo? *[Are you kidding me?]*

> *She looks at MEE-GYUNG.*

Muh-yo? *[Pardon?]*

> *Pause.*

Ah-nee. *[No.]*

> *She gives MEE-GYUNG a look of displeasure, then scares her away.*

Ah-yoo! Na-bbeun-sae-gi! *[Bad child!]*

> *She then speaks into the phone:*

Dear sister… I've been thinking… what if—

> *APBA enters and UMMA stops what she was saying.*

—yes, yes, everything is fine. I should go. I have to go and make dinner. Maybe you can call me tomorrow? Goodbye, Uhn-nee. I miss you.

APBA   Your sister?

UMMA   She called me.

APBA   Did you have a good talk with her?

UMMA   She cares about me. Dinner will be ready soon.

APBA   How was your day?

UMMA   Fine. Someone at work left her husband. He came looking for her. But she wasn't there. The rest of the cleaning ladies and I think she went back to her country. She was never happy in Canada.

APBA   Sounds like a coward to me.

UMMA   I think she's pretty courageous.

APBA   Courageous? No, a selfish coward—otherwise, why would she abandon her husband and cause him such disgrace?

UMMA   She did what's best for herself. Always do what's best for you.

> *UMMA exits.*

SCENE SIX

Flashback to Korea: HALMONEE is waiting. UMMA enters, harried. Slides of protest scenes are projected onto the stage.

HALMONEE   Kyung-Ma, I'm glad you didn't forget about your children.

UMMA   I'm sorry I'm late. Are the kids okay?

HALMONEE   Everyone will be fine once you stop your involvement with the student committee. How dare you put your whole family in danger!

UMMA   What are you talking about?

HALMONEE   Where were you tonight?

UMMA   I told you, I had a meeting at the university.

HALMONEE   You were at the demonstration.

UMMA   There were only speeches.

HALMONEE   How long have you been a member of the student committee?

UMMA   I'm not a member. I support what they're doing.

HALMONEE   Do you know what happens if the government sees you at these demonstrations? They arrest you and put you in jail, where you will be tortured—

UMMA   I was only listening.

HALMONEE   Think of your family.

UMMA   I am.

HALMONEE   You don't understand, do you?

UMMA   Umma, you know what the military did to our family. It's going to happen all over again. Can't you see Park Chung Hee is running a dictatorship? And he's using the threat of communism to instill fear so Koreans will do nothing.

HALMONEE   Kyung-Ma, as long as you continue your involvement with the student committee, I can't call you my daughter.

UMMA   Where are the children?

HALMONEE   Sleeping in your old room.

UMMA   Fine!

SCENE SEVEN

UMMA is cleaning up the house. GYUNG-JUNE is sitting, reading Anne of Green Gables.

UMMA Messmessmessmessmess! Yes, I went through years and years of education. I aspired to do something with my life, to gain respect from my family, from my co-workers, from the Canadian people, so I can be nothing but a maidmaidmaidmaidmaid!

She finds a lunch bag hidden behind a cabinet.

What…? *(finds several more)* Gyung-June, what is this?

She walks up to GYUNG-JUNE and shoves the bag in her face.

What are these? Is this what you do to your lunches?

GYUNG-JUNE just stares at UMMA.

Kee-gee-bae! *[Tramp!]* Do I have to watch you eat your lunches? What is wrong with you? Why are you always hurting me?

GYUNG-JUNE The food embarrasses me.

UMMA Embarrasses you?

GYUNG-JUNE It smells. It isn't normal.

UMMA Normal? What is normal?

GYUNG-JUNE Tuna fish.

UMMA Tuna fish?

GYUNG-JUNE It's what the Canadian kids eat.

UMMA Tuna fish.

GYUNG-JUNE Whenever I bring my lunch to school, I have to eat alone. I don't like being different. I don't like always having to tell people where I'm from. Correcting the pronunciation of my name. Getting confused with English and Korean. Being made fun of all the time. Why are we here? Do you hate me so much to take me away from the only place I know as home? Away from Halmonee?

UMMA Gyung-June-na, let me tell you a story.

GYUNG-JUNE About Halmonee?

UMMA No.

GYUNG-JUNE Umma, I don't want to hear any of your stories.

GYUNG-JUNE walks away. UMMA continues to clean.

SCENE EIGHT

Flashback to Korea: HALMONEE is outside her home. GYUNG-JUNE is nine years old and runs toward her.

GYUNG-JUNE   Halmonee! Halmonee!

HALMONEE   Ah-suh-oh-no-rah *[Come here]*, Gyung-June-na.

GYUNG-JUNE bows.

GYUNG-JUNE   Ahn-yung-ha-sae-yo *[Hello]*, Halmonee.

HALMONEE   What is wrong with my Gyung-June?

GYUNG-JUNE   Your only Gyung-June!

HALMONEE   And still my favourite.

GYUNG-JUNE   Halmonee, how come you haven't visited?

HALMONEE   It is a long story. I'm glad you've come. I've missed you.

GYUNG-JUNE   I've missed you too.

HALMONEE   How is your Umma?

GYUNG-JUNE   Okay. Halmonee, what's Canada?

HALMONEE   It is a country far from here.

GYUNG-JUNE   It really is a place. What's in Canada?

HALMONEE   People. Trees. Cars. Your father's brother lives in Toronto. It is a city in Canada.

GYUNG-JUNE   Is that why we're going there?

HALMONEE   Who is going to Canada?

GYUNG-JUNE   Umma, Apba, Mee-Gyung and… you?

HALMONEE   No.

GYUNG-JUNE   How come you're not coming with us?

HALMONEE   I don't know.

GYUNG-JUNE   Is it really far from here?

HALMONEE   Too far to walk to.

GYUNG-JUNE   They whispered something about an airplane.

HALMONEE   Yes, the best way to travel to Canada is by plane.

GYUNG-JUNE   We're not going for long, are we?

HALMONEE   I don't know, Gyung-June-na.

GYUNG-JUNE   I don't want to go!

HALMONEE   Canada is a beautiful place.

GYUNG-JUNE   Halmonee, let me stay with you. They have Mee-Gyung.

HALMONEE   They need you for Mee-Gyung. To look out for her, as the oldest should. When are you leaving?

GYUNG-JUNE   Soon, I think. It's supposed to be a secret. You won't tell anyone, will you?

HALMONEE   Who would I tell? All of you are so important to me. That will never change. Remember, Gyung-June-na, I will always be with you. Distance means nothing to the heart. You are my only Gyung-June.

GYUNG-JUNE   You are my only Halmonee.

HALMONEE   Umma and Apba love you. Try not to blame them for too much.

GYUNG-JUNE   Halmonee, tell me stories. About your life. So you will never leave me and you'll continue to breathe in front of me as you are now.

HALMONEE   Gyung-June-na, you are such an interesting child. There is no time. I can teach you a song in the meantime, so you will always remember me. When you sing these words, remember the times we've shared in Korea. Don't forget where you're from. Don't forget me, Gyung-June-na.

> *HALMONEE sings "Ah-Ree-Rang."*

SCENE NINE

> *UMMA has a dream.*

UMMA   Kyung-Mei!

HALMONEE   This is where it happened.

UMMA   You never let me go to his funeral.

HALMONEE   There was nothing to see. He was blown away.

> *HALMONEE starts to exit. GYUNG-JUNE runs up to her.*

GYUNG-JUNE   Halmonee, please tell me stories. So I can understand what it's like to be Korean.

> *HALMONEE drops a white rose and exits. "Ah-Ree-Rang" is heard in the background.*

UMMA   There were six children in my family. All but two are in Korea—the two youngest. Me and a brother. *(points to MEE-GYUNG, who is playing*

KYUNG-MEI) His name is Kyung-Mei. *(points to GYUNG-JUNE, who is playing KYUNG-MA, reading a book)* My name is Kyung-Ma. Every summer, the family would have vacations on a beautiful island.

KYUNG-MEI   Kyung-Ma, look at what I found. Are they not beau-ti-ful? Look how they catch the light. Spark! Now it's gone.

KYUNG-MA   Those are bullet shells. Don't touch them, Kyung-Mei.

KYUNG-MA goes back to reading her book.

KYUNG-MEI   There are so many different kinds. From different countries. Here's one from—please read it to me.

KYUNG-MA   They all say the same thing, only in different languages. They don't say, "Made in blank blank country."

KYUNG-MEI   How do you know?

KYUNG-MA   Okay. Fine. Have it your way. *(pretends to read the bullet shells)* Let's see… this one is from France.

KYUNG-MEI   And this one's from Ca-na-da and here's one from U.S.S.R. Kyung-Ma, what's it like to be a soldier?

KYUNG-MA   I don't know.

KYUNG-MEI   I'm going to find one.

KYUNG-MEI runs offstage. UMMA walks across the stage, picks up the bullet shells, kisses them, then puts them in her pocket. KYUNG-MEI returns with a stick, pretending it is a gun. He practises holding the stick in a gun position. A young WHITE DOG looks on, then runs across the stage.

WHITE DOG   *(pretending)* Oww! You shot me! Pain. Pain. *(KYUNG-MEI starts laughing.)* Everywhere. Terrible pain—hey, why are you laughing?

KYUNG-MEI   You're pretending.

WHITE DOG   Play with me, kid. *(pretending)* Ohhh! Owww! My heart! My heart!

KYUNG-MEI   Fine, I'll take you to the butcher.

WHITE DOG jumps up.

WHITE DOG   What!

KYUNG-MEI   Faker.

WHITE DOG   *(offers his paw)* White Dog. Pleased to meet you.

KYUNG-MEI   Kyung-Mei. White Dog, do you know any soldiers?

WHITE DOG   I'm a soldier. I'm anything you want to be, so long as you take me home.

KYUNG-MEI   First, show me a real soldier.

> *KYUNG-MEI and WHITE DOG search all over for a soldier.*
>
> *A NORTH KOREAN SOLDIER enters, tattered and dirty. He dances a short, rural-peasant dance to show poverty and despair. By the time KYUNG-MEI and WHITE DOG approach the SOLDIER, the dance should be more like stylistic, ritual exercises.*

Are you a soldier?

SOLDIER   *(to KYUNG-MEI)* The best.

KYUNG-MEI   How do I know you're a real soldier?

SOLDIER   I can teach you to be a soldier. In my secret place. Only for today.

KYUNG-MEI   *(running to KYUNG-MA)* Kyung-Ma, I found a real soldier! And he said he'll show me his secret place. Can I go? Please?

> *KYUNG-MA is preoccupied with her book and doesn't even look up.*

KYUNG-MA   Just don't go too far.

WHITE DOG   Hey, tell her about me!

KYUNG-MEI   And I got a pet. For all of us. Isn't he cute?

KYUNG-MA   *(head down)* Have fun.

KYUNG-MEI   *(throwing down his stick)* Hold my stick. I'm going to be using a real gun!

> *KYUNG-MEI and WHITE DOG run to the SOLDIER. UMMA walks across the stage and picks up the stick.*

SOLDIER   Some people live in ignorance. They choose to maintain systems and values of dated tradition and fight against natural progression. That's why we have bullet shells littering our beaches.

WHITE DOG   *(to KYUNG-MEI)* Do you understand him?

KYUNG-MEI   No, but he let me touch his gun.

SOLDIER   War is good. It reminds us humans what our natural instincts are. Simply drawing a line to separate north *(indicates himself)* from south *(indicates KYUNG-MEI)* won't separate us emotionally. *(points to KYUNG-MEI)* You. Draw a line down your centre. Right down. Now!

> *The SOLDIER caresses KYUNG-MEI with his gun. WHITE DOG starts to bark and the SOLDIER hits him. WHITE DOG becomes silent.*

What happens if half the body is gone? You die. What sort of reality is half a body? Half a country? *(pause)* You draw a pretty good line.

No line has been drawn. WHITE DOG tries to bite the SOLDIER, who fights back and almost shoots WHITE DOG before WHITE DOG escapes. KYUNG-MEI is frozen.

You stay here. I have a surprise for you.

The SOLDIER exits. An explosion is heard and the lighting imitates a bomb exploding. KYUNG-MEI is blown-up stylistically while UMMA and KYUNG-MA watch. The lighting effect continues until the end of the scene.

UMMA   Firecrackers.

KYUNG-MA   Firecrackers.

UMMA & KYUNG-MA   *(together)* What beautiful firecrackers.

KYUNG-MA   Kyung-Mei, come and look at the sky.

UMMA   Kyung-Mei.

KYUNG-MA   Stop hiding.

UMMA   Kyung-Mei.

KYUNG-MA   Kyung-Mei!

UMMA & KYUNG-MA   *(together)* Kyung-Mei!

The dream moves forward in time. HALMONEE enters.

HALMONEE   It's time to leave, everyone.

UMMA   I'm ready.

HALMONEE   Kyung-Ma, you can't come to the funeral. You're too young.

UMMA   Umma, he's still inside the cave.

HALMONEE   Don't upset me. Stay here with your mother. Now we must go.

UMMA   Umma. Umma! Nah-do chuck-ko-ship-uh-yo. Nah-do chuck-ko-ship-uh-yo. *[I want to die. I want to die.]*

HALMONEE   I want to die too.

HALMONEE exits, then KYUNG-MA. UMMA takes the bullet shells from her pocket.

UMMA   Let's see. This one's from France. Are they not beau-ti-ful? Spark. Look how they catch the light.

Crying, UMMA slowly begins to pack her suitcase. The lighting effect is transformed into a sunrise.

SCENE TEN

Sunrise. APBA is just about to leave for work. UMMA is sitting in the kitchen, waiting for him. She has one suitcase with her.

APBA   Why are you up? *(UMMA doesn't respond.)* Yo bau? Anything wrong? You have to get over this sadness.

UMMA   I'm going on a trip.

APBA   Tell me this tomorrow. I've got to go to work.

UMMA   I'm leaving. I'm going back to Korea. Do you care?

APBA   I'll start caring when you stop acting crazy.

UMMA   There are frozen dinners in the freezer for the children and you. The fridge is stocked with all the Canadian food everyone loves. No more Korean crap for the family.

APBA   What is happening?

UMMA   I'm doing what I have to do.

APBA   Yo bau.

UMMA   I have died, too.

        Pause.

APBA   When are you coming back?

UMMA   I don't know.

SCENE ELEVEN

UMMA is in the children's bedroom to say goodbye. GYUNG-JUNE wakes up.

GYUNG-JUNE   Umma, I had a dream that we were back in Korea. And everyone was waiting for us at the airport—Hyuck-Dong, White Dog and even Halmonee. They were so happy to see us again.

UMMA   Shhh. Gyung-June, go back to sleep. It was just a dream.

GYUNG-JUNE   Umma, how come you're crying?

UMMA   I love you. That's why. Go to sleep, Gyung-June-na. I'm sorry I woke you up. Be a good girl and take care of Apba and Mee-Gyung. Go to sleep, Gyung-June-na. Go to sleep.

GYUNG-JUNE   Umma, where are you going?

UMMA To Korea.

GYUNG-JUNE Umma?

UMMA I'm sorry.

GYUNG-JUNE Can I go with you?

UMMA You want to come with me? Gyung-June... I can't. I can't take you with me. I don't have enough money. I don't. I'm sorry. I'm sorry. Gyung-June-na, you belong here.

GYUNG-JUNE I don't belong anywhere.

SCENE TWELVE

APBA enters the children's bedroom.

APBA Gyung-June-na, you're up. Wake Mee-Gyung up, wake her up and we'll all go to McDonald's.

GYUNG-JUNE I'm not going to McDonald's. I'm not going to Korea. All I'm going to do is stay here. I hate you!

GYUNG-JUNE starts to exit, but APBA stops her.

APBA No! I'm not going to lose you, too.

Pause.

GYUNG-JUNE Wake up, Mee-Gyung.

APBA Mee-Gyung-a, I want to take you somewhere.

MEE-GYUNG wakes up.

MEE-GYUNG Apba?

APBA Do you like McDonald's? Let's go to McDonald's. We can go to all the McDonald's in the city.

MEE-GYUNG What's the catch?

APBA Come on, hurry up. Get dressed.

MEE-GYUNG Apba, how come you're crying?

APBA Because I have two beautiful daughters. I am so lucky.

MEE-GYUNG Apba, where's Umma?

She looks at GYUNG-JUNE. APBA and GYUNG-JUNE do not respond.

SCENE THIRTEEN

APBA, MEE-GYUNG and GYUNG-JUNE at McDonald's.

MEE-GYUNG   Apba, I can't eat anymore. I should be at school.

APBA   Just finish your hamburger, Mee-Gyung-a. Please.

WHITE DOG enters carrying a gun. Only MEE-GYUNG can see him.

WHITE DOG   *(to MEE-GYUNG)* Hey! I want to greet your father.

MEE-GYUNG   I'm warning you—my father's weird. He's weirder today than he normally is.

WHITE DOG   I get along with all sorts.

MEE-GYUNG   We'll see. Apba, White Dog wants to say hi.

WHITE DOG bows to APBA.

WHITE DOG   Ahn-yung-ha-sae-yo. *[Hello.]*

APBA   Mee-Gyung, stop playing games. Eat your hamburger.

WHITE DOG   What's his problem?

MEE-GYUNG   Umma left today.

WHITE DOG   That's too bad.

MEE-GYUNG   I don't care. *(takes the gun from WHITE DOG)* He doesn't need her with me around.

WHITE DOG   Walk low so they can't see you. Hold your gun hard.

MEE-GYUNG   I'll kill anyone who hurts my father. Pow!

WHITE DOG   Why did she leave?

MEE-GYUNG   She's a weakling!

WHITE DOG   How come she didn't take you?

MEE-GYUNG   Stop asking stupid questions!

WHITE DOG   You're angry because she didn't take you with her.

MEE-GYUNG   I'm not angry! I hate her.

WHITE DOG   Don't say that.

MEE-GYUNG   It's true.

WHITE DOG   Hate makes people crazy.

MEE-GYUNG   Apba, you won't leave me, will you?

APBA   No, Mee-Gyung-a. You are my youngest daughter.

MEE-GYUNG   Good. We'll do fine then.

> *MEE-GYUNG salutes WHITE DOG. WHITE DOG salutes MEE-GYUNG.*

SCENE FOURTEEN

> *GYUNG-JUNE's dream. She runs toward HALMONEE's house.*

GYUNG-JUNE   Halmonee! Halmonee!

HALMONEE   Gyung-June-na, come inside and stop yelling.

GYUNG-JUNE   Halmonee, I've missed you.

HALMONEE   Ah, my Gyung-June.

GYUNG-JUNE   Your only Gyung-June.

HALMONEE   Yes, yes, yes. My only Gyung-June. *(She gives her a red rose.)* Here is a flower for my only Gyung-June. Now tell me—how are Umma, Apba and Mee-Gyung?

GYUNG-JUNE   Halmonee, Umma left us.

HALMONEE   Your mother always does what she wants to do.

GYUNG-JUNE   Why didn't she take me? I belong in Korea with you.

HALMONEE   But I do not belong to your world. *(She gives her a white rose.)* Love the country you are destined to live in.

GYUNG-JUNE   My destiny is in Korea. Isn't it?

HALMONEE   I have to go back to my home.

> *HALMONEE walks along a line, then is sprayed with bullets and falls.*

GYUNG-JUNE   Halmonee!

HALMONEE   Go be with Apba and Mee-Gyung.

GYUNG-JUNE   I belong with you.

HALMONEE   You know in your heart where you belong.

> *Pause.*

GYUNG-JUNE   Halmonee, jung-mal-sah-rang-hae-yo. *[I really love you.]*

HALMONEE   Gyung-June-na, I love you too.

SCENE FIFTEEN

MEE-GYUNG and GYUNG-JUNE in their bedroom.

MEE-GYUNG   Cah, can I talk with you?

GYUNG-JUNE   Sure.

MEE-GYUNG   Do you think Umma is coming back?

GYUNG-JUNE   I don't know.

MEE-GYUNG   I don't want her to come back.

GYUNG-JUNE   If she does, she's still our mother.

  Pause.

MEE-GYUNG   Cah, I'm scared.

GYUNG-JUNE   Me too. *(pause)* Mee-Gyung, can I tell you a story?

MEE-GYUNG   About White Dog?

GYUNG-JUNE   No.

MEE-GYUNG   About Umma?

GYUNG-JUNE   Yes. About Umma.

  The lights begin to fade.

Once upon a time, there was an older sister, Kyung-Ma. And she had a younger brother, Kyung-Mei. This was Kyung-Ma's favourite story…

  Lights down.

  The end.

THE PLUM TREE

BY MITCH MIYAGAWA

ABOUT

MITCH MIYAGAWA

Mitch Miyagawa is a writer and filmmaker in Whitehorse, Yukon. His most recent play was *Carnaval*, produced by Nakai Theatre and Gwaandak Theatre Adventures in 2007. He co-owns Up and Away Productions, an independent film company.

ACKNOWLEDGEMENTS

Michael Clark and Nakai Theatre, Patti Fraser, Stephen Hill, Marcus Youssef, Ben Henderson, Patti Flather, Jared Matsunaga-Turnbull, Jovanni Sy, Mary Sloan, John Murrell, Rachel Henessey, Canada Council Quest Program, Yukon Advanced Artist Award, Lise-Ann Johnson, Brian Parkinson, Vanessa Porteous, Vicki Stroich, Bob White, Alberta Theatre Projects, Hiro Kanagawa, Darcy Dunlop, Sarah Stanley, Angela Walkley, Mom, Dad and my aunts and uncles.

The playwright acknowledges the assistance of the 2001 and 2002 Banff playRites Colony—a partnership between the Canada Council for the Arts, the Banff Centre for the Arts and Alberta Theatre Projects.

The Plum Tree was workshopped and received a public reading as part of the National Arts Centre (Ottawa) English Theatre On the Verge Theatre New Works Festival 2002.

The Plum Tree was originally produced in Whitehorse, Yukon, at Nakai Theatre, from March 22–30, 2002, with the following company:

GEORGE   Jared Matsunaga-Turnbull
FRIEDA   Mary Sloan
MAS   Jovanni Sy

Directed by Michael Clark
Set and Costume Design by David Skelton
Sound Design by Daniel Janke
Light Design by Craig Moddle
Stage Management by Dean Eyre

A subsequent revised version of *The Plum Tree* was produced in Calgary, Alberta, at Alberta Theatre Project's' National playRites Festival, January 22 to March 2, 2003, with the following company:

GEORGE   Jared Matsunaga-Turnbull
FRIEDA   Darcy Dunlop
MAS   Hiro Kanagawa

Directed by Sarah Stanley
Set and Prop Design by Scott Reid
Costume Design by Jen Darbellay
Sound Design by Kevin McGugan
Light Design by Terry Middleton
Production Dramaturgy by Vanessa Porteous
Assistant Dramaturgy by Vicki Stroich
Production Stage Management by Dianne Goodman
Stage Management by Rhonda Kambeitz
Assistant Stage Management by Kelly Lunn

CHARACTERS

GEORGE MURAKAMI, age thirty-two. Japanese-Canadian.
FRIEDA WAGNER, age sixty-eight. German-Canadian.
MAS MURAKAMI, age sixty. Japanese-Canadian. George's uncle. Spirit.

SETTING

A U-pick berry farm near Mission, BC, Canada, 1989.

THE PLUM TREE

ACT ONE

SCENE ONE

Mid-morning. MAS sits in the tree. GEORGE enters the clearing. He does not see MAS.

MAS   Boo!

GEORGE   God!

MAS   Got ya.

GEORGE   Uncle?

MAS   Surprised to see me, eh?

GEORGE   Just a little.

> *MAS comes down the tree.*

I've dreamt about you. Waiting here for me.

MAS   Here I am.

GEORGE   Here you are. Is Dad…?

MAS   You think he'd be hanging around here?

GEORGE   Guess not.

MAS   C'mon, George. Here we are. Together. We always talked about coming here. Remember?

GEORGE   It doesn't look like the photo.

MAS   Falling apart. All overgrown.

> *Pause.*

GEORGE   What?

MAS   There's the door, nephew. You remember how to knock.

> *FRIEDA enters. She sees GEORGE and picks up a shovel.*

FRIEDA   Hey. Hey!

GEORGE   Oh. Hello.

FRIEDA   What do you think you're doing?

GEORGE   There was no one here, so I thought—

FRIEDA   —Thought you'd snoop around a little?

GEORGE   No, in fact, I / wanted to—

FRIEDA   *(seeing the basket in GEORGE's hand)* Does this look like the kind of place you can just start picking berries?

GEORGE   Your sign says U-pick, doesn't it?

MAS   Just tell her, George.

FRIEDA   I wasn't expecting any customers today. Should've worn gumboots.

GEORGE   What?

FRIEDA   It's rained every day this week, you know. You drove out from Vancouver?

GEORGE   Yes, but I don't—

FRIEDA   —Drove straight out to my U-pick. Just woke up this morning and thought, my goodness, I could use a bucket of raspberries. Better wear my best shoes.

MAS   Listen to her!

FRIEDA   And rental plates, too.

GEORGE   I flew in this morning, actually. From Winnipeg.

FRIEDA   Even better.

GEORGE   I've got business in the area.

FRIEDA   Business.

GEORGE   Research. I research—

FRIEDA   Oh—oh, I see, research. That's a new one. Snooping around. Seeing how your new strip mall would fit? If you're interested in the open house, just say so.

GEORGE   Open house?

FRIEDA   Yes, open house. As if you didn't know.

GEORGE   I didn't know. Really. There's no sign.

FRIEDA   There was an ad in the paper.

GEORGE   I told you. I flew in from Winnipeg this morning. Look. I have a card. I'm a researcher.

FRIEDA   *(squinting at the card)* Grudge.

GEORGE   George.

FRIEDA   Hmf. Frieda Wagner. This is difficult for me. People coming and going all the time.

GEORGE   You've had a lot of interest in the house?

FRIEDA   I'm not going to sell to just anyone. They've got to have the proper appreciation. Not some vulture from the city out to make a fast buck. They all think I'm just a helpless old lady.

GEORGE   I'm sure they don't think that.

FRIEDA   Kept the place up by myself for ten years. And look at it.

GEORGE   I'd like to.

FRIEDA   What?

GEORGE   I'd like to look at it. The inside.

FRIEDA   Why?

GEORGE   For professional reasons. I'm doing historical research. And this house is obviously—historical.

FRIEDA   I have a lot of work to do.

                    FRIEDA closes the door.

MAS   I don't believe you, nephew. "Historical research."

GEORGE   You saw how suspicious she was. I had to say something.

MAS   Shoulda just been straight. We're samurai. Warriors.

GEORGE   Oh, God.

MAS   Come on. Go in there and tell her.

GEORGE   I'm doing this my way.

MAS   Be straight! Samurai!

GEORGE   If I was "straight," she would think I was after something.

MAS   You are.

                    GEORGE knocks on the door. FRIEDA answers.

GEORGE   Did you have a garden here?

FRIEDA   What?

GEORGE   A garden.

FRIEDA   Where?

GEORGE   I don't know, by the plum tree maybe—

FRIEDA   —Why would you ask a question like that?

GEORGE   Just seems like it would be a nice spot for a garden. Close to the house.

FRIEDA   No. There was nothing there.

MAS   Yes, there was.

GEORGE   You're sure?

FRIEDA   What do you mean, am I sure? Of course I'm sure. It's my property.

MAS   It was right there, George.

> *Sound of trains.*

FRIEDA   Day and night, that rail yard. You damned developers just want to take over the whole valley, bulldoze everything into the ground, plaster Chinese on some apartment building. Sometimes, your people, I don't know what they—

GEORGE   —My people?

FRIEDA   Your kind. Your—you know what I mean.

GEORGE   I'm not Chinese.

FRIEDA   Oh.

GEORGE   I'm Japanese.

FRIEDA   You have to go now.

GEORGE   I'd like to pick some berries.

FRIEDA   Fine. Just don't bother me.

> *FRIEDA slams the door.*

> *Pause. Sound of downpour.*

MAS   It always rains here.

> *GEORGE begins picking.*

Jesus, George.

GEORGE   I said I wanted to pick.

MAS   When I was a kid, we picked so much I couldn't stand the smell of raspberry jam.

GEORGE   Just let me think for a minute.

MAS   Dad used to have this old soya sauce container right here. Mom would put a buncha rice in it. Dad would come along with this big mallet. Wham! Mom would turn the rice with a stick. Wham! Wham! Eh? For mochi. What's wrong, George? How come you're afraid to use the mallet? You're a warrior.

GEORGE   What's the point of being a warrior? What did I ever win?

> *MAS strikes a samurai pose.*

What's that?

MAS   "It is a job promising no pay or reward." Kambei Shimada. The grizzled veteran. *Seven Samurai?* C'mon. We watched that movie a million times.

GEORGE   You talked about this place all the time. And you never came back. I did.

MAS   And how come it took you so long?

GEORGE   I was busy.

MAS   Scared of what your dad might think? Scared he might give you the ol' Frank silent treatment?

GEORGE   I wasn't scared.

MAS   Oh, I know, George. I saw you slam your head against that wall. It was painful to watch. "Hey Dad, I started organizing meetings," "Hey Dad, would you sign this redress petition?", "Aren't you proud of me, Dad?" Nothing. Stonewall Frank. Well, nothing to worry about now, eh?

GEORGE   Uncle. I'm doing this my way.

MAS   Gonna be a wet way. All right then. Let's see what you got.

> *Pause. GEORGE goes to the door and knocks. FRIEDA answers.*

FRIEDA   What is it?

GEORGE   I picked some berries.

FRIEDA   Twenty dollars a bucket.

GEORGE   I haven't picked much. Wrong shoes.

FRIEDA   Half a bucket is twelve.

GEORGE   I've only got a twenty.

FRIEDA   *(taking the money)* That will do.

GEORGE   About your open house…

FRIEDA   The open house is over. Paper printed the wrong address.

GEORGE   Well, if you'd like to talk to me about the house sometime, I'll give you my / card, and—

FRIEDA   *(not taking the card)* / Is there something in your ears? I told you. I'm very busy.

GEORGE   Fine.

> *GEORGE turns to leave.*

FRIEDA   Why are you so interested in this house?

GEORGE   I told you. I research old houses.

FRIEDA   You save these houses?

GEORGE   It depends. On their historical significance.

FRIEDA   And this house?

GEORGE   It's a beautiful place.

FRIEDA   You think so?

GEORGE   Roof needs some work.

FRIEDA   Henry promised to look at it.

GEORGE   Your husband?

FRIEDA   No. My son. My husband had a bad arm from the war, he could never fix that roof. So you think the house is maybe...

GEORGE   I'd have to know more about it. Who built it?

MAS   Jesus, George, will you just tell / her—

GEORGE   / And if there are any significant artifacts. Historical objects.

MAS   Ah, so. Very sly.

FRIEDA   We were immigrants too, you know, my husband and I, just like your parents.

MAS   Immigrants?

GEORGE   My parents were born in Canada.

FRIEDA   Yes, well, you know what I mean. My husband has been dead now for ten years. I kept the place up myself. Henry would help, but he's so busy. I work hard, you know. I know it doesn't look like much, but / I—

GEORGE   / Like I said, it's a beautiful place.

   Pause.

FRIEDA   This work you do. Who is it for?

GEORGE   The Historical Preservation Committee. Of Mission City. The Mission City Historical Preservation Committee.

MAS   The what?

GEORGE   The Committee's very interested in Japanese homes around here. Used to be a big community here, before the war.

FRIEDA   The war was so terrible. Ordinary people had to do terrible things. We heard about what happened, how your people were, what do you call it?

MAS   Trucked out like cattle? Thrown in jail?

GEORGE   Evacuated.

FRIEDA   Yes. I'm sure whoever it was, the people in government, they had no choice.

MAS   You ignorant / kraut.

GEORGE   / If, say, Japanese owned this house at some point, or if there were any artifacts, it might add to the—historical significance of the house. The Committee would make a very generous donation.

FRIEDA   Goodbye.

GEORGE   But—

FRIEDA   —I have to go. I have a meeting with my sister in town. Here is your money. Keep the berries. They are almost rotten anyway.

FRIEDA slams the door.

SCENE TWO

Late afternoon. GEORGE and MAS in the clearing.

MAS   She's not here. Get that shovel. Come on. She could come back any second.

GEORGE gets the shovel.

GEORGE   Where?

MAS   What do you mean, where? By the plum tree.

GEORGE   There's a lot of places by the plum tree.

MAS   I only told you a million times where they were.

GEORGE   You'd only say, "In the garden, right by the plum tree." She said there was no garden.

MAS   Here.

GEORGE   Rock.

MAS   Over there.

GEORGE   Too many roots.

MAS   These goddamned berry bushes. Grow like weeds if you don't control 'em. Old lady really let this place fall apart. I thought "her people" were always tidy. "They had no choice." Gimme a break.

GEORGE   It's not her fault.

MAS   She was going to take a swing at you with that shovel. This would just be a lot easier if you would just ask the old bag.

GEORGE   Think of this as a sneak attack.

MAS   Sneak attack. More like don't rock the boat. Shikataga-nai, eh, George? Same old bull.

GEORGE   Three years. I did my time.

MAS   So why stop now?

GEORGE   Because I'm tired of pushing. Remember those two old Nakashimas on their farm? I showed them a picture of their fishing boat. They both started crying. Old guys had probably never cried in their lives. They were so ashamed.

MAS   'Cause they never stood up for themselves. I could see my family all lined up over there, waiting for that train. Police were stomping around in the bushes. Never woulda found me up in this tree. But then I hear Frank. "I know the trails. I'll show you where he is." My own brother. Plucked me right out of this tree.

GEORGE   He was worried.

MAS   He was scared. Scared my trouble would come down on him.

> *GEORGE puts the shovel by the house.*

GEORGE   And the family. He didn't want you to break up the family.

MAS   He broke it anyway. Sent me straight out to Angler. Wasn't like those cushy camps in the mountains. Guys with guns. Uniforms.

> *Pause.*

We buried them the day before that. They were so beautiful. Golden crane painted on each one. Mom kept them so polished. "Mas," she said, "go help your brother pack up that old rhubarb crate."

> *FRIEDA enters. She puts bags of groceries in front of the door and notices GEORGE. She grabs the shovel.*

Your grandpa said, "Ah, why bother, we'll be back in a month, two maybe." But Mom said, "Go get the shovel."

> *FRIEDA takes a swing at GEORGE and hits him in the arm. She swings again.*

GEORGE   Wait—

FRIEDA   —Get off my land!

MAS   It's war, George!

FRIEDA   My land, you hear!

MAS   You gotta fight. You got no choice. Samurai!

GEORGE   Stop!

>   *GEORGE grabs the shovel.*

FRIEDA   I'm calling the police.

GEORGE   Stop!

>   *GEORGE grabs FRIEDA.*

I forgot my umbrella. I came back to get it.

FRIEDA   Your umbrella?

GEORGE   I left it here when I was picking berries.

FRIEDA   You frightened me. I didn't think. I just—I don't know who you are, are you—?

GEORGE   You almost broke my arm.

FRIEDA   I'm—I'm—let me look at it.

GEORGE   I'm fine.

FRIEDA   Please. It's not so bad, is it? I'm just an old lady, after all.

>   *Short pause.*

The funny thing is that I was wishing you had left me your card.

GEORGE   Why?

FRIEDA   Would you like to come in?

GEORGE   No. That's fine.

>   *Pause.*

FRIEDA   I wanted to talk to you about your work. With this committee. And this house. Supposing this was a—historic house.

GEORGE   Supposing.

FRIEDA   There were Japanese here before the war. We… heard about it from the neighbours.

GEORGE   Was there / anything—

FRIEDA   / It's my sister. She says I can't take care of the place. And now she's given me a week.

GEORGE   For what?

FRIEDA   To sell. Or she'll knock it down. Liesel, my own sister! My own family. Crackers. I bought some, won't / you—?

GEORGE   / No. Thank you.

FRIEDA   It's more for Henry than for me. He still needs a place to call home. Can your committee help me?

GEORGE   Do what?

FRIEDA   I don't know, some kind of protection, something so no one could knock it down, so it would stay the same.

GEORGE   The place needs a lot of work. To get it up to the committee's standards.

FRIEDA   You think that it's possible?

GEORGE   Anything's possible.

       Short pause.

FRIEDA   Maybe you could stay for supper. So we could talk more. About— possibilities.

MAS   Just tell her.

GEORGE   All right.

FRIEDA   Good. Well. What will I cook? I just bought a roast, in case Henry came back tonight, but I think he will not come tonight. Where is your car? I didn't see it.

GEORGE   I parked up the road.

FRIEDA   Oh?

GEORGE   So I could walk here. See all the other properties around here.

FRIEDA   Perhaps you can go for a walk back in the trails. They go all the way down to the rail yard. If you wish, you can use Henry's boots. I will make us a plum pie!

SCENE THREE

       Early evening. After supper.

FRIEDA   More pie?

GEORGE   No. Thank you.

MAS   Isn't this nice, George? How's those plums taste?

GEORGE   You're just like my grandmother.

MAS   Your grandma made wine with those plums. Her plums.

FRIEDA   I ruined that roast. It was so salty.

GEORGE   No, no. It was delicious.

FRIEDA   You're so skinny. Doesn't your wife feed you?

MAS   What's Susan up to now, anyway?

GEORGE   She's not much of a cook.

MAS   Your grandma was a good cook.

FRIEDA   Henry and I, we always have a good meal when he comes home. I guess he will not make it tonight. It's important for families to eat together.

MAS   Ah, family. Used to set the table special at New Year's, George.

FRIEDA   Give me your plate.

MAS   Mom kept our plates so polished. It was like those cranes were on fire. Tell her.

GEORGE   Here. Let me help you.

FRIEDA   No, no.

GEORGE   Please.

MAS   "Let me help you. Please." I'm a very patient person. You know that. I can sit for hours. Hell, that's all we did in Angler Camp.

FRIEDA   Look at this place. Why do I bother?

GEORGE   Why do you?

FRIEDA   What?

GEORGE   Why do you stay?

FRIEDA   My walks in the woods? I don't know. Sometimes I go walking at night. I can see the lights of the house through the woods. Waiting for me. *(getting a picture from her pocket)* Look. Werner and I at the train station the day we left Miessen. I am very fat. Pregnant and happy. It was one of the happiest days of my life. I still think of it when I hear those trains.

> *Pause.*

Meissen was all—broken stones. It's all done now.

GEORGE   It's history.

FRIEDA   That's right.

GEORGE   That's what my father always used to say. It's history, George. Meaning— don't make a fuss. Erase it. But you can't.

FRIEDA   Your father had the right idea.

GEORGE   My father! My father didn't really have ideas. No politics, no talking about issues. Hated it when I got involved in the—we'd argue all the time. Until he just… stopped talking. That's the way he was.

MAS   The Clam King, that Frank.

GEORGE   My uncle, on the other hand. A real inspiration. Started organizing, talking about getting something back for what happened in the war. No one would listen to him. Said there'd be backlash. Turned their backs on him.

FRIEDA   There was an apology from the government. I read it in the paper. Money and an apology.

GEORGE   Yes.

FRIEDA   Your family must have been happy.

MAS   Buncha stones.

GEORGE   They tend to be reserved. It was painful. Brought back a lot of memories.

MAS   Reserved! Buncha stones.

GEORGE   They try to just erase the pain. They even have a saying for it. Shikataga-nai. "Nothing can be done."

MAS   Bull.

FRIEDA   But your uncle must have been happy. With what he got.

GEORGE   No.

FRIEDA   What more did he want?

GEORGE   Something more personal. He's gone, anyway. Lung cancer.

> *MAS lights a cigarette.*

FRIEDA   Let me give you something else. More coffee. Some cookies.

GEORGE   No thank you. I think I should go.

FRIEDA   Wait.

> *Pause.*

This was our new life, you see? For us, for Henry. We had to practically start this farm again, rip everything up, and we found this place in such a mess, especially between the house and the plum tree, where the garden was—

GEORGE   —there was a garden?

FRIEDA   I had forgotten. It was so long ago. I, I never wanted this place. But you have to understand. We had no choice. It was such a confusing time. That's why I want you to help me. To help me save it.

GEORGE   Like I said. Maybe I can help.

FRIEDA   You could talk to your committee.

GEORGE   Yes. I could talk to them.

FRIEDA   Thank you.

GEORGE   You're welcome.

      Pause.

I should go—I don't even have a hotel room yet.

FRIEDA   Stay. Stay here. You can work from here.

GEORGE   I don't know if I would feel right.

FRIEDA   Please. You could stay in Henry's room.

MAS   Frank's room. Your dad's.

GEORGE   All right.

FRIEDA   Good. I'll go make up that room. Your wife won't be jealous, I hope.

GEORGE   We're separated.

FRIEDA   I'm sorry. I say such stupid things.

      FRIEDA turns to go.

It might clear up tonight. We may even see the moon.

SCENE FOUR

Night. Moonlight. A candle glows in the window of the house. Sound of trains. GEORGE is digging under the plum tree.

MAS   That Kurosawa, eh, George? Wish we could watch that movie again. *(enacting Seven Samurai)* The sixteenth century. An age of turbulence. Japan was in the throes of civil war. Farmers everywhere were being crushed under the iron heels of cruel marauders. *(imitating farmers)* Is there no God to protect us? Let's give everything to the invaders and then hang ourselves! Shikataga-nai! *(imitating the old man)* Listen to me. You must hire samurai.

Enter—the two samurai. Me and my disciple. Out to save those poor farmers. And now. Weary from battle. We return. To find—it's all been taken away. Hidden. And so my disciple plans a sneak attack. And then—he eats pie. And when his attack is ready—he washes dishes. And to finish off the enemy—he goes to bed.

GEORGE   —Uncle.

MAS   Eight of us lived in this little house. What's it like?

GEORGE   The house?

MAS   Yeah.

GEORGE   It's very cozy.

MAS   *(looking in the window)* Really falling apart, huh?

GEORGE   Wood in the ceiling is beautiful.

MAS   Dad milled it himself.

GEORGE   There's an old stove in the corner of the living room.

MAS   Might be the same one we had. I can almost smell your Oba-chan's salmon. What else?

GEORGE   Bathroom is just off the kitchen.

MAS   We had an old gasoline drum for a bath.

GEORGE   And then the bedrooms are in the back.

MAS   What's that room like? Frank never let us in there much. He got his own room because he was nee-san. Older brother.

GEORGE   It's just a room. Why don't you go inside and look around.

MAS   Nah. You know. Wouldn't really be the same.

GEORGE   *(indicating a hole)* Nothing.

MAS   Keep going.

GEORGE   There's nothing here.

MAS   Maybe over / there.

GEORGE   / There's nothing here.

> GEORGE begins to put dirt back in the hole.

MAS   How 'bout another story, George? How about Uncle Mas Goes To Camp? You always liked that one.

> MAS climbs the tree halfway and throws plums at GEORGE.

You'll never get me, copper! Hay-ah! Take that! Shoulda seen them. Necks all purple. Got Frank square between the eyes. Heh. Then I tore up my ID card and threw it at their faces. But they dragged me out of this tree. Two weeks on a train to Ontario. Me and the rest of the resisters. Kid with a handful of fruit, a resister. We had to wear red circles on our backs, George. So we were easier targets.

GEORGE   *(simultaneously, as if he's heard the story a million times)* So you were easier targets.

MAS   You remember! And then the big finale. One big bomb and… *(lobbing a plum at GEORGE)* War's over, boys. "Our people" lost. Hooray. We're going home.

GEORGE   Why didn't you ever come back here?

MAS   Wouldn't let us. Wouldn't let us anywhere near the coast. We're island people. We need the ocean.

GEORGE   They lifted the ban. But you never came back.

MAS   It was stay out east or go back to Japan. "Go back," eh George? Good joke. Most've us had never been there! So you know what we did? We went samurai. We attacked with the only thing we had. Our butts.

GEORGE   *(simultaneously)* Your butts.

MAS   We just sat on our butts for weeks. Refused to move, even after they closed the camp. But it was pointless. So I went out to Winnipeg. To my parents and brothers and sisters. The sheep herd. Your dad, of course, was the worst.

GEORGE   You were pushy. You didn't know when to stop.

MAS   Chicken-shit Frank.

GEORGE   Stop it.

MAS   Goddamned Frank—

GEORGE   —Stop it!

MAS   We played cowboys and Indians in those trails. We fished for suckers in the creek. And he didn't lift a finger to get it back. To get anything back. What's enough for you, George? That's the question. Well. You know what they say. It's history.

> *GEORGE picks up the shovel top and begins digging again. FRIEDA can be heard singing offstage. GEORGE hears her and hides. FRIEDA enters in her nightgown, carrying a bucket of berries.*

FRIEDA   Is that you?

> *Short pause.*

Your room's just the same. I kept it all the same. But there's someone in there. I hope you don't mind. A guest. He said he'd help me. Why don't you come down?

> *Short pause.*

Henry! Come down this instant!

> *FRIEDA exits through the house. GEORGE comes back into the clearing.*

MAS   She's nuts. Talking to ghosts.

> *GEORGE leans the shovel back against the house and arranges the bushes to cover the hole completely.*

But George. Maybe if we / tried to—

GEORGE   / I said I'd help her.

SCENE FIVE

The next morning. GEORGE is on a ladder. He inspects the roof of the house.

MAS   Nephew.

> *Short pause.*

George. Nice view up there, huh?

> *Short pause.*

What the hell are you doing? Making a few repairs?

GEORGE   Like you said. Place is pretty rundown.

MAS   So you thought you'd just fix her right up.

GEORGE   I did some shingling once.

MAS   Thought, I'll just do a little roofing.

GEORGE   I'm helping her.

> *FRIEDA comes out of the house.*

FRIEDA   What are you doing?

GEORGE   Thought I'd get a headstart on our "restoration." Start with your leaks.

FRIEDA   You don't have to do that.

GEORGE   I've done some roofing before.

FRIEDA   I've had those leaks so long. This is really very kind of you. I don't know what to say.

GEORGE   Do you have some tools, Frieda? A hammer, some nails?

FRIEDA   Tools? Werner had lots of tools.

GEORGE   Could I use them?

FRIEDA   They're probably all rusty, but I could, I could probably find them. Yes. I think I know where they are. Give me a minute.

GEORGE   No rush.

FRIEDA   It's so nice to have someone who appreciates this place.

> *FRIEDA goes inside the house and looks for some tools.*

MAS   You're getting pretty sweet on that old lady.

GEORGE   Uncle. Aren't you glad to just be here?

> *Pause.*

MAS   Now I get it.

GEORGE   What?

MAS   Ah, nephew, that's more like it!

GEORGE   I don't know what you're talking about.

MAS   Now I see why you're so sweet on her! Get in her good books, "oh, you're just like my grandma," maybe start talking about an offer, and then, when you move in, no more leaks.

GEORGE   It's not like that.

MAS   You're right, George. It's perfect. I thought you were getting soft, but really, you were way ahead of me.

GEORGE   Uncle. All I'm doing is helping her out.

MAS   But you would be helping her. She's right. The house should go to someone who appreciates it. Not someone who'll push everything into the ground for a condo. You'd keep it the same. That's what she wants, right?

GEORGE   That's what she said.

MAS   You buy the house, everyone's happy. Right?

GEORGE   Right.

MAS   But where are you going to get the cash?

> *Pause.*

GEORGE   I've got some money.

MAS   Oh yeah?

GEORGE   Dad gave it to me.

MAS   Perfect!

GEORGE   I want to do something good with it.

MAS   Then do it! Keep doing what you were doing for three years. Educate people. You could turn this into a little museum.

GEORGE   A museum?

MAS   Yeah. With "historical significance."

GEORGE   I don't know. I was thinking I should save the money. Dad was always riding me to give him some grandkids. So maybe someday / I could save—

MAS   / Kids, eh? When you don't live with your wife.

GEORGE   Thanks.

MAS   Where is she, anyways? Last I heard she was moving / out west—

GEORGE   / She's in Vancouver.

MAS   Ah.

GEORGE   So what?

MAS   Dirty trick, leaving you like that.

GEORGE   I was never around.

MAS   You were out fighting the war.

GEORGE   War's over.

MAS   It's never over.

GEORGE   Why are we talking about Susan?

MAS   You're the one who brought up the grandkids. I'm just saying, stick to things you can get. Things you can change.

GEORGE   You never let up, do you?

MAS   Gotta make sure you stay on track. Look, this is something real. This is what you need. This is what we both need.

GEORGE   A museum?

MAS   What a great idea. Why not get it all back?

> *FRIEDA comes out of the house with an old tool belt.*

FRIEDA   I found this old thing.

MAS   *(making train sounds)* Woo-woo! All you gotta do is make the offer. Hey, if you lived here, you'd be a helluva lot closer to Susan. You can almost smell the ocean, eh?

GEORGE   I can fix up a few spots then go to town for some shingles. Just hand it up to me.

FRIEDA   Werner just left them in the rain so much, didn't really take care of them. It will be good to use them again. I made some waffles with raspberries. Why don't you come down?

GEORGE   Better to do it before it rains again.

FRIEDA   Isn't it slippery? Be careful up there, Henry.

GEORGE   What?

FRIEDA   I said be careful up there. Come down and have a cup of coffee at least.

GEORGE   All right.

> *GEORGE comes down the ladder.*

MAS   The offer, George.

GEORGE   Thank you.

FRIEDA   Thank you. This is—well, this is wonderful.

MAS   Train's about to leave.

GEORGE   The house is a lot of work for you. It's a lot to manage.

FRIEDA   Yes, it's hard work, very hard, running this place. But I'm still up to it.

GEORGE   I want to help you, Frieda. I told you that.

FRIEDA   You're helping me already, up there, fixing the roof. And you're going to phone your committee, give the house some kind of, how do you say it, status—

GEORGE   I think I have an idea, Frieda. For a buyer.

FRIEDA   A buyer?

GEORGE   Me.

> *Short pause.*

FRIEDA   You? But what about your committee?

GEORGE   Well—I'd keep everything the way it is.

FRIEDA   You. This is so quick.

> *Pause.*

Well. I don't know what to say.

GEORGE   It would all stay the same. Just like you said, just like we talked about. We could put it in writing.

MAS   Now we're rolling, boy!

GEORGE   I just have a really good feeling about the place. The location.

FRIEDA   It's worth a lot of money, this land, you know. I don't know if you could afford it.

GEORGE   We could talk it over with your sister—

FRIEDA   —and Henry, of course. When he comes home.

GEORGE   We could just start by talking.

FRIEDA   So that's why you're up there looking at the roof. Is that why you offered to help me, just to butter me up—?

GEORGE   —Frieda, you asked me to stay. And I was looking at the roof because I wanted to do something nice for you. Really. The idea just sort of came to me, out of the blue. I wouldn't be in a rush to move in. I wouldn't push you out the door. You'd have time to make arrangements.

FRIEDA   Arrangements.

GEORGE   Your sister.

FRIEDA   Liesel.

GEORGE   She lives around here?

FRIEDA   Across the river.

GEORGE   We could all just talk.

FRIEDA   My sister already meddles so much. I told her I wanted to do this my way.

GEORGE   I want to do it your way.

FRIEDA   You'd keep it the way it is.

GEORGE   Better. I'd fix it up.

FRIEDA   You'd have to keep a candle in the window.

GEORGE   Whatever you want. Listen, Frieda, you said you wanted a buyer who appreciates this place. Well, I—really feel something here. Isn't that what you want?

FRIEDA   I think so.

GEORGE   Why don't you think about it. I could go to town and get some shingles.

MAS   That's some slick grease, nephew. Some slick grease.

FRIEDA   Henry wanted to take those tools. He was going to Israel on this program, young Germans were helping build houses. Shame to let those tools go to waste, he said. Werner would have none of it. He could be such a miserable man. He was in such pain. But still. If only he hadn't hurt his arm. During the war. He was building a bunkhouse. A piece of timber fell on him. He could never fix this house. He could never do anything.

       Pause.

GEORGE   I'll fix the place up, Frieda. I'd make the house the way it was.

FRIEDA   I don't know.

GEORGE   You can come back any time you want. You can go for walks, pick berries. We'll go for walks.

FRIEDA   Perhaps.

GEORGE   I'd refinish the wood on the inside. Replant the garden.

FRIEDA   This was such a beautiful place. But you should cut the tree down. Let more light in.

MAS   Hey, now.

GEORGE   I'd have to think about that.

FRIEDA   You can talk to my sister. She meddles. But she is a very practical woman. Her number is by the phone. Call her. Go and see her.

GEORGE   You would come too.

FRIEDA   No, no, I have no head for numbers. Really, you two can work it out.

GEORGE   Good. Great! Well. Here's to—new beginnings!

FRIEDA   Yes. To new beginnings. You're right. This is a new beginning.

MAS   You've still got the touch with the old ladies, I'll give you that.

MAS climbs up the tree.

FRIEDA   I don't even know your last name.

GEORGE   Oh.

GEORGE gets his card and gives it to FRIEDA.

It's Murakami.

FRIEDA   Murakami. *(recognizing the name)* Murakami.

GEORGE   I should get up there. Before it starts raining again.

GEORGE picks up the tools and climbs the ladder.

FRIEDA   *(softly)* My God. My God.

End of Act One.

ACT TWO

SCENE ONE

The next evening. MAS still sits in the tree. GEORGE stands in the bushes.

GEORGE   *(calling)* Frieda? Frieda?

MAS   Wanna play some cards, George?

GEORGE   I'm busy, Uncle.

MAS   Lady disappeared, eh?

GEORGE   I haven't seen her all day. I went out looking for her. *(calling again)* Frieda!

MAS   What's the big panic?

GEORGE   I'm worried, Uncle. I talked to her sister this morning. About the sale.

MAS   And?

GEORGE   She's very interested. We agreed on a number.

MAS   Way to go, nephew.

GEORGE   So we need to talk to Frieda. But she's disappeared.

MAS   Sounds like trouble. I told you, never trust a white person.

GEORGE   Just shut up, Uncle. I was going to call the police, but what would I say? That I'm a friend? Or, or what?

MAS   Police. Those idiots don't know the trails. I coulda hid up here for days if—

GEORGE   —why don't you help me? You know the trails.

MAS   Can't do that, George.

GEORGE   Why not?

MAS   You know me. I'm more of a motivator.

GEORGE   Please.

MAS   All right, all right. Give me a second.

MAS descends the tree with difficulty.

Just about got stuck up here. Funny place to get stuck, eh? Considering. Cut my arms up pretty good when they hauled me out of here.

GEORGE   This is ridiculous. Why am I doing this?

MAS   Your grandma used to tell us a story. About those dishes. Told us it was an old Japanese legend. She probably just made it up. She'd say: "Once there was this family of cranes who lived on a mountain. And one day, the mountain caught on fire. The whole family left, except one young crane who wouldn't go. His feathers caught on fire. So he flew off to see his family, to see if they would help him." That was what was on those plates. The burning crane flying to see his family. You listening? Mom let us make up our own endings. Me, I figured he made it back. That he found his family by a lake somewhere. They poured water all over his wings, put bandages on his burns. Frank, your dad, he always said the crane just burned up, like a spark in the sky. Just died. Figured it was the crane's fault for staying and he got what he deserved.

GEORGE   Dad was never into happy endings.

MAS   You shoulda seen us bury those dishes. I was swearing up and down, saying I'd kill Mackenzie King. Guess what your Dad said. Nothing! Not a word. But you know, he turned away once or twice, wiping his eyes like he had dirt in them. That's the kicker, George. I knew he loved those dishes. Loved this house. And he wouldn't fight, wouldn't do anything. Goddamned Frank.

GEORGE   Stop calling him that, Uncle.

FRIEDA appears out of the bushes.

Frieda! Where have you been?

FRIEDA   Out for a walk.

GEORGE   You've been gone for twelve hours.

FRIEDA   That long? I didn't notice.

GEORGE   Aren't you—aren't you hungry?

FRIEDA   Oh, I had some raspberries. They are everywhere now. You can't tell where the farm ends and the forest begins.

GEORGE   I talked to Liesel, Frieda. This morning.

FRIEDA   Oh? How is she?

GEORGE   She's very interested in the sale. I think we can work something out.

FRIEDA   Where are those tools? That's how they got all rusty, just leaving them lying around. Someone could step on them, hurt themselves. I should just lock them up.

GEORGE   I need them, Frieda. For the roof.

Short pause.

Liesel wants to talk, Frieda. She wants all of us to talk. She's been worried.

FRIEDA   Worried!

GEORGE   I was worried.

FRIEDA   Really? How sweet of you.

GEORGE   We need to talk about the sale.

FRIEDA   We have to wait until Henry gets home. He hasn't come yet?

GEORGE   No one's here. I've been here all day.

FRIEDA   Well, we'll have to wait.

       Short pause.

All Henry wanted to do was get away from here. He hated this place. Hated, hated, hated.

GEORGE   Frieda, we need to talk. You're going to sell me the house.

FRIEDA   In a minute. Don't push me. Why do you always push me?

GEORGE   I'm not pushing you.

FRIEDA   Why does everybody think there's something wrong with me? Liesel, now you. I'm just fine!

GEORGE   All right, Frieda! I—

MAS   All you want to do is talk.

GEORGE   All I want to do is talk, Frieda.

MAS   You're just trying to help her.

GEORGE   I'm just trying to help you.

       Pause.

FRIEDA   I'm tired.

GEORGE   You were gone a long time.

FRIEDA   It felt like the last time I would see the place. I was trying to say goodbye.

GEORGE   You'd always be welcome back. Whenever you wanted.

FRIEDA   It wouldn't be the same.

GEORGE   Frieda. It would be the same. I promise. I have plans. I want to turn it into a museum.

FRIEDA   A museum?

GEORGE   A kind of memorial. A tribute. To Japanese-Canadians in the area.

FRIEDA   A museum! This is what you—what your committee wants?

GEORGE   Well—

FRIEDA   —this is what you wanted the whole time. This was all some kind of trick.

GEORGE   Frieda—

FRIEDA   —let's phone your committee. I want to talk to your boss. Call him.

GEORGE   Calm down.

FRIEDA   You feel how wet the ground is? Memories. Soaked with them. Not all good. But mine. When I leave—

GEORGE   —you take them with you.

FRIEDA   No. You can't pack them in a suitcase. Some of them stay. Some of them you can't take with you.

    Pause.

This was the promised land for us. A new place. Our new life.

    Pause.

I can't leave.

GEORGE   What do you mean?

FRIEDA   I'm not leaving. I can't.

GEORGE   Frieda. You're tired, you're not yourself.

FRIEDA   I'm not leaving. No one can force me, not you, not Liesel. No matter what she says, how much she threatens me. Says it's her land. Her land! Did she sweat here, picking berries, raising a family? This isn't about a piece of paper. I belong here.

    Pause.

I'm so tired. I'm going to bed.

GEORGE   Frieda! Wait.

    Pause.

This is our land.

MAS   Finally!

FRIEDA   Your land?

GEORGE   My family's. My grandfather built this house. They lived here. They were taken away, on the train. It's ours.

MAS   That's it, George! A little late, but that's it!

GEORGE   My father was born here. My uncle was born here.

FRIEDA   Why didn't you tell me?

GEORGE   I didn't think you'd understand.

FRIEDA   Understand what?

GEORGE   I was afraid you'd think I was after something.

FRIEDA   Aren't you?

MAS   Only what's ours.

GEORGE   It's not like that.

FRIEDA   What's it like, then? You want the house, don't you? Come back to get what's "rightfully" yours?

GEORGE   I didn't come back here expecting any of this.

FRIEDA   Stop it! Stop lying! I knew.

> *Pause.*

I knew this was your family's house. I'm not stupid. A young Jap guy comes around, wants to look around the house because he's doing "research." Wearing his best shoes to pick berries. I was sure you were here looking for something. I saw the way you looked at the place. But you said you would help. You told me about the committee. So I trusted you. But then when you gave me your card there is no "committee".

> *Pause.*

It doesn't change anything. This is my land. Not yours.

MAS   I knew it.

GEORGE   I'm not expecting you to just give it to me.

FRIEDA   We weren't even here when your family was moved. We had nothing to do with it.

GEORGE   That's not the point.

FRIEDA   It wasn't just your people. There were Germans in camps in Canada too, you know.

MAS   You were never in a camp!

GEORGE   *(simultaneously)* You were never in a camp. I don't think "your people" can talk about camps.

FRIEDA   Am I supposed to feel guilty? Is that what you want?

GEORGE   That's why I didn't tell you everything. I was trying not to pressure you.

FRIEDA   You're telling me now.

GEORGE   I had to, you made me.

FRIEDA   Why don't you do like your father does? Just forget about it instead of blaming innocent people? Why do I always have to feel guilty?

GEORGE   You told me you wanted me to buy the house. Now you're changing your mind.

Short pause.

Why don't you call Henry?

FRIEDA   God, we came to this country to get away from the guilt! But no, it followed us from Meissen. It kept following me after Henry—after Werner died, and after Henry—

GEORGE   —where's Henry, Frieda?

Short pause.

Why don't you call him? Go ahead. Go inside and call him.

FRIEDA   Stop it! Why are you doing this? I took you in. I didn't even know you and I invited you to stay.

GEORGE   You almost killed me.

FRIEDA   You said you would help me!

GEORGE   Liesel told me everything, Frieda! Henry's not coming home.

Pause.

FRIEDA   Some days it's raining, and all I do is sit here. I can feel the roof sagging, water pouring through the holes. I think of Henry. I'm waiting. Then the rain lets up. There's just mist. I go walking in that mist. Maybe I see an old footprint in the mud. Maybe I imagine Henry standing right there, under that old plum tree. But that doesn't mean I'm crazy. Do you understand?

Pause.

Now Liesel wants to, to—evacuate me to a nice room somewhere, some place with a view of the mountains.

FRIEDA exits. Pause.

GEORGE   Shikataga-nai.

MAS   What are you doing?

GEORGE   I'm leaving.

MAS   You can't leave.

GEORGE   She's not well. She's sick.

MAS   Don't buy into it, George. All this stuff with her son, it's just an act.

GEORGE starts to leave.

Wait. You can't just forget about all this. You can't just forget about me.

GEORGE   I can try. Shikataga-nai, right? I can let go.

MAS   Not while I'm still around.

GEORGE   I tried, Uncle. I can't do this.

MAS   Where you going? Back to Winnipeg? Back to the flock?

GEORGE   Yes! Back home.

MAS   They'll just tell you how stupid you were, coming here. They just can't stand to see somebody do something. I used to get these letters in Angler. Stop being foolish. Stop embarrassing yourself. Your brother's got a good job at the Bay, he could find you something. Come to Winnipeg.

GEORGE   They just wanted you to come home.

MAS   Home!

GEORGE   Where your family was.

MAS   Some home! I hadn't seen them in six years! Since I was fifteen years old!

      Pause.

I had nothing, not even a shirt. So I went out to Winnipeg, this big flat muddy city. And I sat at the table with them, eating A&W hamburgers, acting like nothing happened, getting married to whites, getting white jobs, smiling white smiles. Out-whiting the whites. And I could still feel this big red circle on my back. So I got up and starting doing something.

GEORGE   You didn't know when to stop.

MAS   Your dad. Your dad, Frank, was the worst. Wouldn't talk to me. Wouldn't let me talk to you.

GEORGE   I can't do this anymore, Uncle.

MAS   The Clam King. The Chicken Shit. Goddamned Frank.

GEORGE   Don't talk about him like that! Everybody's goddamned this, goddamned that. Goddamned Dad. Christ. Goddamn you, Uncle Mas! Goddamned stories stuck in my head. Dad always told me you were a trouble-maker. I never listened to him. Now look where I am. Pushing an old lady off her land. For what? For whom? Just because you turned your back on your family—

MAS   —I turned my back? He turned me in! He put me in Angler. My goddamned brother. They all turned their backs on me. Except for you. At the table, I could hardly see them. They blended in so well with the white walls. This is for them. For the family. So we don't disappear.

GEORGE   We won't disappear.

MAS   Say you and Susan have a kid. Kid grows up sort of beige, eyes a little funny, but nobody can tell. Knows how to use chopsticks. But prefers hamburgers. But you thought about this already, right? That's why you left her.

GEORGE   She left me!

MAS   C'mon. You looked at your wife and you thought about your little imaginary white kid. And then you checked the calendar for the next Redress meeting. She left you, but you were already long gone.

GEORGE   I miss her.

MAS   You had to do something. We both had to do something. We had to fight or disappear into the walls. We had to get something back.

GEORGE   This was it. Here it was. Here it is.

MAS   Exactly.

GEORGE   Then why didn't you come back? If this is what you wanted, why didn't you come back?

MAS   You're braver than me, George. You're the warrior. You're the only one left. The mountain's on fire.

> GEORGE knocks on the door, takes the shovel and begins digging. FRIEDA comes out of the house.

GEORGE   My family buried dishes here. They belong to us.

FRIEDA   They're not here.

GEORGE   You know about them.

FRIEDA   Of course I do.

GEORGE   You found them.

FRIEDA   Yes, we found them. Right there, in an old rhubarb box.

GEORGE   What did you do with them?

FRIEDA   It was so hard back then. We had nothing. And we found those dishes. It was like a gift from God.

GEORGE   What did you do with them!?

FRIEDA   We needed the money so badly.

GEORGE   You sold them.

FRIEDA   No one would give Werner a job. They said it was his arm, but I know it was because we were German. I saw the looks they gave us. What Henry had to put up with in school. The teasing, the names, even from the teachers. What were we supposed to do with them? We didn't know what had happened. We didn't know your family. Otherwise—

GEORGE   —Otherwise what? You would've kept them until now?

            Pause.

You knew.

FRIEDA   We knew that Japanese had lost the land.

GEORGE   Lost it? It wasn't something they just misplaced. The dishes were ours.

FRIEDA   Don't you think I'm sorry?

GEORGE   You lied to me.

FRIEDA   I lied to you?! I didn't pretend to be someone I wasn't.

GEORGE   You were trying to use me.

FRIEDA   I wanted to give you something. I wanted to make you a pie.

GEORGE   Out of guilt.

FRIEDA   I just wanted to give you something. But there was nothing I could give you.

MAS   There's still something.

GEORGE   You're right. You have nothing to give. Because it's not yours to give. It was never yours.

FRIEDA   I'm not leaving.

GEORGE   Yes. You are. And if Henry comes, I'll give him your new address. But somehow I don't think I have to worry about that. He's not coming back, Frieda. That's the truth. This house is falling down. You can't handle the place. That's the truth. You just won't face it.

FRIEDA   I won't face it? You're telling me about the truth? You? You con man! You trick yourself into thinking this is all something moral. You think you're all high and mighty just because your father's family got treated badly. You think that justifies anything? Look at yourself. You're just like those people that kicked out your family. So your father's dead. Your uncle's dead. Your wife left you. Well, getting this house won't bring them back.

GEORGE   Get out!

FRIEDA   You get out! This is my house!

GEORGE   Not for long.

FRIEDA   I'm not leaving.

GEORGE   It's too late.

SCENE TWO

Two days later. MAS is in the tree. GEORGE enters the clearing.

MAS   Hey nephew. There you are. Where'd you disappear to?

GEORGE   Got a motel room.

MAS   You look terrible.

GEORGE   I signed the papers.

MAS   It's ours?

GEORGE   In a week.

MAS   Way to go, nephew. I'm proud of you.

GEORGE   You're proud of me.

MAS   Our land, George. You bought it fair and square. 'Course, it's not those dishes. I was thinking, we could find out who they sold them to. Try to track 'em down. Whaddaya think?

GEORGE   I'm tired. I can't sleep.

MAS   Well, you better get some rest, 'cause we're going to be busy.

GEORGE   "We."

MAS   Oh, I got a million ideas. We could—where are you going?

GEORGE goes to knock on the door.

FRIEDA   What? More research? Your grandmother hid her silverware in the attic? I don't think so. Are you checking up on me already? Making sure I don't set fire to the place or plant land mines under the tree?

GEORGE   I'm going to start on some projects around the yard. Before it gets too cold.

FRIEDA   One week. Do you know how hard it is to pack up a life in one week? You said you'd give me time. To make arrangements.

GEORGE   I'm tired of waiting.

FRIEDA   Just like all the other con men.

GEORGE   There's no one else, Frieda! Nobody wants this place. Liesel said the only other offer was a company who wanted to build a dump. She was going to level the house. I made your sister a fair offer. No, a generous offer. More than I had to.

FRIEDA   It's not about the money!

GEORGE   Would you rather see this place become a dump? This is what you wanted. It's not going to disappear. Look at this place. Really look at it. You can hardly keep it from falling down.

> *Pause.*

This way you'll be near your sister.

FRIEDA   My sister. Puh.

> *FRIEDA comes outside.*

It isn't easy, you know. Keeping up a farm. I hope you don't mind if I take a bucket of your berries. *(tripping over a root)* Damned tree. I wish I had cut it down years ago.

When we first came here, I would stand under that tree. I would hold Henry in my arms. And he'd reach up, with his fat little fingers, for one of the plums, and I would think, thank God, we're out of Meissen. We're out of Germany. Henry will grow up fine. We're in a safe country, a good country. Canada.

GEORGE   Canada!

MAS   Canada, lady. I could tell you about Canada.

GEORGE   What kind of "good country" builds camps for its own people? What kind of people build camps?

FRIEDA   What did Liesel tell you? What did she tell you?

> *Short pause.*

Werner was a man with a job. That's all. He was a carpenter. He didn't know why he was building those bunkhouses. He was told it was a detention centre. That's all.

> *Short pause.*

But Henry couldn't let it go. He couldn't erase it. He knew everything from when he was small.

MAS   He had a right to know.

GEORGE   He had a right to know. You can't deny someone their past. It's not fair.

FRIEDA   Fair? Henry carried that guilt around like it was his own, this giant bucket of guilt. Is that fair?

MAS   You can't just clam up.

GEORGE   The past isn't just yours. You can't just clam up.

FRIEDA   You sound like some speech. Don't you ever get tired of it? Of the same train, going around in circles in your head?

> *Pause.*

Well you have it all now, don't you? This house. Your past and your uncle's. It all belongs to you.

FRIEDA goes back inside the house. Sound of a train whistle.

MAS   Goddamned trains. Woo-woo-woo all the time.

GEORGE   Why are you still here?

MAS   Whaddaya mean?

GEORGE   Why are you still sitting up there?

MAS   I'm still having a few problems with this tree. Branches got me pretty caught. Too bad you can't help me get down.

GEORGE   I am helping you. Don't you get it? I've finished your business. Now you're supposed to leave. That's the way it works.

MAS   You know, I coulda hid up here for / days if—

GEORGE   / Hid? How could you hide?

MAS   What?

GEORGE   What time of the year was it? When they brought the trains?

MAS   Spring. You know / that.

GEORGE   / There were no leaves.

MAS   So?

GEORGE   They would've found you in a second.

MAS   No. It was your goddamned / Dad—

GEORGE   / He was trying to help you too. You said he took the police into the trails. And where did they go?

MAS   Off over there, looking for me.

GEORGE   He led the police away from you.

MAS   No, he / was—

GEORGE   / He was giving you a chance to come down and join the family. To save face. You were scared. You were a scared little kid.

MAS   I was a resister!

GEORGE   Come down, Uncle.

MAS   No! I like it up here. Why don't you come up, George. Damned good view from up here. You and me, we always saw eye to eye. We're here, George. Together. Just like we always wanted.

GEORGE   You lied to me.

MAS   We're going to make it all the same again. I was thinking we could get the farm going again, invite people out, teach them about their roots.

> *FRIEDA comes out of the house. GEORGE does not see her. She watches as GEORGE talks to MAS.*

GEORGE   No.

MAS   What's with all this, this bullshit, George? You got it all.

GEORGE   I don't have anything.

MAS   You've got everything! You got it back!

GEORGE   I've got nothing! Susan's gone. You're gone, Uncle. This isn't the same. Dad. Dad is gone. He would barely talk to me after I started organizing meetings with you.

MAS   The Clam King.

GEORGE   He just wanted you—he just wanted me to forget about all of it. You can't go back, he said. He always said it would bring nothing but pain.

MAS   Bullshit.

GEORGE   A museum? A little history farm? Dad would've knocked it all down first.

MAS   So? It's not his. It's yours.

GEORGE   Do you know where I got the money? *(pulling a cheque from his pocket)* His Redress money. He refused to apply for it—I did it for him. And then, at his funeral, Mom just handed me this envelope. With this.

> *Pause.*

I wanted to do something good with it! And now look what I've done. About to put a down payment on an old shack and talking to my dead uncle. Maybe, Uncle, if you had the guts to come back, to see the place, to find out there's nothing here, you could've let it go. But you didn't, and now here we are. And there's nothing!

FRIEDA   It doesn't help.

> *Pause.*

It doesn't help to yell at them. I know, I've done it for years.

> *Pause.*

Henry sent cheques. From Israel. He got work there, building memorials, houses for Jewish settlers. Sometimes with a short note, sometimes just the cheque. Werner wanted to tear the cheques up. He would go into a rage when another envelope arrived. So I started hiding them. We needed the money.

> *Short pause. FRIEDA takes a picture out of her pocket.*

And then one day—he sent this picture. No cheque. He was standing in front of a big grapefruit tree. In the sunlight. Smiling. He was wearing one of those little black caps they wear there. He was reaching up to pick a grapefruit. My heart just raced when I saw the picture. He's coming home, I thought. He's coming home.

     Pause.

So I waited. I was still waiting when you came that day. In this rotting, cramped, cold, beautiful home.

GEORGE   I just wanted the dishes.

FRIEDA   Those damned dishes! If only you're uncle had taken the money, if he had just told you they weren't there.

GEORGE   My uncle? What are you talking about?

MAS   I never came back.

FRIEDA   It was your uncle. It had to be. You said he wanted something personal.

GEORGE   When did he come back?

FRIEDA   In the sixties sometime.

GEORGE   He never told me he came back. Why wouldn't he tell me? Is it true?

MAS   I never came back!

FRIEDA   Of course it's true! Why would I lie? He wrote us a letter. It was the same name. Murakami. When I saw your card, I knew. We offered him twenty times what they were worth. They weren't worth much, you know. It's not like we made a million dollars.

MAS   She's lying, George!

FRIEDA   People hold on to memories for so long. Look at you. You carry around memories that aren't even yours. You and your Uncle Frank.

GEORGE   Frank?

FRIEDA   You're two of a kind, he and you.

GEORGE   Frank?

MAS   Frank.

FRIEDA   I have the letter. I looked for it the other day when I learned your name. See, here it is.

MAS   That goddamned Frank.

GEORGE   Dad.

FRIEDA   *(not hearing GEORGE)* Here it is. I remember his name so well, because I had just learned it in English. How it meant honest. Well, we were honest with him. We were frank. But it wasn't enough. Money wasn't enough. And we said we were sorry. We apologized over and over again.

GEORGE   You offered him—money and an apology?

FRIEDA   What else could we give him?

> *Pause. Sound of rain.*

Rain, tree, goddamned berries. You get so used to things. Even if they hurt you. *(looking at the photo again)* There was a war in Israel that year. I hope he stayed a while in that orchard. He and Werner used to pick fruit together. I remember.

There were orchards in Miessen, too. And vineyards. Miessen was very beautiful. A big castle on the Elbe. I haven't thought about that place in years. It would be good to go back.

> *Pause.*

George?

GEORGE   Yes. Frieda.

FRIEDA   I really did want to make you a pie. Just because… the plums were sweet.

> *FRIEDA exits into the house.*

SCENE THREE

> *A week or two later. Sunshine. GEORGE is in the tree with MAS. GEORGE holds the letter. Wind chimes hang from the eaves of the house. Sound of wind chimes.*

MAS   You wanna play some cards?

GEORGE   I wish we could.

MAS   You know, you could put that letter in the museum.

GEORGE   It's not going to happen, Uncle.

MAS   Oh.

> *Pause.*

So. What now?

GEORGE   I think I'll spend some time in Vancouver. See the ocean.

MAS   That's a good idea. We're ocean people, George.

> *Short pause.*

Roof's looking pretty rough. Starting to sag. Winter's coming.

Short pause.

Who was that fella that came around this morning?

GEORGE   Native guy. Researching old Indian camps. Left me his card.

GEORGE climbs down tree and begins to dig.

MAS   George. They're gone. The dishes are gone. You can stop now.

GEORGE   I'm not looking for anything anymore.

MAS   What are you doing?

GEORGE   This is for burying something. Don't be scared, Uncle. You can come down now.

The end.

ACKNOWLEDGEMENTS

The Editor is grateful for the help, love, and support of the following individuals who made the process of putting this anthology together possible:

Ric Knowles, Angela Rebeiro, Yvette Nolan, Ella Chan, Jennifer Lau, David Yee, Richard Lee, Leon Aureus, and my beloved and fiercely dedicated anthology reading committee (Byron Abalos, Karl Ang, Leon Aureus, Aura Carcueva, Daniel Christopher Chen, Sandy Chen, Jo Chim, Insurp Choi, Rose Cortez, David Eng, Christina Florencio, Darrel Gamotin, Ramona Katigbak, Justin Kim, Laura Kim, Silver Kim, Camellia Koo, Cyan Kuo, Charmaine Lau, Richard Lee, Sandra Lefrançois, Chase Lo, Susan Lock, Jane Luk, Teza Lwin, Minh Ly, Benny Min, Arlene Paculan, Siobhán Richardson, Brian Sison, Adriano Sobretodo, Lauren Tweedie, David Yee, Norman Yeung, Dale Yim and Maui Zafra).

ABOUT

NINA LEE AQUINO

Nina Lee Aquino is a director, dramaturge, playwright, artistic director of fu-GEN Asian-Canadian Theatre Company and the artistic producer of Factory Theatre's CrossCurrents Festival. Other credits include awards for directing (Ken McDougall Award 2004, Canada Council John Hirsch Prize 2008), and Dora Mavor Moore Award nominations for outstanding direction (*Singkil*, fu-GEN Theatre Company 2007; *People Power*, Carlos Bulosan Theatre 2008). Nina co-wrote *Miss Orient(ed)* (produced by Carlos Bulosan Theatre) and her monologues have been published in *Beyond the Pale* (Yvette Nolan, ed.) and *She Speaks* (Judith Thompson, ed.).

She currently resides in Toronto with her husband, Richard, and their daughter, Eponine.